Highlanders

For Annabel

This 15th-century drawing shows Pharaoh's daughter Scota, from whom the Scots were believed to be descended, leaving Egypt for Ireland with her husband Gaythelos.

Highlanders

A HISTORY OF
THE HIGHLAND CLANS

FITZROY MACLEAN

ADELPHI

Endpapers: map by David Fryer.

The author and publishers wish to thank Alastair Campbell of Airds, Unicorn Poursuivant for his
invaluable advice, Lady Moncreiffe of that Ilk for kindly allowing us to use the information compiled
by the late Sir Ian Moncreiffe of that Ilk for the map of the clans, Hugh Cheape of the National Museums of
Scotland and the many private owners, museums, galleries and libraries who have so
generously allowed us to reproduce objects from their collections.

Picture Research by Caroline Meynell
Designed and typeset by Book Creation Services, London
Printed in Singapore

ADELPHI
Published by David Campbell Publishers Ltd, London

Text copyright © Fitzroy Maclean
© 1995 David Campbell Publishers Ltd
First published 1995
Reprinted 1996 and 1999

ISBN 1-85715-612-9

ADELPHI
GLOUCESTER MANSIONS, 140A SHAFTESBURY AVENUE LONDON WC2H 8HD

Contents

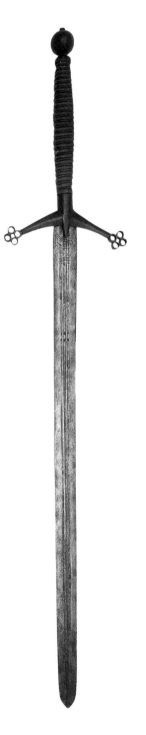

Preface

"To the southern inhabitants of Scotland," remarked Dr Samuel Johnson in the year 1773, "the state of the mountains and the islands is equally known with that of Borneo and Sumatra: of both they have heard little and guess the rest."

Dr Johnson's "Journey to the Hebrides" was a voyage of discovery. With Boswell, who in many ways, though by no means all, was a typical Lowland Scot, he was exploring what to both of them was a foreign country. On their return, like other travellers of their day, they duly wrote up their experiences, describing their adventures, the details of their journey, what they found to eat and drink, the boats they hired, the horses they rode, the beds or bales of straw they slept on, and above all their encounters and conversations with the natives – all in much the same style and tone as a contemporary might have described a journey to Timbuctoo or the North West Frontier of India.

Today you can take a package tour to Sumatra. You can likewise now travel in considerable comfort through the Highlands and Islands of Scotland, fraternise freely with the natives and, for that matter, see for yourself what is undoubtedly some of the most magnificent scenery in the world. And yet, for all that, the Highlands and even more the Islands, however easily reached, remain in many respects a world apart, still retaining much of the mystery and remoteness they possessed in Johnson's day. To grasp why this is, to gain some understanding of the Highlands you need first and foremost to know something of Highland history, a history very different from that of England or, as Dr Johnson was quick to grasp, from Lowland Scotland.

In the Highlands and perhaps even more in the Islands' history and myth, fact and legend, mingle and overlap. Hard facts are not everything. The clan bard or *senachie* was an essential, indeed in many ways the most important, member of every Chief's retinue or tail, his duty being to witness and chronicle for posterity his Chief's heroic deeds and those of his clansmen. His office was as often as not hereditary, the stories he told being repeated in much the same words from one generation to another, which lent them a century or two later all the immediacy of an eye-witness account.

More than thirty years ago, at dinner at Inveraray, I remember listening spellbound to the (for a Maclean) tragic story of the Battle of Traigh Ghruinnard, recounted, first in Gaelic and then in English, by old Donald Morrison from the Isle of Mull, himself the direct descendant of a long line of story-tellers. It was like listening to someone who

MacDonald of the Isles in his ceremonial costume. 19th-century engraving by McIan, from James Logan's "The Clans of the Scottish Highlands", 1845.

Contemporary miniature sketch and signature of Prince Charles Edward Stewart.

had himself taken part in the battle when it was fought in August 1598. He told, for instance, of the basket-loads of fingers and thumbs, cut off as the Macleans sought vainly to board the MacDonalds' oncoming war galleys (or vice versa) and picked up from the shore once the fighting was over and the swords and axes cleaned and put away. These and other grisly details he described as if he had seen them with his own eyes.

I remember, too, sitting not so long ago in the parlour of what was once MacDonald of Clanranald's house at Nunton on Benbecula, where in June 1746 the finishing touches were put by Lady Clanranald (Lady Clan, as she was known) to the gown of blue-sprigged calico which Prince Charlie was to wear in the character of Flora MacDonald's Irish maid Betty Burke, and listening to its present and extremely voluble occupant, by profession the island's undertaker, recounting how, on opening up some panelling in the stairway, he had come on a couple of rusty old swords and some faded red tunics, dating back no doubt to the Fortyfive. How they had come to be there, one could only guess – hidden away in all probability after their owners' throats had been cut. After which, over a dram, our host, drawing on his childhood memories, went on to describe how in his father's day, when he was no more than a wee boy, a mermaid had been washed up on the shore, dead, and after some debate it had been decided that she must be given a proper Christian funeral. Which was duly done, with himself looking on.

And then there is the story, which anyone will tell you, of the nondescript little house which stands just above the famous cockle strand in Eriskay, where in July 1745 Prince Charlie first set foot on Scottish soil. To this day it stands empty and seems likely to remain so, the last man who spent the night there (for a bet) having emerged from the experience stark staring mad. Just what it was that sent him mad is hard to discover. But, after much questioning, it appeared that what he had seen or thought he had seen

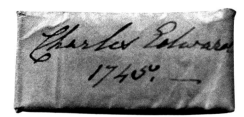

was a revelation, not of anything that had already happened, but of some entirely horrifiying event that is due to take place there at some unspecified time in the future.

But what stirred my imagination most of all was the discovery I made late one night in a deedbox of recently inherited family papers of a small, twice-folded sheet of frayed and yellowing paper bearing in faded ink the inscription "Prince Charles Edward 1745 – given to my Grandfather's care by another Jacobite gentleman who was afraid to have the portrait found on him".

The little packet was no more than a couple of inches long. What kind of portrait could it possibly contain? Carefully unfolding first one and then a second flimsy layer of paper, I came at last on two tiny representations of the Prince, a fraction of an inch square, bearing, on either side of his head, the letters "P.C." for Prince Charles. All at once I felt immensely excited. Clearly these were secret tokens carried on their person by loyal Jacobites – in the back of a watch or some such safe place – and discreetly displayed to a like-minded person, whom, rightly or wrongly, they thought they could trust.

I felt myself carried back two centuries to the anxious weeks and months before and after the Rising, when, apart from the hazards of the battlefield, any chance indiscretion could lead to hanging, drawing and quartering at Tyburn or on Tower Hill. For me it was to be the beginning of an enduring fascination with the history of the Highlands and of my own family and clan.

Of all the senachie's duties, the most important was, of course, to celebrate the heroic deeds of the Chief and his ancestors. Not only did the clan bards entertain their Chief while he was at table, "rousing his own and his followers' courage by their powerful recitations", they continued their ministrations on the actual field of battle, where they helped maintain morale, says General Stewart of Garth, by "eulogising the fame resulting from a glorious death . . . as well as the disgrace attending dastardly conduct or cowardly retreat". "It was", wrote James Logan in 1831, "not only useful to the living to extol the virtues of former heroes as an excitement to their imitation, but was reckoned extremely pleasing to the deceased – it was indeed thought the means of assisting the spirit to a state of happiness and became consequently a religious duty".

Embodying as they clearly did the essence of the clan spirit, both the bards and the Gaelic tongue became a natural target for *miorun mor nan Gall*, the Lowlander's historic detestation of the Highlander. Already in the time of King James VI and I, in the course of his deliberate Daunting of the Isles, determined efforts were made to stamp out the

John Francis Campbell, the famous folklorist, and Hector MacLean of Ballygrant, taking down a Gaelic folk tale recited by Lachlin MacNeill in 1870.

*Highlanders, drawing by
David Wilkie.*

Gaelic or, as it was called, the Irish language. And in 1695, after the so called Glorious Revolution and the Massacre of Glencoe, an act was passed for the "erecting of English Schools for rooting out the Irish language and other pious uses".

But, for all this, the ancient traditions did not die easily. In the Highlands and Islands the old tales continued to be told. "In every cluster of houses", wrote J.F. Campbell in 1860, "is some one man famed as good at *sgialachdan* (storytelling) whose house is a winter evening's resort. I visited these and listened, often with wonder at the extraordinary power of memory shown by untaught old men". In this way the Highlander's sense of history and regard for the past have been kept alive.

It is this tortuous and blood-stained history, the history in its essence of a tribal society full of devious and manifold ramifications, that I have tried to piece together and bring alive in this book. "History", remarked Henry Ford, "is bunk". And much more recently the egregious Mr Francis Fukuyama proclaimed in his turn, to my mind a trifle prematurely, "The End of History". But for Highlanders history still possesses an immediacy and a relevance which it lacks (or is thought to lack) for dwellers in most other parts of the modern world.

All the more reason, when one is as directly involved as I am, to make due allowance to aim off, as it were, for innate prejudice and try to keep sufficient balance to make one's account acceptable to readers who may well have built in prejudices and preferences of their own.

Every Highlander naturally knows something of the history of his own clan, but usually a good deal less about that of other clans, except that they were, in contrast to his own, of course, treacherous and bloodthirsty. This one-sided approach, however reassuring to the individual clansman or woman, is apt to give most of us a narrow and not very well-balanced picture of our country's past.

For my own part I was brought up from an early age on *An Account of Clan Maclean by a Senachie*, published in 1832 under the auspices of my great-great-uncle Charles. Its concluding paragraph, which runs as follows, conveys well enough its general drift and shows that the Senachie had been left in no doubt where his duty lay.

"In the preceding pages it will be observed that the Macleans (for several ages the most powerful family in the Isles) were no less celebrated for their stedfast and distinterested loyalty than for their struggles with fortune, resulting (though the fact is singular enough) from the constancy of their loyalty. Selfishness they ever despised; time-serving principles they knew not. This naturally made the selfish and the cunning their determined foes. Dissimilarity of principles made them ever be regarded with dislike by the time-serving and calculating house of Argyle; and by the circumventing wiles of that house they were at length brought to the verge of ruin. Nevertheless the descendants of Gillean still hold a high position in the land. In the service of the sovereign and in defence of the country few names even at the present day can produce more distinguished individuals than that name, once the dread of it's foes, the beloved and revered of it's friends, and the universally respected of the honourable and good – THE NAME OF MACLEAN."

Writing a hundred and sixty years later, I have tried to take a wider and more balanced look at Highland history and have found it an enlightening and rewarding experience. By considering the individual clans, not in isolation, but in relation to their neighbours and contemporaries and to what was happening at the time in Scotland as a whole, by taking as it were a synoptic view, one gains a new insight into the character and motivation of each clan and a clearer understanding of the reasons for which at any given moment they behaved as they did.

One of the charges most frequently brought against this clan or that is of treachery or disloyalty. But disloyalty to whom or to what? Seen simply as subjects of the Scottish Crown, of the House of Stewart or the House of Hanover, there are occasions when the conduct of any Clan may appear reprehensible. But this is to misunderstand the whole character of the Clan. In its essence the Highland Clan was an independent principality, a group of individuals owing loyalty to no one but their Chief, while it was the duty of the Chief, like the monarch of an independent state, to pursue whatever line of conduct corresponded most closely to the interests of his Clan.

The author Sir Fitzroy Maclean of Dunconnel, Knight of the Thistle.

Looked at in this way, Highland history takes on a different aspect. Sudden changes of front, the sudden abandonment of one ally for another, the elimination of an adversary by whatever means came to hand can all be readily explained as acts of policy dictated by more or less enlightened self-interest. While perhaps difficult to excuse morally, even the old Highland practice of setting light to a church with the congregation inside was something that any competent senachie would with a little thought be able to justify on military, political or even theological grounds.

F.M.

CHAPTER I

Origins

The Clan is in its essence a Celtic and Highland concept. For that reason this book is concerned first and foremost with the Highlands rather than the Lowlands of Scotland, though clearly, if it is to make sense, the story of the clans cannot well be separated from the main stream of Scottish history.

What do we mean by the Highlands? It is hard to define them exactly, but roughly speaking, the Highland Line or Highland Escarpment, dividing the Highlands from the Lowlands, can be said to run diagonally across Scotland from, say, Stonehaven in the East to Helensburgh in the West. To the north of this line, often not very clearly defined, the Eastern Highlands are divided from the Western by Drumalban, the Ridge of Scotland, stretching from Ben Hope in the far north by way of Ben Nevis to Ben Lomond in the South, and, over a shorter distance, by Glen Mor, the Great Glen, linking Loch Ness and Loch Linnhe with the Moray Firth. East of Drumalban rises the great mountain mass known since mediaeval times as the Mounth, comprising Badenoch, Atholl and Breadalbane and reaching from the Forest of Atholl westwards to Ben Nevis and eastwards to the coast. To the west, dramatically different from the massive uplands and more orderly coastline of the east, are the rocky peaks, the deeply indented seaboard and successive sea-lochs of the Western Highlands with, beyond them again, and, as it were, repeating them, the tangled pattern of the Western Isles.

Nor are the differences between Highlands and Lowlands, between North and South, East and West, purely a matter of geography. They are also, to a great extent, racial, social, cultural and above all temperamental. At various times during the thousand years which preceded the Christian era and in particular during the seventh century before Christ, the British Isles were overrun by a succession of warlike Celtic tribes, some say of Scythian origin, who, reaching Britain from Asia by way of the continent of Europe, in due course replaced or assimilated that country's earlier Stone and Bronze Age inhabitants of whom our knowledge is necessarily limited. The Romans, who for close on four centuries occupied the whole of England and considerable parts of Scotland or Alba, as it was then called, never penetrated any great distance into the Highlands. In 84AD, it is true, they defeated the Caledonians, which was their name for the Celts of Alba, in a savage battle at Mons Graupius, possibly the Hill of Moncreiffe in Perthshire, but shortly after that withdrew, not to return, leaving the inhabitants to their own devices.

Celtic Cross, Iona Abbey.

A Pictish stone from Invergowrie in Angus, dating from the early 10th century, depicting a warrior drinking from a horn. The eagle-head symbolises power.

With the final departure of the Romans three and a half centuries later, Britain as a whole found itself at the mercy of the Angles and Saxons, barbaric Teuton invaders from across the North Sea who, taking over most of what is now England, drove the native Celtic population back westwards into Wales and Cornwall and northwards into Scotland, in particular into the Western Highlands and Islands. There the older Celtic civilisation and Gaelic language were to survive long after England and much of Eastern and Southern Scotland had been more or less completely anglicised. By the beginning of the sixth century what we now call Scotland was divided up between four different races. Of these the most numerous were the Picts, of Celtic stock, who held sway from Caithness in the North to the Firth of Forth in the South. Another Celtic tribe, the Britons of Strathclyde, controlled from their capital at Dumbarton, literally the Fortress of the Britons, an area reaching from the Clyde to the Solway and beyond that into Cumbria. To the east, the country south of the Forth as far as Northumbria was occupied by Anglo Saxons who, like their kinsmen further south, had come originally from the lands lying between the mouth of the Rhine and the Baltic. Finally, to the west, embracing what is now Argyll and the Isles and stretching as far north as Applecross, lay the Kingdom of Dalriada, founded in the third and fourth centuries of our era by the *Scotti* or Scots, warlike Celts who had originally come there from a region of the same name in Northern Ireland.

Over the centuries the Scots in Alba retained their links with their fellow Scots – the name is said by some to have signified brigands or bandits – across the sea in Irish Dalriada. Then, in about 500 came a fresh invasion or migration from Northern Ireland, led this time by the three sons of Erc, King of Irish Dalriada, Fergus, Angus and Lorne MacErc, who under Fergus Mor MacErc now established a new Scottish dynasty taking as their capital the rock-fortress of Dunadd, rising steeply from the water-meadows, near Crinan. There to this day you may see, carved in the solid rock, the wild boar that was their heraldic and dynastic symbol and the footmarks where successive monarchs stood to be crowned.

Gold Torques, or armlets, over four thousand years old, discovered on a Highland estate in 1861 and still worn as an ornament by their present owner.

True to the tribal system they had brought with them from Ireland, the sons of Erc and their descendants divided the kingdom they had conquered between families and groups of families. These were called *tuath* or *cinel*, meaning kindred, or *clann*, meaning children. In this manner the kindred of Angus MacErc took the offshore islands of Islay and Jura as their tribal territory, while those of Lorne occupied what is now Lorne. Soon a fresh generation appeared on the scene. One son of Fergus, Comghall, established himself in the Cowal peninsula. Another, Gabran, took Knapdale and Kintyre. Later still the *Cinelbado*n or tribe of Baodan, who was one of Lorne's grandsons, made their home in Morvern. Thus, in time, the Scots of Dalriada gained possession of the entire western seaboard and islands as far north as Applecross, while eastwards their territories reached to Drumalban. To this whole region was given the name *Oirer Ghaideal* or Argyll, the Coastland of the Gael.

Though individual Christian communities had existed in Southern Scotland since Roman times, it was from Ireland that towards the middle of the sixth century the first Christian missionaries came to Dalriada. Of these the most famous and most effective was St Columba, who, establishing himself on the little offshore island of Iona, formerly a shrine of local Druids, used it as a jumping-off place for missions to the mainland and to the adjacent islands. As a prince of the royal house of Tirconaill in Ireland, descended from Niall of the Nine Hostages, High King of Ireland, when the Romans were still in Britain, Columba was of royal descent. His impact, in addition to being spiritual, was also to a high degree political. He arrived at a time when the morale of the Scots was low. Only recently they had suffered a severe defeat at the hands of the more numerous Picts and their very independence was now seriously threatened. Columba did more than preach the Gospel. In response to a divine vision, he took urgent and effective action to strengthen the monarchy, replacing the rightful, but ineffectual heir to the throne by Aidan the False, an astute and resourceful ruler. Soon, thanks to their combined efforts, the Scots were more than holding their own against their Pictish neighbours. Nor did Columba confine his activities to Dalriada alone. Penetrating by way of the Great Glen deep into northern Pictland, he successfully quelled a monster he came on by the shores of Loch Ness and dealt no less faithfully with the local Druids he encountered at the court of the Pictish King, Brude.

Interior of a chambered cairn at Nether Largie, Kilmartin, Argyll (opposite).

By the time of Columba's death in 579, Dunadd, with its symbolic rock carvings, was the capital of a firmly established independent state, while the sacred Isle of Iona had become a flourishing religious centre, whence more and more missions set forth to preach the gospel to the still benighted Angles and Picts. Before the end of the seventh century all four kingdoms of Alba had been converted to Christianity – their own kind of Christianity, for doctrinally the early Celtic Church was not always at one with Rome

These chessmen, carved from walrus ivory in the mid-13th century, probably originate from Skye. Each mail-clad figure holds a sword in his right hand and a shield over his left.

Book of Deer (9th century) from St Columba's monastery at Deer. An early example of a Gaelic manuscript. Deer was a 6th-century Celtic monastic foundation in Buchan, Aberdeenshire. The main text of the Book is in Latin. It contains the complete gospel of St John and a number of fragments from other Gospels.

and in the Highlands these divergencies, with their pagan undertones, were to persist for many more hundreds of years. Towards the end of the eighth century came the first seaborne incursions of the dreaded pagan Norsemen or Vikings, who, descending on Scotland in their longships from their bases in Scandinavia, raping, burning and massacring as they came, soon gained a foothold and then more than a foothold on the islands and on the coastal areas of the mainland. Though by this time all nominally Christian, the four Kingdoms of Alba were anything but united in the face of this fearsome new menace. Regardless of the danger that threatened all of them alike, Picts and Scots, Britons and Angles still continued to bicker vainly among themselves. Before long the Norse invaders had conquered Orkney, Shetland and the Western Isles. Caithness and Sutherland soon followed.

Silver "chapes", used to decorate the tips of sword scabbards. These formed part of a Pictish treasure buried on St Ninian's Isle in the Shetlands, dating from the 9th century. Loot such as this attracted the Norsemen time and again in raids.

Only in 843 was a greater measure of unity achieved between neighbours, when Kenneth MacAlpin, King of the Scots of Dalriada, who, through his mother, also had claims on the Pictish throne, fell upon the Picts, now weakened by the raids of the Norsemen and, having utterly defeated them, made himself King of all Scottish and Pictish territories north of the Forth, being subsequently crowned *Ard-righ Albainn*, High King of both nations, at Scone. From Dunadd Kenneth now moved his capital inland to Forteviot, at the same time shifting the religious centre of his kingdom to nearby Dunkeld, whither for good measure he now took the remains of St Columba. At Scone nearby, he and his successors were henceforth crowned on the sacred Stone of Destiny, brought there, it was said, from Tara in Ireland by Fergus MacErc. "And so," says the Huntingdon Chronicle, "he was the first of the Scots to rule over the whole of Albania, which is now called Scotia." In the north and north-west, meanwhile, the Norsemen were more firmly established than ever.

Two troubled centuries later, in 1057, Kenneth MacAlpin's direct descendant, Malcolm Ceann Mor or Bighead, ascended the Scottish throne as King Malcolm III, after first overthrowing and supplanting his predecessor Macbeth (who had killed Malcolm's father Duncan seventeen years earlier) and Macbeth's wife, Queen Gruoch.

In contrast to Shakespeare's picture of him, Macbeth, formerly King of the more or less independent Celtic Kingdom of Moray, had been an able and reasonably benevolent ruler who, on his wife's as well as on his own behalf, had at least as strong a claim to the Scottish throne as his successor. Nor was the latest change particularly beneficial in other respects. Though, like him, of Celtic stock, Macbeth's supplanter, Malcolm Ceann Mor, had been brought up in England and had, as his second wife, married Margaret, an English princess. A pious, strong-willed young woman, later to be canonized, Margaret, with the approval of her English-educated husband, at once set about introducing more and more English customs and English fashions. She also did much to Anglicise, in other words to Romanise the Scottish church, at any rate in the Lowlands. Under her influence, the centre of Scottish culture and civilisation gradually shifted away from the Celtic north and west of Scotland to the Anglo-Saxon south.

By this time the Norman Conquest of England had given Scottish history a new dimension. In 1071, five years after conquering England, William the Norman invaded Scotland in strength and at Abernethy in Perthshire forced King Malcolm to pay him homage, thus establishing a thereafter constantly exploited but also strongly contested tradition of ascendancy over his northern neighbour.

A score of years later, in 1093, Malcolm, who periodically still sought to assert his independence, was killed in a clash with the Normans and for the next thirty years Scotland was in turmoil. Malcolm's brother and successor, Donald Ban, who unlike Malcolm had grown up in the Western Isles, did something to restore his country's ancient Celtic traditions and way of life. But this did not meet with the approval of the Anglo-Normans. Soon, Donald was overthrown by a strong force from south of the Border and Malcolm and Margaret's half-English son Edgar made King in his place. For this Edgar rewarded his Anglo-Norman sponsors by encouraging large numbers of them to settle in southern Scotland, whence, with time, many were to move further north.

In 1098, following a fresh Norwegian invasion of Scotland, Edgar, a born appeaser, also came to terms with the King of Norway, Magnus Barelegs, by formally ceding to him Kintyre and the Hebrides, already largely in Norwegian hands. Even St Columba's sanctuary of Iona, for so long the burial place of

The Hunterston brooch shows the brilliance and sophistication of Celtic craftsmen. Possibly made as early as 700 AD, it is decorated with interlacing animals and spiral filligrees. It serves as a reminder of the close ties between Celtic Scotland and Ireland, where similar brooches existed.

the old Celtic kings, now became Norwegian territory, Donald Ban being the last of his dynasty to be buried there. In 1107 Edgar was succeeded as King of Scots by his brother Alexander. Leaving Argyll, Ross and Moray to the mercy of the Norsemen, Alexander only ruled over the land between the Forth and the Spey, while Scotland south of the Forth was entrusted to the care of his younger brother David, who, following Alexander's death in 1124, succeeded him as King of Scots. David's reign was to prove a period of further anglicisation. On coming to the throne, the new King, who, like his brothers, had been educated in England, and was indeed Premier Baron of that Kingdom, proceeded in his turn to distribute large estates among his Anglo-Norman friends and associates. Among these were Walter FitzAlan, his High Steward, a Breton and progenitor of the Stewarts, de Brus, progenitor of the Bruces, de Bailleul or Balliol and finally de Comines or Comyn. Like the others, Comyn had come to Scotland with King David and his descendants and, thanks to cleverly planned marriages with Celtic heiresses, had later established themselves in Buchan, Badenoch and Lochaber, becoming in due course Earls of Buchan. The first Comyn to settle in Scotland had been William de Comines, Bishop of Durham and chancellor of Scotland under David I, from whose nephew Richard were descended the Comyn Lords of Badenoch. Before long each of these families, Stewarts, Comyns, Balliols and Bruces, could claim links of kinship with the Royal House, as well as with each other. It was thus that in the Lowlands

The Brogdar Ring of standing stones on the mainland of the Orkneys is the largest in Scotland. Of its sixty original stones, twenty-seven are still standing. The stones form part of a Neolithic sacred area, and are placed with mathematical accuracy.

a new feudal system, founded on a French-speaking, Anglo-Norman aristocracy, soon took the place of the older, more patriarchal Celtic traditions and way of life.

In the Highlands, meanwhile, the old system still persisted and the King's writ counted in effect for little. Thus, in what before its conquest by the Scots had once been Northern Pictland was the still more or less autonomous Kingdom or Earldom of Moray, with boundaries to the north and west which, extending far beyond the limits of present day Morayshire and Ross-shire and marching on the west with Argyll, also comprised most of what is now Central and eastern Inverness-shire. Virtually independent of the Kingdom of Scotland, it was ruled over by its own line of Celtic Mormaers or Earls, of whom, before becoming King of all Scotland, Macbeth had been one. Over the years these native rulers stoutly defended their country against the incursions both of the Scottish Kings and of the Norse invaders from across the seas. At this time the Mormaer of Moray was Angus, a direct descendant of Queen Gruoch (in other words Lady Macbeth), through her son Lulach, and therefore as strong a claimant to the Scottish throne as any kin of Malcolm Canmore.

Here, clearly, was a potential, indeed a certain source of trouble. Nor was the trouble slow in coming, set off in this instance by a rising in Moray,

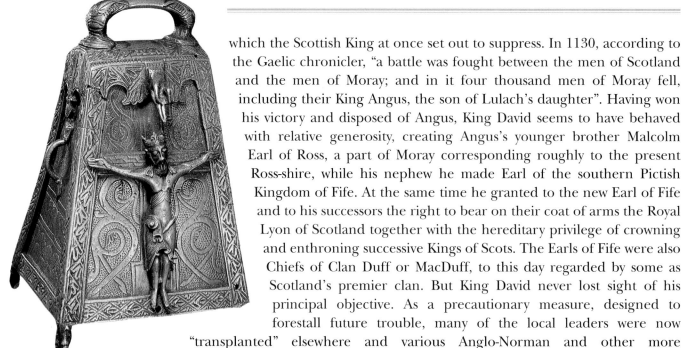

Bell shrine found at Kilmichael Glassary in Argyll, c.1814. Constructed of bronze plates it dates from the 12th century. Very little metalwork of this quality survives in Scotland from that period.

The Broch of Mousa stands on the tiny islet of Mousa just off the main island in the Shetlands. It is the finest and best preserved of all Scottish brochs – fortified homestead towers built for the purposes of defence.

which the Scottish King at once set out to suppress. In 1130, according to the Gaelic chronicler, "a battle was fought between the men of Scotland and the men of Moray; and in it four thousand men of Moray fell, including their King Angus, the son of Lulach's daughter". Having won his victory and disposed of Angus, King David seems to have behaved with relative generosity, creating Angus's younger brother Malcolm Earl of Ross, a part of Moray corresponding roughly to the present Ross-shire, while his nephew he made Earl of the southern Pictish Kingdom of Fife. At the same time he granted to the new Earl of Fife and to his successors the right to bear on their coat of arms the Royal Lyon of Scotland together with the hereditary privilege of crowning and enthroning successive Kings of Scots. The Earls of Fife were also Chiefs of Clan Duff or MacDuff, to this day regarded by some as Scotland's premier clan. But King David never lost sight of his principal objective. As a precautionary measure, designed to forestall future trouble, many of the local leaders were now "transplanted" elsewhere and various Anglo-Norman and other more dependable incomers settled in Moray in their place.

King David I died in 1153 and, his son Henry having predeceased him, was succeeded as King of Scots by his grandson Malcolm, a boy of twelve, to be known as Malcolm IV or Malcolm the Maiden. Taking advantage of this tempting opportunity, the Celts of Moray now rose once more against the Scottish Crown in support of a claimant of their own choosing and it was a full three years before they could be quelled and further dependable incomers settled in Moray.

In their latest rebellion against the Crown the men of Moray had for a time enjoyed the support of an ally from the West, the part-Celt, part-Norse Somhairle or Somerled, King, as he styled himself, of Morvern, Lochaber, Argyll and the Southern Hebrides, who, like them, was always ready to demonstrate his independence of the Scottish royal house. Although in 1140 Somerled had married Ragnhild, daughter of the Norse King Olaf of Man, neither this, nor his own Norse blood nor, for that

Pictish incised stone carvings are simple and effective. This bull comes from Burghead, Morayshire (6th–8th century).

matter, his theoretical allegiance to the King of Norway prevented him from resisting Norse encroachment or prosecuting his own dynastic interests to the maximum of his ability. Having successfully driven the Norsemen out of Lochaber, Morvern and Northern Argyll and made himself ruler of the whole area, Somerled, after giving such help as he could to the men of Moray, now left his eastern allies to fend for themselves and, turning once more on the Norsemen, in 1156 decisively defeated his wife Ragnhild's brother Godfred, by this time King of Man, in a great sea-battle off the island of Islay in the Inner Hebrides. Nor in the years that followed did he show any greater respect for Malcolm King of Scots, but, sailing boldly up the Firth of Clyde, seized the strategically situated isles of Arran and Bute and in 1164 put the city of Glasgow to the sack.

For Somerled, however, this was to be the end of the road. At Renfrew, where he encountered in battle a royal army led by Walter Fitzalan, Hereditary High Steward of Scotland, his caterans were overwhelmingly defeated and he himself killed – stabbed, some said, by a traitor in his tent. To this day the event is commemorated by Barochan Cross, an ancient stone cross which stands near the site of the battle.

Following Somerled's death, his considerable dominions were divided between his sons. From his eldest son, Dugald, heir to Lorne, Morvern and Ardnamurchan, sprang the MacDougall Lords of Lorne, whose strategically sited castles of Dunollie and Dunstaffnage effectively commanded the Firth of Lorne. From his younger son, Ranald, or rather from Ranald's son Donald, who inherited Islay, the adjoining islands and part of Kintyre, sprang Clan Donald, the MacDonalds of Islay, later to assume the proud title of Lords of the Isles, while to Donald's younger brother Roderick or Ruari and his offspring, the MacRuaris, went Arran, Bute and further north the coastal area of Garmoran, including Morvern, Moidart and Knoydart. Such were the origins of two great West Highland clans, though in accordance with the general practice of the time neither MacDonald nor MacDougall was used as a surname until much later. As for the MacRuaris, following the marriage a couple of centuries later of the MacRuari heiress Amy to John MacDonald of the Isles, their inheritance was in the end added to that of Clan Donald.

Malcolm IV of Scotland died young. He was succeeded in 1165 by his livelier and more enterprising brother, William the Lion, who on coming to the throne, at once concluded a formal alliance with France, to be known as the Auld Alliance. After a stormy start he also managed in the end to establish a more stable relationship with England. It was to be the beginning of a hundred years of relative peace between the two countries.

For centuries the Western Isles had been disputed territory. But by now the years of Norse invasion and encroachment were coming to an end. Soon after his accession to the Scottish throne in 1249 William the Lion's grandson Alexander III launched a series of raids against the Norse-held Hebrides. In retaliation, King Hakon of Norway set sail for Scotland in the summer of 1263 with a mighty armada. By cleverly opening negotiations with the enemy, the Scottish King managed to delay an encounter until October of that year, when, as he had hoped might happen, a sudden autumn gale caught Hakon's fleet where it lay at anchor in the Firth of Clyde and played havoc with it. Having with difficulty fought their way ashore at Largs on the Firth of Clyde, the Norwegians were now defeated on land as well as at sea and withdrew in confusion. Old King Hakon died on his way back to Norway at Kirkwall in the Orkneys and not long after his son Magnus signed a treaty of peace under which the Inner and Outer Hebrides became part of Scotland, though Orkney and Shetland were to continue in Norwegian hands for another two hundred years. In practice, however, the Hebrides and large areas of the adjoining mainland remained for many years to come autonomous principalities, ruled over by the MacDougalls of Lorne and the MacDonalds of Islay, who paid no more heed to their Scottish than they formerly had to their Norwegian overlords.

Silver plaques incised with Pictish symbols, dating from the 7th century. These were found 200 years ago at Norrie's Law, Fife.

CHAPTER II

Robert The Bruce and Bannockburn

It is now, in the second half of the thirteenth century, that we first find firm evidence of the emergence in the Western Highlands of a number of other clans, each with its own part-historical, part-mythical background and traditions and descended for the most part from the Scots of Dalriada or, in some cases, from the Norse invaders. On the mainland south of the Kyle of Lochalsh, were the Macleods, of mainly Norse origin, claiming to descend through their name-father, Leod, from Magnus, the last King of Man; in Kintail the O'Beolan Earls of Ross and their vassals the Mackenzies; on the isles of Gigha and, later, of Barra and Colonsay, the MacNeils, springing probably from Hy Nial, an ancient race of Irish kings; in Cowal the MacLachlans, whose forebear Lachlan Mor was already living at Castle Lachlan on Loch Fyne in the thirteenth century, and the Lamonts, both springing from the same long line of Irish kings as the MacNeils. Further north, in Glen Orchy, were the MacGregors; to the west, in Morvern and Mull, the Macleans, descended from Gillean of the Battle Axe, a hero of the Battle of Largs, and, through him and Cinelbadom, from the old Kings of Dalriada; and between Loch Fyne and Lochawe, Clan Nechtan, the MacNaughtons. Last but by no means least, Clan Diarmid, the Campbells, likewise claiming descent from a succession of Irish and Dalriadic Kings and heroes, notably from Diarmid O'Duibhne, slayer of the Great Boar of Caledon, were by the latter part of the thirteenth century firmly established on Lochaweside. From his island stronghold of Innischonnaill or Inchconnell their Chief Cailean Mor, Colin the Great, was already effectively dominating Lochawe and its surroundings in the very heart of Argyll. It is from Great Colin, who was to meet his death in 1294 in a fight with the MacDougalls of Lorne and lies buried at nearby Kilchrenan, that subsequent Campbell Chiefs take their resounding patronymic, MacCailean Mor.

By the late thirteenth century, following the battle of Largs, the Norse threat to Scotland had receded and the English menace became paramount. And it was now, in 1286, that the death of King Alexander III plunged Scotland into sudden turmoil. Alexander's heir apparent was his grandchild Margaret, the infant daughter of the King of Norway. Margaret, it had been agreed, would eventually marry the heir to the English throne and so unite the crowns of the two countries. But before she could reach Scotland little Margaret had died, of seasickness, it was said, and with her death the old Celtic line of Kings came to a sudden end, leaving the succession open to half a

A 15th-century drawing with Stirling and its castle in the background, showing the encounter between the English Knight Sir Henry de Bohun and Robert the Bruce, King of Scots, before the Battle of Bannockburn.

Tomb slab from Iona. Effigy of an armed warrior known as Macquarie.

dozen candidates, all connected by kinship or marriage with the Royal house. Of these, the two strongest claimants to the throne were Robert Bruce and John Balliol, both nobles of Anglo-Norman origin, whose forebears had first come to Scotland a century or two earlier and who still possessed large estates in England and France as well as in Scotland. The rivalries of these and other claimants offered a clear opening to King Edward I of England, a formidable, ruthless man, whose declared purpose it was, by one means or another, to bring Scotland under his sway. Invited to come to Scotland to keep the peace and help choose a King, Edward awarded the throne to Balliol in the belief that he would prove more amenable than Bruce. But even Balliol rejected the terms Edward sought to impose on him and early in 1296, after repudiating his allegiance to the English crown and concluding with England's old enemy France an allegiance which was to endure for close on three hundred years, advanced into England.

Two days later Edward invaded Scotland in strength. During the wars that followed Robert Bruce's grandson, also Robert, soon emerged as the main Scottish leader, with a strong claim to the throne. On Palm Sunday 1306 Bruce took a bold initiative. He raised the Royal Standard at Scone and there, in the presence of three bishops, St Andrews, Glasgow and Moray, caused himself to be crowned King of Scots. Edward at once responded to Bruce's act of defiance by sending against him a strong army which soundly defeated him at Methven and scattered his allies far and wide. Though Edward hanged three of Bruce's brothers and many of his leading supporters, the

On the dramatic rock of Dunadd in Argyll, the Scots established their capital of Dalriada amidst hostile Picts in AD 500. An important fortress since the Iron Age, it became the birthplace of the modern Scottish nation. The single carved footprint in the rock is associated with the inaugural ceremonies of the Kings of Dalriada.

The charter of Kelso Abbey bears portraits in miniature of its founder, David I (1124–53), and his heir and grandson, Malcolm (1153–65).

17

new Scottish king was not dismayed. He rallied his forces and fought on, gradually turning the tide of Edward's power.

By the beginning of 1309 Bruce already controlled most of Scotland north of the Forth and Clyde. In 1311, after the Pope had yet again excommunicated him, he invaded Northern England, sacking Durham and Hartlepool, and during the three years that followed drove the English garrisons from Perth, Dundee, Dumfries, Roxburgh and Edinburgh. Only the great stronghold of Stirling strategically poised between Highlands and Lowlands, still remained in English hands. Edward now felt bound to bestir himself. Marching with a strong force to the relief of Stirling, he found Bruce waiting for him.

On 24 June 1314 the two armies met by the nearby Bannock Burn. Battle was joined at sunrise. "Now's the time and now's the hour," remarked Sir Alexander Seton, a canny Scottish knight who after a prolonged period of collaboration with the English, had chosen that moment to join Bruce. By midday the English, outmanoeuvred by the more mobile Scots, were in full flight. Among the English dead lay the Red

A Pictish reliquary of the 8th century, thought to have held the relics of St Columba. William the Lion (1165–1214) gave the casket to the monks of Arbroath, whose abbot carried it to the battle of Bannockburn in 1314. Soon after, the Grants of Monymusk in Aberdeenshire became its hereditary keepers, hence its name the Monymusk reliquary.

Castle Sween, probably the earliest stone castle in Scotland; built c.1200, when the area west of Kintyre was under Norse rule. It was held by the MacNeils of Gigha for the Macdonalds until 1481.

Comyn's only son, killed fighting for his country's enemies against his father's murderer. After Bannockburn the war dragged on in a desultory manner for another fourteen years. But the English had by now lost the will to win and in 1328 a treaty of peace was signed, formally recognising Scotland as an independent Kingdom and Robert the Bruce as King Robert I.

As we have seen, serving in Bruce's army were the chiefs of several of the great Highland clans, while others fought for the English, as their interests and loyalties demanded. Long before his victory at Bannockburn Bruce had begun to reward his allies at the expense of those who had sided against him, notably the Comyns and their MacDougall kinsmen. The Comyns having by this time been driven from Buchan, Badenoch and Lochaber, the remainder of their lands, including their castle of Slains on the coast of Buchan, were now allocated to Sir Gilbert Hay, a nobleman of Norman descent, who was at the same time rewarded for his support of Bruce with the office of hereditary High Constable of Scotland, still held to this day by his descendant Lord Errol, the present Chief of Clan Hay. After their defeat by Bruce and the Black Douglas in the Pass of Brander, the MacDougalls had been deprived of the Lordship of Lorne and

Scotland's first gold coin, David II's noble, was struck in 1357.

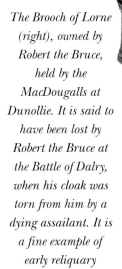

St Fillan's bronze and silver crozier, 8th century (right).

The Brooch of Lorne (right), owned by Robert the Bruce, held by the MacDougalls at Dunollie. It is said to have been lost by Robert the Bruce at the Battle of Dalry, when his cloak was torn from him by a dying assailant. It is a fine example of early reliquary brooches.

of their great stronghold of Dunstaffnage on the Firth of Lorne. This Bruce bestowed instead on the Campbells, who, having once joined him, had supported him loyally and whose Chief Neil had married his sister Mary. For the time being Dunstaffnage was placed under the constabulary of Sir Arthur Campbell of Strachur, becoming Campbell property in 1470.

Meanwhile, the Mac-Dougalls though evicted from Dunstaffnage and a number of their other possessions, nevertheless managed to retain their other castle of Dunolly likewise looking out across the Firth of Lorne, where their Chief still resides today in a castle built in the fifteenth century.

Moreover, after their Seventh Chief had married Bruce's grand-daughter, the Lordship of Lorne was also restored to them by Bruce's son King David II, later, however, passing by marriage to the Stewarts and from them to the Campbells.

Robert the Bruce died in 1329, possibly of leprosy, which to his dying day he firmly believed himself to have been stricken with as divine retribution for having slain the Red Comyn. In twenty years this Anglo-Norman noble had given the people of Scotland a new sense of nationhood. But much of what he had achieved was undone during the years of tumult that followed his death.

Bruce's five year old son having duly succeeded him as King David II, the Regency was now assumed by his nephew and former comrade at arms, Thomas Randolph, Earl of Moray. Three years later, in August 1332, a number of disgruntled Scottish nobles, disinherited by Bruce and led by old John Balliol's son Edward, now in his turn a claimant to the throne, landed with English encouragement in Fife.

Thence they marched on Perth. Moray advanced to meet them, but died before battle was joined and the Regency passed to another of Bruce's nephews, Donald Earl of Mar. But at Dupplin Moor in Perthshire Mar was defeated and killed; the invaders took Perth; and Edward Balliol, after being crowned King of Scots at Scone, immediately offered Berwickshire to his English benefactors. Before he could do anything else, however, a number of his angry subjects, led by Good Sir James Douglas's brother Archibald, promptly chased him across the border hastily arrayed in his shirt and one boot. The situation clearly invited English intervention. In the summer of 1333, King Edward III of England, who had succeeded his ineffectual father six years earlier, marched on Berwick in strength, dispersed a fleet sent by Scotland's ally France to relieve it, and crushingly defeated the Scots at Halidon Hill. Not for the first time, a number of Scottish nobles, from the Highlands as well as from the Lowlands, chose now to change sides, notably Angus Og's son, Good John MacDonald of Islay. The Lowlands were easily overrun and garrisoned by the English while Edward Balliol readily recognised the English King as Lord Paramount.

In this disturbing situation little King David II was sent to France for safety and Bruce's seventeen year old grandson Robert Stewart formally appointed regent. Robert Stewart now rallied such resistance as he could. In 1339, with French help, he took

Dunstaffnage Castle, Argyll, built by the MacDougalls of Lorn and captured by Bruce in 1309.

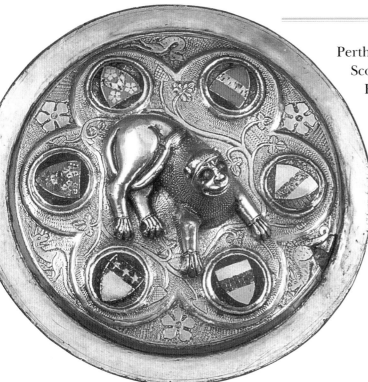

Perth. The following year he cleared Scotland of the English north of the Forth and in 1341 felt able to call his fat young uncle David back from France.

The English by this time heavily involved in their Hundred Years War with France, already had their hands full. Stirling and Edinburgh were recaptured and for a space the Scots enjoyed a badly needed respite. But, hard pressed at Crécy in 1346, the French called on their Scottish allies for a diversion and King

The Horn of Leys (opposite) was presented to Alexander Burnard or Burnett by Robert the Bruce.

Lid of the Bute or Bannatyne mazer or communal drinking cup (left).

Robert the Bruce from the 16th-century Seton Armorial (below).

David, who had none of his father's military qualities, set out with an army to invade England, where he was heavily defeated and himself taken prisoner at Neville's Cross.

David, who as it happened enjoyed life in England, spent the next twelve years there as a prisoner at the court of King Edward III, while Robert Stewart again undertook the Regency and the war dragged out its desultory course. In 1357, however, King Edward III, having defeated the French at Poitiers, offered the Scots a truce, pensioned off Edward Balliol and sent King David back to Scotland in return for a crippling ransom, thus imposing a heavy burden on the Scottish Exchequer. Unpopular with his own people, and perpetually intent on ingratiating himself with the English, David reigned for another fourteen years, dying without a direct heir in 1371. On his death, he was succeeded as King by his nephew the former Regent, Robert Stewart, the son of his sister Marjory and of Walter Fitzalan, 6th Hereditary High Steward of Scotland, a nobleman of Breton origin, who, as Walter the Steward or Walter Stewart, thus gave his name to the new dynasty which now ascended the Scottish throne.

CHAPTER III

The Emergence of
the Western Clans

In the years that followed Bannockburn the Highland clans began to assume what was to be their ultimate character, each, according to its circumstances, developing in its own way and after its own individual fashion. Clan Campbell, for example, whose Chief, Neil, had married Bruce's sister Mary, had by this time already achieved a position of considerable strength on Lochaweside and were well placed to extend their influence still further. In common with Bruce's other allies they had been generously rewarded for their services to him by grants of land previously held by the Comyns, the MacDougalls and other of his enemies. To Sir Neil of Lochawe and Mary, his spouse, and to their son John, went many of the lands in Perthshire which had formerly belonged to David, Earl of Atholl whose title was now bestowed on John Campbell. Neil was later appointed Constable of the Royal Castle of Dunoon on the Clyde in Cowal, while another charter made over to Arthur Campbell the lands of Torrinturk in Lorne "with many others". Further south, Sir Duncan Campbell, a grandson of Cailein Mor, obtained by his marriage to Susanna Crawford of Loudon, the rich lands of Loudon and Stevenston in green, fertile Ayrshire on the Firth of Clyde, which, later becoming the heritage of the future Campbell Earls of Loudon, gave Clan Dairmid a foothold in the Lowlands (Menstri had been in Campbell hands since 1263). To Ivar Campbell went in 1334 Rosneath, likewise pleasantly situated on the banks of the River Clyde. On succeeding his father Neil as Chief, Colin Oig was duly confirmed in his ownership of the Campbell heartland of Lochawe. Colin's son Archibald, who succeeded him in 1343, was, in his turn, given still more forfeited lands as a reward for his loyalty to David II. Less than half a century after Bannockburn the Campbells were already a force to be reckoned with.

Clan Donald for their part had benefited to an even greater extent from their loyalty to Robert Bruce. After the death of his rather less loyal elder brother Alexander, Angus Og MacDonald of Islay, now Chief of Clan Donald, had been awarded Morvern and Ardnamurchan, the islands of Mull, Coll, Tiree and part of the former Comyn lands in Lochaber, being at the same time confirmed in the possession of his existing territories of Islay, Jura, Gigha and Colonsay. Under Bruce's successors, the MacDonalds continued to add to their possessions. In 1343, to regain his wavering loyalty, David II made a grant of the Isle of Lewis to Angus Og's son and successor Good John of Islay, who ten years earlier had briefly sided with Edward Balliol. In 1346, John inherited

Kisimul Castle – the picturesque yet impenetrable stronghold of the MacNeills of Barra. Cut into rock alongside the castle is the berth for the famous "Kisimul's Gallery", featured in Gaelic song. The Great Hall has a peat-burning central hearth of a type dating back to Viking times, with no chimney, so the smoke must find its own way out. The castle is still inhabited by the present chief.

*St Martin's Cross, Iona,
early 9th century.*

*Iona Cathedral
(St Mary's Abbey).
Somerled's son Ranald,
Lord of the Isles,
established a Benedictine
Community on Iona in
about 1200. The Abbey
Church, dedicated to the
Virgin Mary, was
extended over the
centuries and became the
Cathedral of the Bishops
of the Isles in 1507.*

through his wife Amy, heiress of his cousins the MacRuaris, descendants of Somerled's grandson Ruari or Roderick, the remainder of Lochaber, Garmoran and, in the Outer Hebrides, the islands of North and South Uist, Benbecula, Eigg and Rum. Next, having in 1354 discarded Amy (but kept her inheritance) and shrewdly married Margaret, daughter of the future King Robert II, Good John, so known, we are told, on account of his piety, assumed the lofty title of *Dominus Insularum*, Lord of the Isles or King of the Hebrides, subsequently adding Kintyre and half of the former MacSween territory in Knapdale to his already extensive dominions.

His father's marriage to Margaret Stewart having given him a close and advantageous connection with the Scottish Royal family, John's son, Donald, who succeeded him in 1380 as Second Lord of the Isles, soon made an equally clever marriage, taking as his wife Mary, sister of Alexander Earl of Ross, the possessor of vast domains in the north. Meanwhile to Ranald, his son by Amy, Good John had left the whole of her very considerable inheritance, to be held by him as a vassal of his younger half-brother Donald. While the Lordship of the Isles continued in what now became the senior branch, from Ranald were to spring two important branches of Clan Donald, namely Clanranald and its younger branch, the MacDonells of Glengarry. Donald's younger brother Iain Mor, the Tanist, married the heiress of the Bissets of the Glens of Antrim. From their union sprang Clan Donald South, the MacDonalds of Islay and Kintyre, as well as the McDonnell Earls of Antrim, while from another brother, Alasdair Carrach, came the Macdonells of Keppoch.

Other clans in their turn benefited from their links with the MacDonalds. Even before the days of Angus Og MacDonald of Islay, Clan Gillean, the Macleans, already long established in Morvern and Mull, had enjoyed close family and other connections with Clan Donald. Fighting at Bannockburn under their Chief Malcolm, they had,

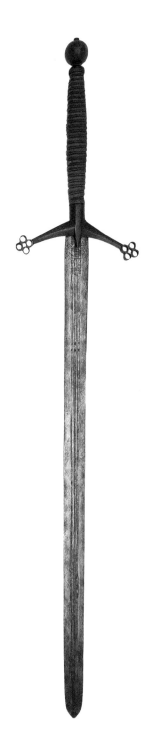

Double-handed sword or claymore, said to have belonged to William Wallace, hero of the Scottish Wars of Independence at the end of the 13th century.

with Angus Og, supported Bruce, and with him had reaped their reward. In 1366 Lachlan Lubanach, Lachlan the Wily, reckoned Fifth Chief from Gillean of the Battle-Axe, name-father of the Clan, had married Good John's daughter Mairi. As her dowry, Mairi brought with her much of Mull and a number of the nearby islands, thus helping to make the Macleans, those "Spartans of the North" as they have been called, a formidable sea-power in their own right. As his principal stronghold Lachlan Lubanach picked the mighty fortress of Duart, the Black Headland, standing high on its crag above the Sound of Mull. At the same time Lachlan was appointed High Admiral and Lieutenant-General of the Kingdom of the Isles, a position of no little authority.

Lachlan Lubanach had won Mairi's hand and all that went with it by what Skene has called "one of the most daring actions ever recorded of any Highland chief", namely by carrying off Good John of the Isles in the latter's own galleon, holding him a prisoner on the precipitous and strongly fortified island of Dunconnel in the Isles of the Sea and refusing to let him go again until he had agreed to accept him as his son-in-law and bestow on him the lands and honours due to a chief of his standing. After which, to make doubly sure, he escorted his future father-in-law to Iona and there caused him to repeat his previous undertakings, while seated on that island's sacred Black Stone, (thus called, not so much because of its colour, but because of the black doom which overtook those who went back on their given word).

But Good John seems to have borne his son-in-law no ill will for his rough and ready approach. On the contrary, the transaction thus concluded marked the beginning of almost two centuries of friendship between the two clans and their respective chiefs. To Lachlan Lubanach Maclean's younger brother Euchunn or Hector, who had helped kidnap him, Good John now gave Lochbuidhe on the southern coast of Mull, while on the mainland his grandson Alexander, Third of the Isles, later bestowed the lands of Ardgour on Loch Linnhe on Donald, son of Lachlan Bronnach of Duart, and the Isle of Coll on another of his sons, Iain Garbh. From Hector of Lochbuidhe's son Tearlach or Charles sprang the Macleans of Dochgarroch in Inverness-shire, to be known as the Macleans of the North. More than six hundred years later, not only the mighty fortress of Duart and the lands of Ardgour, but also the rocky stronghold of Dunconnel are, after various vicissitudes, all safely in Maclean hands.

Many of the lands held by the Macleans in the north of Mull had previously belonged to Clan Fingon, the Mackinnons, as to whose loyalty the Lords of the Isles had in the course of the 14th century come to entertain serious doubts. A prominent and rather equivocal part in the events leading up to this change of ownership seems to have been played by the Mackinnon Chief's brother Fingon. Known as the Green Abbot and described by the Chroniclers of the Isles as "a subtle and wicked councillor", Fingon appears to have encouraged his brother and Chief, Niall MacGillebride Mackinnon, to plot against the Lordship. Though in its essence political, the intrigue also had ecclesiastical overtones. Like their neighbours the Macleans, the Mackinnons quartered in their arms a hand bearing a cross, indicating that they were of the Kin of Saint Columba. This gave them considerable standing in church affairs. In 1358 Fingon had been made (or had made himself) Mitred Abbot of Iona in the teeth of active opposition from the Vatican and from the Lords of the Isles, who would both have

LORD OF ÞE ILLIS

preferred to see monks of the Benedictine order installed in Iona. The Green Abbot, for his part, chose to follow the precepts of the old Celtic church which, unlike the more orthodox Benedictines, sanctioned, amongst other things, married clergy. Indeed he himself had in his time fathered a number of children by "the lady of his choice". And so it befell that in the end Niall Mackinnon was done to death by the Macleans, always ready to demonstrate their loyalty to the House of the Isles, more especially when it also brought them substantial territorial advantage.

Thereafter the Mackinnons, having lost much of their lands in Mull to the Macleans, moved to Skye, though still retaining Mishnish and their castle of Dunara in Mull. As for the Green Abbot he stuck to his guns and some forty years later, in 1397, was confirmed by the Pope as Mitred Abbot of Iona. We learn, too, that in 1426 one of his many grandsons, Fyngonius Fyngonii, having acquired a concubine ("with her mother's full consent") managed to infiltrate himself into the Iona monastery, where he "proceeded to lay violent hands on the goods of the said monastery", including some forty cows which he generously made over to his mistress.

With the growing power of the Lords of the Isles, ever more Western clans drifted or were brought under their hegemony, among them the Mackenzies. Like their neighbours and kinsmen the O'Beolan Earls of Ross, Clan Kenneth claimed descent from a local 12th century Celtic potentate known as *Gilleoin na h'Airde* or Gilleoin of the Aird, himself descended, or so it was said, from the ancient royal house of Lorne, forebears likewise of the Celtic Kings of Moray. By 1267, the founder and name-father of the clan, Coinneach or Kenneth, literally the Bright One, was already firmly established in Kintail in his stronghold of Eilean Donan at the mouth of Loch Duich. The Mackenzies were at this time vassals of the Earls of Ross. But though the Earl of the day was no friend of Robert the Bruce, this had not prevented Kenneth's son John from giving the royal fugitive shelter when pursued by his enemies – a generous gesture which, in the long run, was to bring great benefits to Clan Kenneth.

Kintail, across the water from Skye, where the Seven Sisters look down on Loch Duich, was the Mackenzies' heartland. Thence they were over the years to reach out northwards up the coast as far as

Ranald (top left), founder of Clan Ranald, eldest surviving son of Eoin MacDonald, Lord of the Isles, by his first marriage to Amy MacRuari. Died at Eilean Tioram Castle in 1386 and was buried in Iona.

Arms of the Lords of the Isles (above) about 1623.

Bricius MacKinnon, effigy from Iona Abbey Museum, from the 14th century.

The charm stone of the family of Stewart of Ardshiel (above) and the Glenorchy stone (below). Charm stones were credited with magical healing powers.

Andrew Macpherson of Cluny, 17th century, by Richard Waitt (opposite). The tartans of the jacket, plaid and trews are all different.

Coigach and Ullapool, westwards to the Isle of Lewis in the Outer Hebrides and, later still, eastwards right across Scotland to the rich shores of the Cromarty Firth. Meanwhile, with the eventual transfer of the Earldom of Ross from the O'Beolans to the MacDonalds, the Mackenzies found themselves vassals of the Lords of the Isles.

Among other vassals of the MacDonalds were the MacLeods, who proudly claimed descent from Liotr, a younger son of Olaf the Black, Norse King of Man and the Northern Isles from 1187 to 1237, but who, from the Nordic beginnings, were, in the words of their clan historian, eventually to be "absorbed into Gaeldom". From their original clan lands on the mainland, south of the Kyle of Lochalsh, they were later to move to Skye and to the Outer Isles.

At about the same time, the MacNeils, whose main stronghold had by this time become the great castle of Kisimul on Barra in the Outer Hebrides, likewise came to be vassals of the MacDonalds from whom Gilleonan MacNeil received a charter of Barra in 1427. After this MacNeil of Barra was generally recognised as Chief of his Clan and in 1495, after the downfall of the Lords of the Isles, received a further Charter from the Scottish Crown, confirming him in his possession of Barra and his neighbouring territories. The MacNeil Chiefs had, for their part, a proper sense of their own importance. Once MacNeil had dined it was the custom for a herald to make the following proclamation: "Hear all ye people and hark all ye nations! The great MacNeil of Barra having finished his dinner, the Princes of the earth may now dine." A century later the MacNeil Chief was Ruari Og, described by a contemporary as "a Scot that usually maketh his summer's course to steal what he can", and who in 1591, jointly with the Macleans, led a famous and extremely successful raid on County Mayo in Ireland. His successor, known as Ruari the Tartar and described as "an hereditary outlaw", carried on in the same tradition. Nor was Ruari's private life any less reprehensible. Having had several sons by Maclean of Duart's sister, he simply discarded her and married the Captain of Clanranald's sister by whom he had several more sons. This was asking for trouble. In 1610 the conflict which not unnaturally broke out between his two groups of sons was brought to a head, when Duart's nephews, armed with "weapons invasive", seized the old Chief's stronghold of Kisimul Castle, chained up their father and half-brothers and installed their eldest brother Neil Og as Chief.

It was Neil Og who made Barra the staunchly Roman Catholic island which it still remains today. In 1652 Father Duggan, a Catholic Missionary reported back as follows to his ecclesiastical superiors: "MacNeill, Laird of the Island of Barra, having heard of me, sent a gentleman to beg me to do his island the same service as I had done for the Laird of Clanranald." Eighteen months later he wrote in a further report of the Barra people he had baptised: "Amongst these were some troubled and annoyed by ghosts or evil spirits, who were completely delivered from them after Baptism and never saw them again." But, whether Catholics or Protestants, the MacNeils still continued to show the same "hie and proud contempt" for convention and indeed for the central government.

Other MacDonald vassals were the progenitors of Clan Cameron, who by the fourteenth century had already gained a foothold in Lochaber.

There they were soon at odds with their neighbours the MacKintoshes, contesting the latters' claim to Glen Loy and Loch Arkaig and as early as 1370 raiding Badenoch, by now cleared of Comyns. The Cameron Chief at the beginning of the fifteenth century was the great warrior *Domnhuill Dubh* or Black Donald, from whom his successors were to take their patronymic *MacDomnhuill Duibh* and whose famous *pibroch* was to serve as a march both for the Clan and much later for the Queen's Own Cameron Highlanders. From the Gaelic *Camshron* or Wry-nose was to come, it is said, the name Cameron.

In the north-eastern Highlands Bruce had found no more loyal supporter than Angus, 6th Chief of Clan MacKintosh. The MacKintosh chiefs had been established in the former Kingdom of Moray since very early times. Purely Celtic by origin, they traced their descent from one Shaw Macduff, the founder and name-father of their clan, and through him from the royal Earls of Fife. For helping King Malcolm IV defeat the men of Moray in 1163 Shaw had been made Keeper of the Royal Castle of Inverness and rewarded with grants of land nearby, notably the lands of Strathdearn and Petty, which have remained the Clan's *duthus* or heartland ever since. From Shaw they took the name of Mackintosh, derived from the Gaelic *Mac-an-Toisich*, son of the Chief or Thane.

In 1291 Shaw's descendant Angus, Sixth Chief of the Mackintoshes, married Eva, daughter and heiress of the Sixth Captain or Chief of Clan Chattan in Lochaber, whose successor he accordingly became. Clan Chattan, signifying in Gaelic the Children of the Cat, was a confederation of neighbouring clans, held together by ties of kinship and by an urgent and enduring need for mutual defence. Eva's forebears claimed descent from Gillechattan Mor, a shadowy figure, whose name they variously interpreted as meaning the Servant or Son of Saint Chattan, or of the Cat, and who may in some way have been connected with the ancient Priory of Ardchattan on Loch Etive in Argyll, latterly in Campbell hands. The Chiefs or Captains of Clan Chattan also owned lands in Glenloy and near Loch Arkaig, to the West of the Great Glen, which were claimed and partly occupied by the Camerons, with whom they were consequently at feud. As well as the Mackintoshes, other neighbouring clans belonging to Clan Chattan, largely for geopolitical reasons, were: the Macleans of Dochgarroch, who from Argyll had made their way to Inverness-shire; the MacQueens; and the Macphersons of Cluny, who, claiming to be even more directly descended from Gillechattan Mor than the Mackintoshes themselves,

Dunollie Castle, Argyll, stronghold of the MacDougalls. Inherited by King Dougall in 1164, it is today owned by his descendants. The castle was besieged in 1646, and again in 1715, as the MacDougalls were Royalists and Jacobites.

periodically disputed the latters' leadership of the confederation. On the death of the 28th Chief of Clan Mackintosh and Captain of Clan Chattan in 1938, the Captaincy of Clan Chattan passed first to his grand-daughter Arbell and then in 1942 to his cousin Duncan Alexander Mackintosh of Torcastle and to the latter's heirs, while the Mackintosh Chiefship went to his kinsman Admiral Lachlan Mackintosh.

During the first dozen years of the fourteenth century, when Robert the Bruce was contending with the Comyns and his other enemies, Angus, sixth Chief of Clan Mackintosh had, despite his family links with the Comyns, given him all possible help, fighting for him at Bannockburn and throughout the War of Independence. For this he was rewarded in 1319 by the grant of large parts of former Comyn territory in Badenoch. It was thus that by the end of the Middle Ages the Mackintoshes, with the backing of the rest of Clan Chattan, held sway over an area reaching from Strathnairn through Badenoch as far as Deeside. By 1345 William Mackintosh, who in that year succeeded his father Angus as 7th Chief, had acquired from the Bishop of Moray the Barony of Moy, near Inverness, where his descendant, the Thirtieth Chief, Commander Lachlan Mackintosh, still lives today.

William had also been confirmed in his right to the lands of Glenloy and Loch Arkaig, by this time however firmly occupied by the Camerons. This was the beginning of a feud with Clan Cameron which was to last for the next three hundred years, one famous episode in it being a set battle fought in 1396 on the North Inch in Perth by thirty champions from the two clans in the presence of King Robert III at a total cost to the Exchequer of fourteen pounds two shillings and elevenpence. This historic and not unduly costly encounter proved, it is said, an overwhelming victory for Clan Chattan, who suffered only one casualty, while their adversaries were, for their part, left with a single survivor, who in the end only escaped annihilation by successfully swimming the river Tay.* After his father's death William also secured from the Bishop of Moray a fresh lease of Rothiemurchus, which in the long run was to prove yet another bone of contention, being likewise claimed by the neighbouring Grants, an Anglo-Norman clan already established in Inverness-shire for the past century or more.

* There is, it appears, some doubt as to the identity of the contestants, some authorities claiming that they were in fact not the Camerons, but the Comyns and the Mackintoshes.

CHAPTER IV

Clans of the Central and Eastern Highlands

Over the centuries that followed, the Highland clans continued to evolve each after its own fashion. In its original Celtic form the clan had been a patriarchal form of society, with its own patriarchal laws of succession and land tenure. The clansmen followed their chief not so much as their feudal superior, but rather as the representative of their common ancestors. Each clan had its own branches and septs who, while sometimes quarrelling among themselves, more often joined forces against a common enemy. Though in theory accepting the concept of a national monarchy, they were not bound to it by the same close feudal ties as were their Lowland neighbours. With them local and personal considerations counted for more.

Until the thirteenth century the central and eastern Highlands had continued to be ruled over by a number of native Celtic earls, Mar and Moray, Atholl, Angus, Buchan, Fife and, on the southern fringes, Lennox and Menteith. By the fourteenth century the original Celtic lines of all of these, save Mar, had failed, the old titles being bestowed by the Scottish kings on members of the Royal Family or on Anglo-Norman newcomers whom they wished to ennoble. Thus, early in the 13th century, the Comyns had, by marriage with a native heiress, become Earls of Buchan. In 1312 the Celtic Earldom of Moray, which, as we have seen, had been forfeited in the twelfth century, was bestowed by King Robert the Bruce on his nephew Randolph, while the Celtic Earls of Atholl and Angus were succeeded by incomers who had married Celtic heiresses. Finally, in 1377, the male line of the Celtic Earls of Mar had also failed and their inheritance, too, had passed into Anglo-Norman hands, the heiress being more or less forcibly married to the King's cousin, Alexander Stewart, who thus became Earl of Mar.

With the disappearance of the old Celtic earldoms, what could be called new clans now emerged on what had once been their clan territory, groups of families held together by community of descent or interest or by the simple fact that they lived in the same area. "By pretense of blude or place of thare dwelling," was the way the Scottish Parliament phrased it. In contrast to the older-established Celtic clans of the West, whose traditions went back to a largely patriarchal system and whose clansmen could with some justification claim to be of the same kin as their chiefs, these new clans possessed a quasi-feudal character, which in some ways offered greater stability than the

Genealogical tree of the Campbells of Glenorchy, by George Jamesone, 1635.

35

Highland army on the march in Flanders, 1743. A mounted Captain, a Lieutenant (followed by his wife) and an ensign carrying the Regimental Colour appear on the left of three panels. Gentlemen volunteers often joined the early Highland regiments, accompanied by their ghillies and servants.

less precise bonds of real or imagined kinship. As time went on and the power of the central monarchy increased, there came to be a virtue, too, in land held under a royal charter or parchment rather than by mere tradition, however ancient.

In the event, however, the two systems were to grow more and more alike, both providing land and protection to the members of a clan and in return ensuring by one method or another their loyalty and obedience to their chief. Whereas the Western clans, being of Celtic or Norse descent, had by origin been tribal and patriarchal and only later acquired feudal characteristics, in the Eastern and Central Highlands the process was reversed. Thus in Moray in the twelfth century Malcolm IV had deliberately encouraged settlement by "a personally devoted and peaceful people", mainly of Anglo-Norman origin, as feudal superiors, with the existing Celtic population as their vassals. But, though feudal in origin, these communities in time developed many of the fundamental characteristics of clanship.

Such new clans were the Frasers, the Chisholms, the Grants, the Roses, the Hays, the Inneses and the Gordons, their chiefs being all of Anglo-Norman origin. In Caithness,

Clothing, weapons and musical instruments are clearly shown, as well as a vehicle for the sick and wounded and a baggage horse, but no pipers.

too, were the Sinclairs and the Sutherlands, the latter of Flemish origin, the Menzies in Perthshire and, further West, the Stewart Lords of Lorne, kinsmen of the new Royal Family who replaced the Macdougalls and were the ancestors of the Stewarts of Appin. With time these alien landlords gradually adjusted themselves to the local way of life, to the pastoral environment, the Gaelic speech and ancient Celtic traditions of their clansmen, until they too became completely assimilated and thoroughly Celtic in their customs and outlook. In this way they won in the end from their native dependents as well as from their own kith and kin (and with the years, by fosterage and interbreeding the two quickly became inextricably intermingled) the loyalty due to a clan chief in addition to that demanded by a feudal superior.

For example the records show that in 1160 a Norman knight in the Lowlands of Scotland bore the name of La Frèzelière. A century or so later his descendants, by now known as Fraser, moved to Aberdeenshire. In the fourteenth century, having been rewarded for their loyal services to the Crown with lands in the Highlands, they moved still further north. And by the end of the century there is already evidence that Fraser of Lovat in Inverness-shire was known by his own clansmen neither as Fraser nor as Lovat, but by his Gaelic patronymic, *MacShimidh*, son of Simon.

The Frasers had by this time become a considerable force in the northern Highlands. Their clan lands extended on either side of the Great Glen and the River Ness. To the west lay the Aird, sometimes known as *Aird Mhic Shimi*, comprising the coastal strip along the south shore of the Beauly Firth and its wilder hinterland, rising abruptly to a height of 2000 feet and including most of Strathglass and Strathfarrar as far as Loch Morar. This was the Fraser heartland. On the southern shore of the estuary of the Beauly, a famous salmon-river, stood the Tower of Lovat, from which the Fraser Chiefs take their title, while a couple of miles upstream is Beaufort Castle, for more than four centuries their seat and adjoining the site of Castle Downie and other still earlier strongholds, including one destroyed by the English in the War of Independence. Between the two is Beauly with its

ancient ruined priory (promptly seized by the enthusiastically Protestant Frasers at the time of the Reformation), where many of the early chiefs lie buried, and the late seventeenth-century Fraser mausoleum of Wardlaw.

To the east of the Great Glen the Fraser lands originally stretched almost thirty miles from the Burgh of Inverness, southwards along the shore of Loch Ness to Kilchuimein (known since 1731 as Fort Augustus in honour of the infant Duke of Cumberland). Here are Stratherrick and, further south, Abertarff, where arable land of a kind mingles with crag and moorland. A few miles to the south of Fort Augustus the strategically important Pass of Corrieyairack leads from the Great Glen to the headwaters of the Spey.

Such was the territory of the Frasers from the beginning of the fifteenth until the middle of the eighteenth century. Much of it is still held by them today. They had, as we have seen, come here from the south, having owned land in England and the Borders since the twelfth and thirteenth centuries and in France before that. As early as 1160 one Simon Fraser gave land to the monks of Kelso. In 1306 Sir Simon Fraser of Oliver Castle in Peeblesshire, a leading supporter of William Wallace and Robert the Bruce, was captured by the English at Methven and later executed in London. Another Simon Fraser fought at Bannockburn and was later killed with two of his brothers at Halidon Hill. His elder brother, Sir Alexander, who likewise fought at Bannockburn and became Chamberlain of Scotland, was a close friend of Robert the Bruce and later married his sister Mary, widow of Neil Campbell of Lochow. From a son of this marriage are descended the Frasers of Saltoun and a number of other Fraser families who later settled in Aberdeenshire and thereabouts.

Yet another Sir Simon Fraser, probably Alexander's brother, having married an heiress of the Bissets, a great Anglo-Norman family who early in the thirteenth century owned Lovat and the Aird and founded Beauly Priory, seems to have established himself in those parts in 1254. Certainly a document dated 12 September 1367 describes one Hugh Fraser, who also owned land in Peeblesshire and was possibly the son or grandson of the Simon killed at Halidon Hill, as *Dominus de Loveth et portionarius de la Ard* and it is from that the subsequent Lovat chiefs undoubtedly descend. In 1416 this Hugh's son, likewise named Hugh, married Janet de Fenton, a Bisset grand-daughter, thus securing for his family still more of the much coveted Bisset inheritance. By this time the Gaelic patronymic MacShimi seems already to have been in current use locally, pointing to an earlier forebear named Simon as well as to the increasing Celticisation of an

The MacDonald boys playing golf, by Jeremiah Davison. Golf has been played in Scotland since the 13th century.

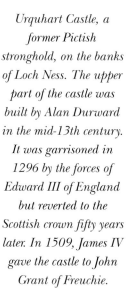

Anglo-Norman family. This Hugh also obtained, possibly from the Earls of Moray, some land in Stratherrick and one third of Glenelg on the Sound of Sleat (on the West coast opposite Skye), later to become a cause of dispute with the MacLeods. In about 1460 his grandson, yet another Hugh, was created Lord Fraser of Lovat, having married Margaret or Violetta Lyon, of the House of Glamis, described as a famous huntress and killer of wolves. So close was Violetta to the Scottish Court that it was said of Hugh that, thanks to her, "his ear could hear at Lovat what was whispered at Holyroodhouse".

Like the Frasers, the ancient family of Sinclair reached the Northern Highlands in more than one stage. Henri de Saint Clair from Normandy held land in the Lothians as early as 1162. More than two hundred years later his descendants became Earls of Orkney and later Caithness in succession through marriage to a long line of Norse earls or *jarls* and in 1395 Henry Sinclair, Jarl of Orkney, after first conquering the Faroe Islands, seems to have sailed on across the Atlantic and, with the help of a skilled Venetian navigator called Antonio Zeno, to have discovered America a full century before Columbus.

Similarly, from the marriage to a Celtic heiress of William de la Haye, who also arrived in Scotland in about 1160, springs the present twenty-fourth Earl of Errol, 33rd Chief of Clan Hay and Hereditary High Constable of Scotland, who still resides at Slains on the coast of Buchan on the former Comyn lands granted to his forefathers as a reward for his ancestor Sir Gilbert Hay's exploits at Bannockburn.

Of probable Anglo-Norman origin, too, are the Gordons, who first appear in Berwickshire in the reign of King David I. Having fought for the

English, they later changed sides and supported Bruce against Balliol, fighting under his command at Bannockburn. In 1320 Sir Adam, Lord of Gordon in Berwickshire, was one of the two Scottish envoys who journeyed to Rome in order to present to the Pope the famous Declaration of Arbroath which finally led him to annul his excommunication of Robert Bruce. In return for these and other services, Sir Adam was granted the lands of Strathbogie in Banffshire which had formerly belonged to Earl David of Atholl, who, being connected by marriage with the Comyns had, in company with others so connected, been summarily dispossessed.

Thereafter Strathbogie or Huntly became the Gordon heartland, stretching from the high hills of the south-west to where its rivers flow down through fertile farmland into the Moray Firth. To Strathbogie were added over the years, by marriage rather than conquest, the district of Aboyne on Deeside and an area to the north of the great city of Aberdeen, which itself long enjoyed the patronage and protection of Clan Gordon. As often happened, the Gordons' geographical position was important in determining their clan's development and history. Cut off by the Grampians in this borderland of the north-east, they lived on the edge of the Lowlands. Though their clan lands reached far into the great mountain mass of the central Highlands, they also included the fertile farmland of the coastal areas, while their proximity to the rich burgh of Aberdeen brought numerous mutual advantages to both.

Harder to determine than those of the Anglo-Norman clans are the origins of the Mackays or MacAoidhs of Strathnaver, the vast, barren, mountainous area which lies west of Caithness and north of the Earldom of Ross and which had in the tenth century been very largely settled by the Norsemen. By the fourteenth century the MacKays could, it is known, already muster four thousand fighting men. What is more, their Chiefs were by now of sufficient standing to intermarry with the Lords of the Isles and in about 1415 Donald of the Isles gave his sister Elizabeth in marriage to Angus Dubh Mackay, though only three or four years before they had fought on opposing sides. Whence they originally came is not entirely clear, but it seems at least possible that they had moved north to Strathnaver from Moray in the twelfth century, at the time when the old Kingdom of Moray was cleared of its native inhabitants and resettled by King David I with more dependable Anglo-Normans from the south.

The Mackays themselves claim to be of Celtic origin and to descend from the old Royal House of Moray. Certainly, in 1160, at the time of the Moray Plantation, when King Malcolm IV of Scotland in his turn drove out the men of Moray and put his own henchmen in their place, many of those thus driven out took refuge in the south and west, while others moved northwards into what is now Caithness and Sutherland, then still under Norse rule. There the MacEths, with whom Mackays claim kinship, became leaders of local resistance to the Scottish Crown, among them Malcolm MacAedh or MacEth, whose daughter had married a Norse Earl of Caithness, killed fighting the Scottish King in 1198 at Dalharold in Strathnaver.

With the disappearance from the scene of the MacEths, the Mackays make their appearance, which again points to some link between them. Though his family seem to have owned lands in Durness from an earlier date, Iye Mackay is known to have been Chief of his Clan from about 1330 until 1370 and in 1415 a charter from Donald Lord of the Isles, bestowing on his brother-in-law Angus Dubh Mackay the lands of Ferincaskry and Strathalladale, describes him as "of Strathnaver", a term then used to describe the greater part of Sutherland. A dozen years later Angus was "leader of four thousand Strathnaver men" and therefore a Chief of some consequence.

Of possibly Pictish origin are the Brodies whose name it has been suggested could be derived from Brude, as the old Pictish Kings were called long before the advent of Kenneth MacAlpin in 843. Some say that through the centuries the Brodies kept somewhat apart from the turbulent mainstream of Scottish history out of a lingering resentment at the treatment their forebears suffered at the hands of MacAlpin and his invading Scots more than eleven hundred years ago. For Highlanders, whether Pictish, Scottish, or Norse in origin, have long memories. But it seems on the whole more likely that the Brodies, whose Chiefs have lived in their Castle of Brodie near Nairn on the Moray Firth for over 800 years and who trace their descent directly from Malcolm Thane of Brodie, who died in 1285, were in fact one of the loyal Celtic tribes who were rewarded with lands in Moray by King Malcolm IV in 1164 after he had finally crushed the rebellious Moraymen.

The magnificent tombslab of Murchard of Colosay, Chief of Clan Macfie, who died in 1539.

THE GERMANE SEA

A Scotch Woman

A Highland woman

Performed by John Speed and are to be sold by Roger Rea ye Elder & younger at ye Golden Crosse in Cornhill against the Exchange

A Scotch Man

A Highland Man

Highlander and Lowlander male and female dress. From John Speed's map of the Kingdoms of Scotland, 1662.

Two centuries after Bruce's death, life in the Highlands was to continue much as it had before and much as it would for several more centuries to come. Here what happened in the Lowlands still had little relevance; the hold of Church and State alike was tenuous. Different loyalties and different standards prevailed. The Chief was father of his people. He was, in theory and sometimes in fact, of the same blood as they were. He, rather than the King, had power of life and death over them and of this he made full use. By one means or another he managed to command their loyalty. His land, in a sense, was their land; their cattle were his cattle; his quarrels, above all, were their quarrels.

To the Highlander, land, the barren land of the Highlands; cattle, the stunted little black beasts that somehow got a living from it and from which he in his turn got a living; and men, men at arms to guard the land and the cattle, were what mattered. In its ancient form the clan was founded on the deeply-rooted Celtic principle of *kindness*, a mixture of kinship and tradition, stronger than any written law. By ancestral right, the clan lands were held by the chief and by him distributed among the members of his family and the men of his clan. The cattle were the most prized possession of chief and clansmen alike, the source of their livelihood and social standing, the source, too, of unending strife.

In time of war the chief and those of his own blood led the clan in battle against their common enemy, whoever he might be. When their Chief sent out the fiery cross, it was the inescapable duty of his clansmen to follow. In peace as in war he had absolute power over them, being, by ancient custom, both law-giver and judge, standing midway between them and God, settling their disputes, helping them when they were in need,

Bas-reliefs from Iona Cathedral, showing rural scenes.

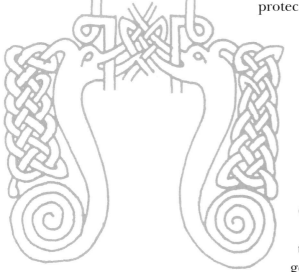

protecting them and their cattle against their enemies. Bauchaille nan Eilannan, the Shepherd of the Isles, was the Gaelic title of the Macdonald chiefs. With his chief the humblest clansman shared an extraordinary pride of race. All who bore their chief's name liked to believe themselves – and often were – descended, as he was, from the name-father of the clan, from Somerled, from Gillean of the Battleaxe, from Calum Mor, from Olaf the Black or Gregor of the Golden Bridles, and, through them, from countless generations of Norse or Irish kings. "Though poor," ran an old and constantly repeated saying, "I am noble. Thank God I am a Maclean."

Small wonder, then, that from their mountain or island fastnesses the great chiefs and chieftains of the north and north-west, surrounded by their loyal clansmen, should through the ages have paid but little heed to the edicts of kings or parliaments or officers of state from south of the Highland Line, regarding these only as potential allies or enemies in their own, more personal struggles for power. Which is why, in seeking to follow the successive twists and turns of Highland history, it is essential to think, not in terms of a clan's loyalty or disloyalty to this or that monarch or dynasty or government, but rather of a system of ever-shifting alliances and conflicts of interest between a number of independent or semi-independent princes and principalities.

CHAPTER V

The Lords of the Isles and Clan Wars

King Robert II of Scotland, formerly Regent and later first of the Stewart Kings, succeeded his uncle David II on the latter's death in 1371. An adequate Regent, he proved a weak King, his reign being disturbed throughout, in the Highlands as in the Lowlands, by the incessant brawling of the great nobles. Though of noble birth, he was of Norman origin and did not command the authority that flowed from eight centuries and more of Celtic kingship. His son, Robert III, who came to the throne nineteen years later, fared no better. A well-meaning cripple, he virtually abdicated in 1399. For the remainder of his reign Scotland was ruled over by Regents, notably by his able and ambitious half-brother, Robert Stewart, Duke of Albany, who had for a time already served as Regent in the previous reign. Seven years after King Robert's withdrawal, in 1406, his son and heir, James, had the misfortune to fall into the hands of the English, Robert himself died from the shock and James I, now nominally King, spent the first eighteen years of his reign a prisoner in England, while his uncle, Robert of Albany, continued to rule as Regent in his place. In addition to Robert III, Robert II had fathered a large number of sons, both legitimate and illegitimate. Of these by far the ablest was Albany, who served as Regent during the greater part of three reigns, those of his father, Robert II, his brother Robert III and finally his nephew James I. A ruthless and determined man, it was widely rumoured that, having no wish to relinquish the Regency any sooner than he needed to, he now deliberately prolonged his negotiations with the English for his nephew's release, while himself remaining comfortably in power.

Of the many trouble-makers who in those days disturbed the peace of the realm, none was more notorious than the Regent Albany's brother, Robert II's fourth son, Alexander Stewart Earl of Buchan and Justiciary of the Northern Lowlands, known, with good reason, as the Wolf of Badenoch. In 1390, after the Bishop of Moray had dared excommunicate him for deserting his wife in favour of his mistress, the Wolf showed his displeasure at the Bishop's insolence by burning to the ground, with the ready help of a band of "wild, wykked Heland-men", both his Cathedral of Elgin and the neighbouring town of Forres. By some it is claimed that after a period of richly deserved imprisonment the Wolf in the end mended his ways. Be that as it may, a handsome black marble monument, standing immediately behind the altar in Dunkeld Cathedral, to this day euphemistically describes him as being "*bonae memoriae*", of good

Duart Castle, on Mull, stronghold of the Macleans, by Paul Sandby, 1748.

47

memory. Of the Wolf's numerous bastards the most famous was Alexander Stewart, Earl of Mar, a worthy son of his father who had won the Earldom of Mar by first murdering the heiress's husband and then besieging her in her castle and forcibly making her his wife. The time was propitious for men of his stamp and he was later to prove himself a not ineffective military leader. From the Wolf's various other bastards are descended numerous well regarded families of Stewarts still living in Atholl, Aberdeenshire, Banffshire and Moray.

From another of Robert II's natural sons springs another line of Stewarts, the Crichton-Stuart Earls and Marquesses of Bute, whose Crusader ancestor Alexander, 4th High Steward of Scotland, married in the thirteenth century the daughter of Seaumas MacAngus, Lord of Bute, of the ancient royal house of the Isles, and who can thus be said to have held their lands in Bute by direct descent for more than a thousand years.

Yet another famous branch of the family made their way to Appin in Argyll, where in time they became a Highland clan in their own right. In 1386 Robert Stewart, a direct descendant of Walter Stewart and his wife Marjory Bruce, through their son Alexander the 7th High Steward, had married the daughter of John MacAlan de Ergadia, heiress of the Macdougalls of Lorne, thus securing for his family the Lordship of Lorne. The Lordship having, however, subsequently passed to Colin, First Earl of Argyll, by his marriage to Isabel, heiress to John Stewart, Lord of Lorne, and thus, like so much else, became a Campbell prerogative, the former Stewarts of Lorne thereafter had to content themselves with the lands of Appin in Upper Lorne, adopting the style Stewart of Appin. Described by one early writer as "the best sort of Stewartes", their pride of race is neatly illustrated by their clan motto: "Not we from Kings, but Kings from us". During these troublous times the great nobles of the Lowlands, like the chiefs of most

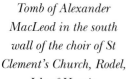

Tomb of Alexander MacLeod in the south wall of the choir of St Clement's Church, Rodel, Isle of Harris.

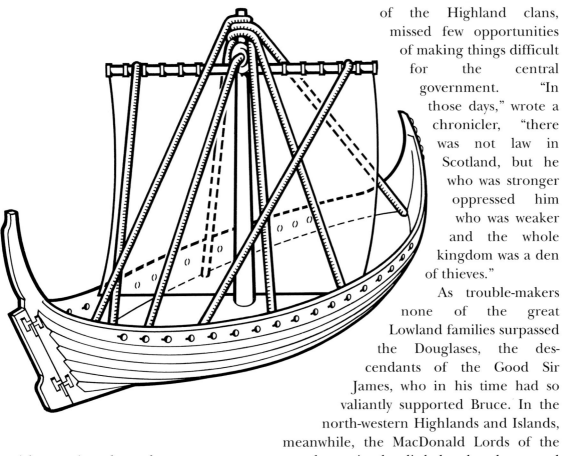

of the Highland clans, missed few opportunities of making things difficult for the central government. "In those days," wrote a chronicler, "there was not law in Scotland, but he who was stronger oppressed him who was weaker and the whole kingdom was a den of thieves."

As trouble-makers none of the great Lowland families surpassed the Douglases, the descendants of the Good Sir James, who in his time had so valiantly supported Bruce. In the north-western Highlands and Islands, meanwhile, the MacDonald Lords of the isles continued to rule as autonomous monarchs, paying but little heed to the central government or to anyone else. With their kinsmen the Macleans and a number of other Western clans, they had, it is true, fought bravely with Bruce against the English at Bannockburn. But they had done so as allies rather than as subjects. Now the scene changed and in pursuance of their own personal and dynastic aims, they allied themselves instead with successive Kings of England by a series of treaties negotiated as between sovereign states. It was thus that in 1388 the Oxford-educated Donald of the Isles revisited England with his brother Iain Mor for the purpose of signing a regular alliance with King Richard II and that twelve years later, in 1400, after Richard had abdicated, Donald and his brother were received by Richard's successor Henry IV of England and a further defensive alliance concluded. In 1408 this alliance with Scotland's hereditary enemy was further strengthened when King Henry sent a special embassy to sign a fresh treaty with Donald. In addition to the Isles, Donald by this time held sway over much of the western seaboard. An opportunity now offered to extend his authority and his dominions still further. His wife Mary was, as we have seen, the sister of Alexander, Earl of Ross, the last of a long line of Celtic or possibly Norse Earls who for the past two hundred years or more had ruled over both Easter and Wester Ross and much else besides. On Alexander of Ross's death in 1402 he left as his heir a sickly only daughter, Euphemia, who, entering a convent in 1411, renounced the Earldom and estates she had inherited. This left Donald's wife with a

In the Highlands and Islands the galley provided a vital means of transport, with surprising mobility. It was used to import silks and wines. The standard drink in the Highlands in earlier times was claret.

strong claim to her late brother's lands and Earldom which, were they added to the Lordship of the Isles, would make Donald master of most of northern Scotland. A counter-claim was, however, now advanced by no less a person than the Regent Albany himself on behalf of his own son, John Stewart, presently Earl of Buchan, who was likewise Euphemia's uncle by marriage. Enraged by this and egged on by promises of help from his ally Henry IV of England, Donald now led an army of 10,000 Islesmen right across Scotland for the purpose of forcibly asserting his claim to the Earldom and, if possible, sacking the temptingly rich city of Aberdeen into the bargain. In this ambitious venture he was loyally supported by the Macleans under their Chief, Red Hector of the Battles; by the Macleods, led by Fierce Ian of Dunvegan; by the Camerons under the great Donald Dubh and the Mackintoshes under their tenth Chief, Calum Beg.

After first laying waste the Royal Burgh of Inverness and defeating the Mackays and the Frasers, who had sought to check their progress being both relatively loyal to the Crown, the Islesmen encountered on 24 July at Harlaw on the Ury, some twenty miles north-west of Aberdeen, a mixed force sent to meet them by the Regent under the command of his nephew, Alexander

Castle Tioram in Loch Moidart, a stronghold of Clanranald, built in the 13th century.

Stewart Earl of Mar, bastard son of the notorious Wolf of Badenoch who, as it happened, was Donald's own first cousin. With Mar were Sir James Scrymgeour, the Royal Standard Bearer and Constable of Dundee, Sir Alexander Ogilvy, Chief of that name and Hereditary Sheriff of Angus, and Sir Robert Davidson, Provost of Aberdeen, vigorously supported by the armed burgesses of the city, who not unnaturally viewed the sudden advent of the Islesmen with grave concern. He also enjoyed the wholehearted support of the neighbouring Gordons, and finally of the Mackenzies who, though nominally vassals of Clan Donald, discerned in the invasion a threat to their own dynastic interests.

As the opposing armies came to the shock, the right wing of Donald's army was led by Red Hector Maclean of Duart and the left by Calum Beg Mackintosh. Donald himself commanded the main body, supported by Fierce Ian Macleod of Dunvegan. The ensuing conflict, known from the amount of blood shed as the Red Harlaw, was savagely contested, both Maclean of Duart and Macleod of Dunvegan losing their lives. Though militarily inconclusive, the battle ended in the withdrawal westward of Donald and his allies, with the result that Buchan held the disputed Earldom of Ross until his death in 1424, when it was resumed by the Crown. Though renouncing none of his claims, Donald, for his part, remained relatively quiet until his death in 1420, while his English allies, having in the event done nothing to help him, made their peace with Regent Albany. Had the Lord of the Isles, with English help, decisively

defeated the Royal Army at Harlaw, the course of Scottish history could well have been markedly different.

In the event, the status quo remained undisturbed. Having ruled Scotland in fact if not in name for half a century, the Regent Albany died in 1420. He was succeeded both as Duke and regent by his feeble son Murdoch. It was not, however, until four years after that that the new Regent finally negotiated the return from England of King James, by now a sturdy, well built, active man of thirty, who while in England had received a good education and learned something both of statecraft and of matters military. He had also married the English King's cousin, Lady Joan Beaufort, daughter of the Earl of Somerset, of whom he had first caught sight from his prison window "walking under the toure the fairest or the freschest yonge floure that ever I sawe, methoght, before that house."

Having thus at long last entered into his inheritance, James I lost no time in asserting his authority, introducing numerous much needed reforms and taking drastic measures to restore order. "If God gives me but the life of a dog," he declared confidently, "I will make the key keep the castle and the bracken-bush the cow." As a first step, he vented his accumulated hatred on the House of Albany by ordering the execution on the Heading Hill of Stirling of his cousin the Regent Murdoch, of two of the latter's sons and of Murdoch's old father-in-law, the Earl of Lennox. The only one of Murdoch's brood lucky enough to escape the slaughter was James Mor Stewart, from whom are descended the Stewarts of Ardvorlich by Loch Earn.

Not long after his return to Scotland King James, in the hope possibly of conciliating the MacDonalds, handed over the disputed Earldom of Ross, vacant since Buchan's death, to Mary, the widow of Donald of the Isles, thereby formally recognising her claim to it. From Mary it passed to her son Alexander, who by now had succeeded his father Donald as Third Lord of the Isles. The Earldom added greatly to the territories of the Lordship. In addition to the fertile eastern coastlands of Ross, the possession of both Sleat in Skye of neighbouring Loch Alsh now gave the Lord of the Isles control of the strategically important sheltered sea-passage to Lewis between Skye and the mainland. But greater possessions brought more problems. Clan Chattan and Clan Cameron, both vassals of the Lordship, were constantly at loggerheads with each other, and the difficulty of maintaining any degree of control over either was considerable.

If by giving the Earldom of Ross to Alexander of the Isles the King had hoped to guarantee his temporary obedience to the Crown, he was destined to be disappointed. Within a couple of years of his return from England, there was fresh trouble in the Highlands and in 1427 James, resorting to drastic means, summoned some fifty Highland Chiefs to Inverness on the pretext of holding a parliament, arrested forty or more of them, including his own cousin Alexander of the Isles, and put three to death. Nor was this all. While Alexander of the Isles was in prison, the King, who sometimes preferred a rather less direct approach, sent a certain James Campbell to visit Alexander's uncle, his father Donald of the Isles' brother, Iain Mor MacDonald the Tanister, who had wisely refused to come to Inverness when summoned and whose loyalty he evidently doubted. Whatever the true purpose of their meeting, Iain Mor did not survive it, being killed, in the time-honoured phrase, while resisting arrest.

At this there was a great outcry in the West. Whereupon the King, resourceful as ever, quickly charged James Campbell with murder. Campbell, as was to be expected, maintained that he had been acting on the King's instructions. But in the event this did not save him. "Because," says the chronicler, "Campbell had no written order from the King to produce in his defence, he was taken and beheaded." "Which," adds the chronicler reflectively, "shows the dangerous consequences of undertaking such a service without due circumspection."

The two-handed sword known as the Claymore or Great Sword, used well into the 17th century.

After the battle of Harlaw, Mar, as Justiciary of the North, had been directed to build a "fortalice at Inverness for the utility of the Kingdom against the said Lord of the Isles". But more than a single fortalice was needed to quell the turbulent Islesmen and the Highland problem as such still remained largely unsolved. On his release from prison two years later, Alexander of the Isles showed his resentment at the treatment he had received at the hands of the Crown by immediately marching on Inverness with a force of 10,000 men and burning it to the ground fortalice and all. After which he withdrew into Lochaber. There, King James, having mustered a strong force, in the end overtook him and managed to defeat him. On this occasion the King enjoyed the support of the MacKenzies, who, though vassals of the Lordship, had already fought against the Islesmen at Harlaw, and of the Camerons and Mackintoshes under their respective chiefs, Donald Dubh and Malcolm, both of whom had eighteen years earlier fought with the Islesmen against Mar at Harlaw, but now for one reason or another transferred their allegiance to the Crown.

Following his defeat, Alexander of the Isles gave himself up and was again imprisoned, this time at Tantallon in East Lothian, having first made a dramatic act of contrition and submission before the high altar of the chapel royal at Holyrood. Thereafter he was confirmed by the Crown in his possession of the Earldom of Ross and for the time being remained quiet. On Mar's death four years later, Alexander was

Inverlochy Castle, built about 1270–80 by the Comyn Lord of Badenoch. From the Comyns it passed to the Bruces and the Gordons. Near it was fought the Battle of Inverlochy in 1645 when Montrose led the Highlanders to victory over Argyll's Covenanters.

appointed to succeed him as Justiciary of the North, a post which ironically enough carried with it the Keepership of Inverness Castle, which he himself had destroyed not many years before.

A clan who, following their timely shift of allegiance, at this time won royal favour were the Mackenzies. Among the chiefs invited to Inverness by King James I in 1427 had been young Alexander Mackenzie of Kintail who, though a vassal of the Lord of the Isles, had of late refused to support the latter against the Crown. In recognition of this, King James, instead of imprisoning Alexander with his fellow chiefs, had carried him off to school in Perth, where he himself often held court. In this manner he managed to win his friendship and loyalty for the Crown, so that, when the following year the Lord of the Isles launched a fresh rebellion against the King, the Mackenzies had refused to join it.

In return for this, Alexander of Kintail, henceforth to be known, rightly or wrongly, as *Ionraic* or the Upright, was granted royal charters for his lands in Kintail, first as a vassal of the Earls of Ross and later directly from the King, who likewise granted him charters in respect of certain lands in Strathconan and Strathgarve in Ross-shire, thus extending his possessions a long way eastwards. It was to prove a further important step in his clan's rise to power. Soon, however, there was fresh trouble in the West. In 1431, resenting what he regarded as his cousin Alexander of the Isles' submissive attitude to the Crown, Donald Balloch, son of the murdered Iain Mor the Tanister, who had been brought up on Mull by his bellicose kinsmen the Macleans, raised a fresh rebellion on Alexander's behalf and in a hardfought contest half way up the Great Glen at Inverlochy at the head of Loch Linnhe, heavily defeated Mar, Caithness,

The Dunvegan Cup was presented to Ruairidh Mor MacLeod (1562–1624) by Shane O'Neill in recognition of his efforts on behalf of the Gaelic cause in Ireland. The cup is made of wood and is adorned with mountings of silver and precious stones.

The Book of Clanranald. This 17th-century manuscript records in classical Gaelic verse the heroic virtues of the Chief of Clanranald.

Huntly and the Frasers, whom the King had sent against him, at the same time savagely revenging himself on the Camerons and Mackintoshes for what he with good reason regarded as their treachery of two years before. But again King James now took command himself and, thanks to superior numbers and armament, succeeded in more or less restoring the situation. After this set-back Donald Balloch, laden with loot, fled to Ireland, where he conveniently took refuge with O'Neil of Connaught. On being invited by King James to

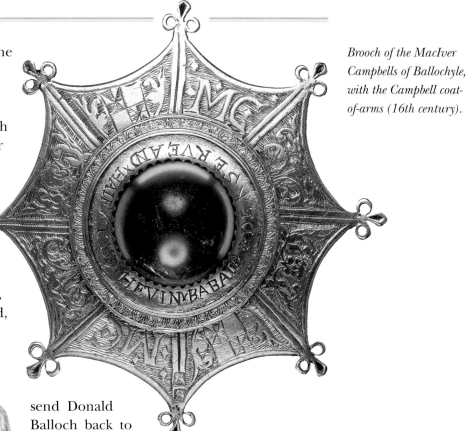

Brooch of the MacIver Campbells of Ballochyle, with the Campbell coat-of-arms (16th century).

send Donald Balloch back to Scotland dead or alive, O'Neil, after some delay, sent him a single severed and somewhat mutilated head, which, he assured him, was Donald's and which seemed to satisfy the King. In fact, however, Donald, who in the meanwhile had married O'Neil's daughter, was in the best of health. In Lochaber, meantime, the constant bickering of Clan Cameron and Clan Chattan continued to disturb the peace.

CHAPTER VI
The early Stuarts

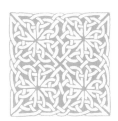

It was only natural that a King as able and as active as James I should make enemies. In February 1437 he was brutally assassinated by a number of these in Perth in the presence of his English Queen. The chief conspirators were his own uncle, the seventy-five year old Walter, Earl of Atholl, a surviving brother of Albany and of the Wolf of Badenoch; and Atholl's grandson Sir Robert Stewart, both of whom wanted the throne for themselves. Another was their cousin, Sir Robert Graham. They did not, however, achieve their ultimate object. James was promptly succeeded by his six year old son as James II, while Queen Joan, his "milk white dove", as her husband had called her, saw to it that his assassins suffered an even more unpleasant fate than their victim. After being tortured in public for three days the aged Earl of Atholl was, on the Queen's specific instructions, crowned with a crown of red hot iron to recall his royal ambitions, while his grandson suffered a scarcely less disagreeable death. After attempting to escape, the third conspirator, Sir Robert Graham, was in the end also successfully hunted down and seized by Good Grizzled Robert of Struan, Fourth Chief of Clan Donnachaidh and name father of the Robertsons of Struan, who handed him over to the widowed Queen in chains to meet the terrible fate she had especially devised for him. Struan's capture of Graham greatly enhanced his standing at Court. "For the capture of that most vile traitor, the late Robert the Graham," Grizzled Robert's lands were now erected into the Barony of Struan and Clan Donnachaidh's prestige and power thereby greatly increased. His exploit is aptly recalled by a chained man shown under the Struan coat of arms and by that family's crest which consists of a hand firmly supporting a royal crown. Unfortunately, by the time these honours were bestowed upon him, Grizzled Robert was himself dying from wounds received in an encounter with a nephew of the Bishop of Dunkeld, whose bishopric he had recently chosen to lay waste. This anti-clerical tradition was vigorously continued by his successor Alexander, Fifth of Struan, who not long after caused his clansmen to shower arrows on a subsequent Bishop of Dunkeld while the latter was at Mass in Dunkeld Cathedral, and who only escaped excommunication or worse thanks to the timely intervention of his father-in-law, Lord Glamis.

After her husband's death and her son James's succession to the throne, the widowed Queen married another Stewart, Sir James Stewart of Lorne. Of their three sons, half-brothers to young King James II, one was to become Earl of Atholl, another

Castle of Moy, Mull, built by Hector Maclean in the 15th century. It was involved in the Maclean–Campbell struggle of the 1670's and then abandoned in the next century.

Perth, the ancient capital of Scotland up to the 15th century. Engraving by John Slezer, 1693.

James I (1406–37), second son of Robert III, was born in Dunfermline in 1394 but spent nearly half his life as a guest of the English. He was murdered in 1437.

Earl of Buchan and the third Bishop of Moray. Some thirty years later, in 1465, one of Atholl's daughters, Elizabeth Stewart, became betrothed to Grizzled Robert's grandson Duncan, the son of Alexander Robertson, Fifth of Struan. But before Duncan could marry her he died, whereupon his old father, boldly bridging a sizeable generation gap, married her himself. Their union which was happily fruitful, was to mark the beginning of a long alliance between the Stewarts of Atholl and the Robertsons of Struan, who over the centuries often helped each other keep order in Atholl, for example against the marauding MacGregors, but no less frequently combined to wreak havoc. With time, Struan's position was firmly established as leader of Clan Donnachaidh and in due course a majority of Robertson Chieftains formally declared their loyalty to him as "thair Cheiff". Today his descendant, whose forebears moved a couple of centuries ago to Jamaica, has returned to Struan to resume the Chiefship.

James II was barely six at the time of his father's murder. Again there was a Regency, the Regent being this time the immensely powerful Earl of Douglas. Douglas, however, died in 1439, leaving two young sons, and the Regency passed to Sir William Crichton, Keeper of Edinburgh Castle. Seeing a chance to break the power of the Douglases, Crichton now invited the fourteen-year-old Earl and his brother to dinner with the nine-year-old King in the Great Hall of Edinburgh Castle and,

having set before them a symbolic Black Bull's Head, signifying death, murdered them both.

Edinburgh Castle, towne and toure, sang the poet.

God grant thae sink for sinne!
And that even for the black dinoir
Earl Douglas got therein.

But Crichton's "black dinoir" fell short of the final solution he had hoped for. By 1446, when King James II, now nineteen, assumed control of his kingdom, an alliance highly dangerous to the Crown had sprung up between the young Eighth Earl of Douglas, a cousin of the murdered boy, well known to be in touch with the English, the "Tiger Earl" of Crawford, at this time the most powerful noble in the east, and John of the Isles, still resentful at the treatment his father had received from James I.

The young King, in some ways as able and resourceful as his father, first sought to conciliate Douglas. But Douglas rejected his advances, while his allies, the Islesmen, despite Fraser of Lovat's strenuous efforts to stop them, promptly seized the Royal Burgh of Inverness. Finally in 1452 James, exasperated and consciously or unconsciously re-enacting a familiar scene from his childhood, invited Douglas to dine with him under a safe-conduct at Stirling Castle and then, over dinner, stabbed him to death with his own hand, dirking him in the neck and "down in the body", while leaving nothing to chance an attendant, standing by with a pole-axe, beat out his brains. "The Earl," Parliament tactfully concluded, "was guilty of his own death by resisting the King's gentle persuasion."

For a time it seemed as though Douglas's four surviving brothers might, with English encouragement, successfully defy the King. In 1455, however, James, forcing the issue, marched against them in strength and defeated them decisively at Arkinholm on the River Esk. There three of the brothers were killed, while the fourth, now the ninth Earl, fled first to the Isles and then to England. The power of the Black Douglases had at last been broken. The "Tiger Earl" of Crawford had by this time come to terms with the Crown, while James, by heaping favours on John of the Isles had won at any rate his temporary allegiance. For a time the country was at peace.

In England, meanwhile, the Wars of the Roses were raging and James,

James II (1437–60). He stabbed the Regent Douglas with his own hand.

having concluded a temporary truce with the English King Henry VI, chose this moment to intervene on his side against the usurper York. The border stronghold of Roxburgh, which for the past century had been in English hands, was held at the time by a henchman of York's. In the summer of 1460 King James, with the active support, strangely enough, of John of the Isles, laid siege to it. As he was observing his cannon bombarding it, one of them, a great hooped gun called the Lion, suddenly exploded and killed the watching monarch – "mair curious", writes a contemporary, "nor became the majesty of ane King".

With James II's death the Scottish crown passed yet again to a minor, this time to the nine year old James III, and yet again a Regency was declared. Taking rapid advantage of the government's temporary weakness, John of the Isles was soon once more in open rebellion. During the English Wars of the Roses the Scots had, as we have seen, given their support to the Lancastrian faction. In 1461 Edward IV, having won the throne of England for the House of York and resenting such blatant Scottish intervention in English affairs, at once turned his agile mind to the congenial task of stirring up trouble for his northern neighbour. In the Earl of Douglas, who had taken refuge at his court, and in John of the Isles he found willing allies. In 1462 they together drew up and signed the Treaty of Westminster-Ardtornish, under which John, his cousin, another Donald Balloch, and the new Earl of Douglas expressly acknowledged the English King as their Liege Lord, took his money and agreed that, once he had with their help conquered Scotland, they would divide their country up between them, John of the Isles and Balloch sharing the north and west, while Douglas ruled over the south. As a first step, John of the Isles, having publicly declared himself King of the Hebrides, boldly moved his seat of government right across Scotland from Ardtornish to Inverness.

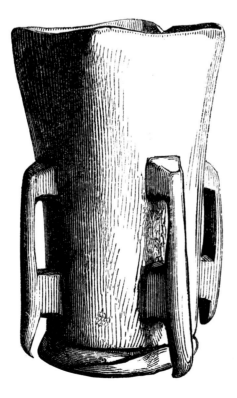

Wooden mether. A four-sided medieval Highland drinking cup.

In the long run, however, little was to come of this ambitious scheme. After attempting to raise a rebellion in the Lowlands, Douglas was in the end captured and despatched to a monastery. "A man who can do no better must become a monk," he ruefully remarked as they led him away, while for the next ten or twelve years his associate John of the Isles stayed at home, prudently ignoring successive summons to appear before the Estates of the Realm.

During the latter part of the fourteenth and first half of the fifteenth centuries Clan Campbell's royal connections and well developed political sense continued to stand them in good stead. Under Robert III, Colin Oig of Lochawe, son of Sir Neil, had been succeeded in the barony of Lochawe by his son, another Colin, known as *Iongantach* or the Wonderful. While James I was still a prisoner in England and Robert of Albany

Regent, Colin Iongantach's son and successor Duncan, known as *Abn Adh*, the Fortunate, had married as his first wife the Regent Albany's daughter Marjory Stewart and had been raised to the peerage as Lord Campbell of Lochawe. Having succeeded his father as Chief in about 1410 Lucky Duncan was in the event fortunate enough to avoid the consequences of what after the young King's return could have become an embarrassing connexion with the House of Albany, by now in deep disgrace. But, after bearing him a son and heir, Archibald Roy, Marjory had conveniently died and as his second wife Duncan now married Margaret Stewart, daughter of Sir John Stewart of Ardgowan on the Clyde in Renfrewshire, a natural son of Robert III. From their son, Colin Dubh, were to spring the Campbells of Glenorchy, later Earls and Marquesses of Breadalbane.

The Glenlyon brooch.

A great benefactor of Holy Church, Lucky Duncan founded the Collegiate Church of Kilmun on the northern shore of the Holy Loch and bestowed various lands in Knapdale on the Cistercian Abbey of Saddell in Kintyre. On his death in 1453 he was succeeded as Chief by his grandson, Archibald Roy's son Colin, who four years later, in 1457, was created Earl of Argyll by King James II.

During young Colin of Argyll's minority, his uncle, Black Colin of Glenorchy, had acted as his guardian, displaying towards his ward a "kyndness and fidelity" described by the chronicler as "exemplarily remarkable". It was Black Colin who at this time built the town and Castle of Inveraray, which thereafter became the Campbell Chiefs' main dwelling-place and stronghold, giving their galleys ready and strategically invaluable access by way of Loch Fyne to the open sea and its islands. For his own residence Colin Dubh took Kilchurn Castle near the northeastern end of Lochawe, built, it was said, by his wife Margaret, the daughter of John Stewart of Lorne, while her husband was away on a prolonged pilgrimage to Rome. By reason of this pilgrimage Colin was for the rest of his days to be known as *Colin dubh na Rhoime*, Black Colin of Rome.

In 1475 King James III, in his search for a solution to what had become the perennial problem of the Isles, appointed Colin of Argyll to be Royal Lieutenant with far reaching powers and particular authority to prosecute a decree of forfeiture against John of the Isles. It was an appointment which for Colin clearly held considerable promise. In 1481 he also received a grant of much of Knapdale, including the Keepership of Castle Sween; by marrying his aunt Margaret's sister, Isabella, the heiress of John Stewart of Lorne, he gained for his family the ancient Lordship of Lorne, subsequently quartering the Galley of Lorne in his arms and taking the title of Lord Lorne for the heir to the Earldom which had by now been bestowed on him.

In the North the Mackintoshes had likewise gained by their loyalty to the Crown. During the latter part of the fifteenth century, Duncan, who succeeded his father Malcolm as eleventh Chief in 1464 and is described by the clan historian as not only "mild and gentle" but also "prudent and vigorous", somehow contrived to keep on good terms both with the Crown and with the Lord of the Isles, receiving from the latter in 1466 charters for considerable areas of land including Glen Roy and Glen

Portrait of James III (right). He "fell into the hands of vile persons and was slain at Sauchieburn in 1488".

Portrait of James IV: a "glittering and tragic King", he was killed at the Battle of Flodden in 1513 with the flower of the Scottish nobility.

Spean in Inverness-shire, as well as the heritable Stewardship of all Lochaber, much of which was however already claimed by the Camerons. Following the eventual forfeiture of the Lordship of the Isles, Duncan prudently resigned the lands of Brae Lochaber into the hands of King James III, being subsequently rewarded for his good conduct by a new Royal Charter in respect of them.

For a number of years John of the Isles managed to escape retribution for his part in the rebellion of 1462. In 1476, however, following the conclusion of peace with England, the Earls of Crawford, Atholl, Huntly and Argyll, acting on behalf of the Crown as Royal Lieutenants, together invaded his mainland territories and by the decree of forfeiture which had been issued against him the year before forced him to surrender the Earldom of Ross (which was now once more annexed to the Crown) as well as his lands in Kintyre and the Castles of Inverness and Nairn. As a vassal of the Scottish Crown, he was then appointed a Lord of Parliament and, the better to emphasize his subordinate status, expressly granted by the Crown a formal title to the remainder of his lands. Even so, it was not long before trouble again broke out in the Isles. John's apparent submission to the Scottish Crown and its Lieutenants was deeply resented by many of his own more turbulent dependents. Putting himself at their head, his bastard son, Angus Og, a man of singularly violent and bloodthirsty character, who not long before had married a daughter of the newly created Earl of Argyll, declared war, not only on the King, but on his own father, whom he now sought to supplant as

Lord of the Isles. At the Battle of *Badh na Fola* or the Bloody Bay near Tobermory on the Sound of Mull in 1484, Angus encountered his father, the latter's two principal lieutenants, Hector Maclean of Duart and Ewen Maclean of Ardgour, and the Macleods, who were also supporting John. The Earl of Atholl and Angus's father in law, the Earl of Argyll, who together had helped mount the expedition against him, preferred for one reason or another to take no part in the proceedings. In his great war-galley Maclean of Ardgour led the attack on the rebel fleet, supported by Macleod of Harris, while the MacDonalds of Sleat and Moidart, for their part, came to the help

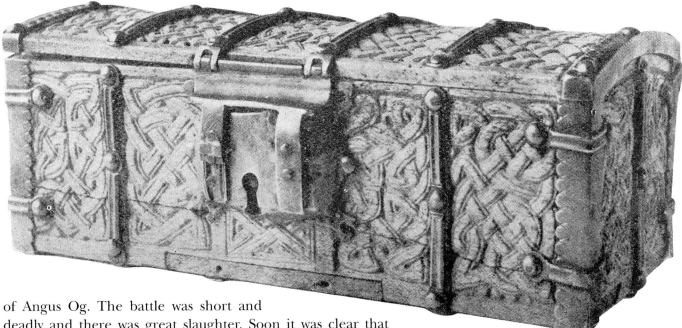

of Angus Og. The battle was short and
deadly and there was great slaughter. Soon it was clear that
Angus had won the day. Macleod of Harris had been mortally wounded and John
of the Isles taken prisoner along with the Chiefs of Duart and Ardgour. Ardgour was
lucky to escape with his life. Just as one of Angus's henchmen was preparing to
despatch him, MacDonald of Moidart who valued Ardgour as a sparring partner
intervened on his behalf. "If Maclean were gone," he asked anxiously, "who should I
have to bicker with?" And so in the end Ardgour's life was spared, as were those of
Duart and of Angus's own father.

Casket of carved whalebone bound with strips of bronze. The style of its interlace design indicates its early West Highland origin.

For a time Angus effectively displaced his father as Captain of Clan Donald. In the
end, however, the latter who, while making his submission to the Crown, had also kept
in touch with the English and retained the loyalty of the Macleans, the Macleods, the
MacNeils and the Mackenzies, somehow succeeded in re-establishing his position. As
for Angus Og, he continued to cause trouble in one way or another until in 1490 his
throat was cut in Inverness, under somewhat obscure circumstances, by his own Irish
harper, O'Carby or MacCaibhre. According to one account, the minstrel in question
had conceived a violent passion for the daughter of Mackenzie of Kintail, who
happened to be at feud with Angus Og. Another of Angus's enemies was Clanranald's
wife, the Lady of Moidart, who for reasons of her own likewise wished to see him dead.
With this in mind, she induced Kintail to promise his daughter's hand in marriage to
the simple-minded O'Carby on condition that he did away with Angus. And so, picking
his occasion, the harper crept into his master's bedroom one night while he was asleep
and cut his throat. But O'Carby was destined to be disappointed. In the event, he
failed to win his affianced's hand. On the contrary a singularly unpleasant fate awaited
him. "According to the cruel custom of the time," says the Chronicler, "the harper was
torn asunder, limb from limb, by wild horses." By his Campbell wife Angus Og left a
young son, named Donald, to be known as *Domnhall Dubh* or Donald the Black whom,
however, his grandfather Argyll prudently removed for safekeeping to his own castle of

Innischonaill in the middle of Loch Awe.

King James III, it must be said, did not in the long run fulfil his early promise as a man of action. To its very end his reign continued to be punctuated by plots and counterplots, an active part in which was played not only by the Islesmen, but by the English, by his own brothers, Albany and Mar, and by Archibald Douglas Earl of Angus, head of the Red Douglases who, "rising upon the ruins of the Black", quickly succeeded them as a major menace to the Crown. All this shook the royal authority and in 1488 the Campbell Chief, Earl Colin of Argyll, though Chancellor of Scotland, Royal Lieutenant for the West and Master of the King's Household, readily joined the Douglas Earl of Angus, the Homes and the Hepburns, in a plot to overthrow the King, who, we are told, "happinit to be slain", in the confusion which followed an encounter with the rebels at Sauchieburn near Stirling.* James's fifteen year old son was now set on the throne in his place as King James IV. While wearing an iron chain about his body as a penance for his own part in the plot against his father, the young King had, in a way, good reason to be grateful to Colin of Argyll who, as a new reign began, thus found himself in a stronger position than ever.

* It seems probable that he was in fact stabbed to death by William Striveling or Stirling of Keir, masquerading as a priest.

Jacob von gots.
genaden küing.
von Schottland

CHAPTER VII
Flodden

Not surprisingly, one of the first problems to confront the new King and his advisers was a fresh recrudescence of trouble in the Western Isles. This time the rebellion was led, with Cameron support, by John of the Isles' ambitious nephew, Alexander of Lochalsh, who, like his cousin Angus Og before him, resented the settlement imposed on the Lordship by the Crown. In 1491, in a fresh attempt to regain the long disputed Earldom of Ross, Alexander seized Inverness. He also ravaged the lands of his neighbours the Mackenzies of Kintail who, however, having by this time firmly transferred their allegiance to the Crown, soundly defeated him and took him prisoner at the Battle of Park (*Blair na Park*) by the river Connan in Ross-shire, not far from what is now Strathpeffer.

James IV was now eighteen. He was to prove a man of a different calibre from his predecessors, a true Renaissance prince, courageous and decisive, with wide interests and a multitude of talents. His reaction to Alexander's rebellion and to the discovery that John of the Isles had again been intriguing with the English, was simply to forfeit the Lordship of the Isles once and for all. In 1493 he annexed it to the Crown and the following year old John finally gave in, to die some years later as a pauper in a common lodging house in Dundee, after which he was buried in Paisley Abbey and the cost of his funeral charged to the Treasury. King James's decision marked the end of an era. "It is no joy without Clan Donald," sang the MacDonald bard gloomily. "It is no strength to be without them." Whether he realised it or not, the step the King had taken was a fateful one. By his action he was not simply quelling a troublesome chief. He was disrupting a whole ancient world, leaving in its place a dangerous void and giving free scope to the conflicting interests and ambitions of the variously motivated successors who sought to fill it.

Nor was this all. With the forfeiture of the Lordship, began the disintegration of Clan Donald, until then greatest of all the clans. The Chiefship itself was disputed, being claimed both by MacDonald of Lochalsh and by Donald Dubh, the young son of the deplorable Angus Og. In the same way, the chieftains of the Clan's different branches, notably Clanranald and Glengarry, could now claim that they held their lands directly from the Crown instead of from the Lord of the Isles and were therefore Chiefs in their own right. Equally, the Chiefs of the other island clans, Macleans, Macleods, MacNeils and, on the mainland, of the Camerons and Clan Chattan, all

James II as a young man. Illumination by Jorg von Ehingen. In 1449 James, now nineteen, took control of affairs. He was to rule for just eleven years. During the reign of his grandson James IV, the Mackenzie Chiefs gave a stag as an annual tribute to their king.

The quality of Scottish craftmanship spans the centuries. The bronze shield (above), from the 8th century BC, was used mostly for ceremonial purposes and is the forerunner of the Highland targe. The 16th-century silver gilt Galloway Mazer (right), with a finely engraved scrolling foliate design on a hatched ground, belonged to Archibald Stewart, Lord Provost of Edinburgh in 1578. Scottish mazers of this period were of finer quality than their southern counterparts.

former vassals of the Lordship, followed suit, the charters under which they held their lands being removed and confirmed by the Crown, so that they, too, became completely independent clans with well defined interests and policies of their own. Clearly, the possibilities of trouble were endless.

In 1493 King James appointed as Chamberlain of the Isles his cousin Duncan Stewart of Appin, who now established Castle Stalker on the Cormorant's Rock in the Sound of Lorne as his own strategically placed stronghold. The following year, arriving with a strong naval force under Sir Andrew Wood, James posted a garrison in Dunaverty Castle on a headland near the Mull of Kintyre. This was, however, almost immediately recaptured by John MacDonald of Dunniveg in Islay who added insult to injury by hanging its newly appointed Royal Keeper before the King's very eyes. But the old allegiances no longer held good. The MacDonalds of Ardnamurchan, whose new-found loyalty to the Crown now considerably outweighed their loyalty to their fellow-clansmen, quickly recovered the castle for the Crown and, having captured the offending John of Islay and four of his sons, despatched them to Edinburgh where in due course they were hanged. "A sad deed," wailed the compiler of the Annals of Ulster for 1499, no doubt himself a MacDonald, "was done in this year by the King of Scotland, James Stewart. Eoin MacDomhnaill, King of the Foreigners' Isles and Eoin the Warlike, his son, and Raghnall the Red and Domhnall the Freckled were all executed on one gallows in the month before Lammas." And when Alexander of Lochalsh next rebelled against the King, it was once again his kinsman MacDonald of Ardnamurchan who came out against him, this time defeating and killing him.

One Western clan who gained considerably by the latest turn of events were the Mackenzies. Following their timely change of allegiance and the valuable service they had rendered by defeating Alexander MacDonald of Lochalsh at Blair na Park, they were generously rewarded in the ensuing redistribution of territory. Freed from any allegiance they had ever accorded to the Lordship of the Isles, they had by this time firmly established themselves as an independent clan with the best of prospects. A succession of able chiefs further contributed to this happy result. Upright Alexander's son, Kenneth of the Battle, so called for his part in the overthrow of Alexander of Lochalsh, sensibly followed the course set for him by his father. He died in 1491 and was buried in Beauly Priory. Of Kenneth's son, John, it was said to be doubtful whether his predecessor's courage or his own prudence had contributed most to the rise of his family's fortunes. A score of years later his own mountainous region of Kintail, where the River Shiel flows into Loch Duich, was duly constituted a feudal barony, giving its chief full judicial powers over his clan. Thereafter, as their tribute to the King, the Mackenzie Chiefs delivered to him each year a fine stag, heraldically represented by the stag's head in their coat of arms and echoed by their Gaelic title: *Caberfeidh* or Deer's Antlers. Though the Macleods remained loyal to the Lordship to the end and readily joined in successive attempts to restore it, they had in fact little reason to regret its passing. Despite their loyalty to the MacDonalds, the latter had not hesitated to distribute Sleat, Uist and other former MacLeod lands among members of their own family and clan. By the end of the fifteenth century Siol Tormod, the MacLeods of Dunvegan, having gained their independence, had become a powerful clan in their own right and, with the other Western clans, still shared a healthy disregard for any central authority. "Alexander MacLeod," ran a legal document of the period, "dwelleth in ye isles, whear ye officers of ye law dare not pass for hazard of their lives." By this time the MacLeod Chiefs had for three centuries or more dwelt on Skye in their great castle of Dunvegan, parts of which, they claimed, had been built by their famous Norse name-father Leod himself. Its massive keep was believed to date from the fourteenth century and to be the work of Malcolm, the Third Chief. At Dunvegan the MacLeods religiously preserved the famous Fairy Flag, on which were said to depend the fortunes of both Chief and Clan. This had been kept at Dunvegan since at least the fourteenth century and was believed by some to have been brought back from the East by an early Norse forebear. Over the centuries it was regularly carried into battle as a standard and, if waved at the right moment, was believed to possess the power of saving the clan from disaster – but not more than three times, two such occasions being by now already in

A MacDonald targe, depicting double-headed eagles, from the end of the 17th century. Leather shields were more effective than metal against swords.

Dunottar Castle (overleaf), stronghold of the Keiths, Earls Marischal. On landing here in June 1650 Charles II was received by William Keith, the 7th Earl Marischal, who served him plentiful fresh salmon. Following the Earl Marischal's participation in the Jacobite Rising of 1715 his castle was forfeited and dismantled.

Kenneth Sutherland, 3rd Lord Duffus (died 1734), by Richard Waitt. The Viking Southland was made an Earldom in the 13th century in favour of William of Duffus, the descendant of a Flemish noble whose family later adopted the name Sutherland.

the past at Glendale in 1490 and at Trumpan in 1597, having one to come. According to one prophecy a MacLeod Chief by the name of John will regain the lands lost by his clan over the centuries and lead the MacLeods on to yet greater glory. The present Chief, it may be observed, himself bears that name, but has not, as yet, regained any lost lands for his clan.

Having assumed the Lordship of the Isles for himself, James IV, a civilised and relatively humane man, attempted a rather gentler and more constructive approach to the Western Highlands. He learned Gaelic ("The King even speaks the language of the savages who live in some parts of Scotland and the Islands," wrote the Spanish Ambassador at his Court), and from time to time would himself actually visit the Highlands and Islands, hunting and feasting with the Chiefs and encouraging the

clansmen to engage in fishing, shipbuilding and other supposedly worthwhile pursuits. In 1493, in forgiving mood, he even confirmed the Cameron Chief, Ewen, in his possession of certain lands in the neighbourhood of Lochalsh and Locheil, only recently granted to him by John of the Isles in return for his active support against the Crown in the rising of 1491. With the lands of Glen Loy and Loch Arkaig, these were later erected into the Barony of Locheil, from which Ewen and his successors in due course assumed the style of Cameron of Lochiel.

In the long run, however, King James's attempts to pacify the West met with but little success and the chaos which had followed the disintegration of the Lordship continued unabated. Accordingly in 1498 he resorted once more to the classic feudal approach adopted by his father some twenty years earlier, making Archibald Campbell, who in 1493 had succeeded his father Colin as Second Earl of Argyll, Lieutenant of the Isles, with powers to revoke charters and feu lands, a position of strength of which Archibald, who was also Justice-General, not surprisingly made the fullest use. James meanwhile had appointed the Gordon Chief, Huntly, whose father had held the same post before him, to be his Lieutenant for the North, with powers which extended from the Forth to the Orkneys. In this manner he in effect divided the Highlands and Islands between two viceroys, at the same time shrewdly establishing a rough balance of power between them.

Over the previous hundred years the Gordons had gained greatly in influence and power. In 1411 they had with other north-eastern clans fought against the Lord of the Isles at Harlaw and had by the middle of the century achieved a position of considerable strength in the north east. In 1402, Sir Adam Gordon of Gordon and Strathbogie had died leaving no male heir. But Alexander, his daughter Elizabeth's eldest son by her marriage to Sir William Seton of Seton (a descendant of the quick-thinking Sir Alexander Seton who had so timeously changed sides at Bannockburn) had taken the name and arms of Gordon and so continued the line of Gordon Chiefs, being in 1445 created Earl of Huntly. Meanwhile Elizabeth's bastard first cousins, Jock and Tam, sons of her uncle John by a handfast marriage, continued the male line less officially. From them descend many well regarded local families of Gordons, who over the centuries have proved an important source of strength to their clan. They include the Earls and Marquesses of Aberdeen. In 1451, possibly to balance the reviving power of the Douglases, King James II had added the old Comyn Lordship of Badenoch to Huntly's already considerable possessions and, when the following year the Earls of Crawford and Ross raised an army to march against the King, it was Huntly who in 1452 helped defeat the rebels in battle at Brechin. His victory there left him one of the most powerful nobles in Scotland and this King James III recognised when in 1476 he made

Norman, 22nd Chief of Clan MacLeod (1748), by Allan Ramsay. Norman succeeded his young brother in 1706 thus becoming a Chief in his cradle. He is shown wearing trews and a plaid, often worn by Chiefs as riding dress in preference to the kilt.

Rory Mor's Horn, the ancestral drinking vessel of the MacLeod Chiefs. On coming of age the Chief's heir had to drain a full horn of claret – equivalent to one and two-thirds of a bottle – at a draught "without setting down or falling down". The present Chief performed this feat successfully in 1965. His time was one minute fifty-seven seconds.

George, the second Earl, his Lieutenant for Northern Scotland or, as he was popularly called, Cock of the North, the same appointment being bestowed on several later Gordon Chiefs. Indeed, between 1475 and 1557 successive Earls of Huntly were to be given control of the North of Scotland from the Forth to the Orkneys at least half a dozen times.

In the absence of a standing army the principal duty of a Royal Lieutenant was to keep order in the area under his jurisdiction. For this purpose Argyll and Huntly alike used the men at arms of their own clans, taking full advantage of the opportunity thus offered to further their own interests and pay off old scores. It is therefore scarcely surprising that in both regions the practice should have given rise to enduring feuds between them and their neighbours, feuds not necessarily unwelcome to the central government as a means of maintaining a kind of uneasy balance of power in the Highlands.

Archibald of Argyll's appointment as a Royal Lieutenant with vice-regal authority in the West marked another decisive stage in the rise to pre-eminence of Clan Campbell, who throughout

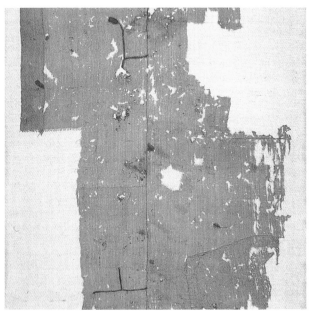

Dunvegan Castle, the Sea Gate entrance. Until 1745, the only access to the castle was by sea gate through the curtain wall and along a narrow entrance passage.

The MacLeods' Fairy Flag (right) came from the East and may date from the 7th century. A possible link is through Harald Hardrada, King of Norway, who had in his youth commanded the Varangian Guard of the Emperor in Constantinople. It is believed to hold protective powers that have saved the Clan from peril on more than one occasion.

Dunvegan Castle, an engraving by Thomas Pennant.

the fifteenth century had steadily and methodically extended their territories and influence in Cowal, in Knapdale, in Lorne and, latterly, at the expense of the Fletchers and MacGregors who had formerly dwelt there, in neighbouring Glenorchy. During the next twenty years Earl Archibald, who, like his father, held many high offices of state, did everything he could, as Lieutenant of the Isles, to establish the greatest possible measure of control over the Western Highlands and Islands, while at the same time progressively strengthening his own position and that of his clan. With the decline of Clan Donald, the Campbells were to play an ever more important part in Highland affairs, usually, though not invariably, in support of established authority.

At the turn of the century Archibald of Argyll contrived by an unusually clever stratagem to extend his clan's influence deep into north-eastern Scotland, far outside its usual sphere of action. Not many weeks after the death in 1495 of John, Thane of Cawdor, the latter's ancient inheritance passed to his posthumous daughter Muriel. In the ensuing confusion, Archibald, who happened to be Justice General, managed, without too much difficulty, to secure the child's wardship for himself. At the same time

Targe of MacDonald of Keppoch with his heraldic achievements. He was killed at Culloden.

he found means of bringing pressure to bear on Muriel's maternal grandfather, Rose of Kilravock, a neighbouring Nairnshire chieftain, who happened at the time to be facing a charge of armed robbery. Four years after this, in 1499, he sent sixty Campbell clansmen to Cawdor to carry off little Muriel, now a red-haired child of four. Characteristically, he had foreseen every contingency and, when someone naively suggested that, if Muriel were to die, his carefully laid plan might fall through, his interrogator at once received the assurance that, "so long as a red-haired lass could be found in Campbell country", little Muriel would never die. In fact the true Muriel, whom her mother had prudently branded with a red hot key, while her devoted old nurse had bitten off the end of one of her fingers to make her even more readily identifiable, remained alive and in due course actually married Archibald of Argyll's third son John, who thus became the first Campbell of Cawdor. To this day, his direct descendant, the present Earl of that Ilk, still resides in the fine castle which Muriel's

Standard of the Earl Marischal of Scotland, carried at Flodden Field. It is 8 feet, 8 inches long.

grandfather, the Thane, built for himself in 1454 on the spot, it is said, where a wandering donkey laden with a box of gold had conveniently come to rest.

But, despite such occasional forays further afield, the West remained the true Campbell heartland and, as part of an overall strategy, Campbell marriages were usually planned with a view to consolidating and extending Campbell influence there. With this purpose in mind, Earl Archibald's daughter Catherine had shortly before been married to the not entirely estimable Lachlan Cattanach Maclean of Duart. But Shaggy Lachlan, later wishing for reasons of his own to be rid of her, "without his hand causing her death",

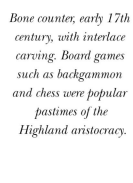

Bone counter, early 17th century, with interlace carving. Board games such as backgammon and chess were popular pastimes of the Highland aristocracy.

simply left her on a low rock in the Sound of Lorne to be drowned by the rising tide. As chance would have it, however, she was rescued from this unpleasant predicament by her brother, John of Cawdor, who happened to be passing that way and many years later murdered his former brother-in-law in bed in Edinburgh. The rock, only visible at low tide, has been known ever since as The Lady's Rock. In the far North, as elsewhere, King James IV sought to play one clan off against the other, thereby in the long run perpetuating old feuds and generating fresh bitterness. In 1499, in return for helping to capture the recently outlawed Sutherland of Dirled, he granted to the latter's neighbour, Odo Mackay, a large proportion of Dirled's lands. Soon after this he confirmed Odo in the possession of Strathnaver and his own Mackay heartland, *Duthaich Mhic Aoidh*, which, while consisting partly of barren mountain country, also contained good salmon rivers and convenient

stretches of the adjacent coast, Strathnaver itself being the most fertile valley of all and the most populous.

The Sutherland Chiefs, who since 1519 had by marriage become Gordons, had long been the hereditary enemies of Clan Mackay over whom, greatly to the latter's resentment, they claimed superiority. In 1370 Iye Mackay had been involved in a dispute with the then Earl of Sutherland, who, having greatly to his own advantage married the King's sister, bluntly declared the Mackays to be his "ancient enemies". In the end Sutherland neatly settled the dispute by murdering both Mackay and his son, just, it was said, as they had succeeded in conclusively proving their case. After this the trouble between the two clans continued intermittently through the centuries, losing none of its bitterness and leading to innumerable reciprocal acts of violence and terror.

In the century and a half between 1400 and 1550, successive Mackay Chiefs, described in the mid-14th century as leaders of 4000 men, fought on their own account no less than ten pitched battles and, when not otherwise occupied, were always glad to undertake Commissions of Fire and Sword on behalf of the Crown. One of their more notable forays was against the outlawed Torquil Macleod of Lewis, whom they captured in 1506, after besieging and successfully storming his island stronghold of Stornoway, a feat of arms for which they were generously rewarded at his expense. As far back as the 8th century *Sagard Ruadh*, the famous Red Friar of Strathnaver, sometimes identified with St Maeprubha himself, had prophesied doom for the Mackays if one of their Chiefs should ever marry into the detested House of Sutherland. Several centuries later, however, in 1589, the Gordon Earl of Sutherland of the day, disregarding the feud between their respective clans and urgently needing the Mackays' support as allies, offered their then Chief, Huisdean Dubh Mackay, £50,000 Scots and his daughter Jane's hand in marriage in return for all the help he could give him, an offer which Black Huisdean, being in acute financial difficulties at the time, promptly accepted. This in spite of already being married to the daughter of the Sinclair Earl of Caithness. But despite the Red Friar's prophecy of doom, Donald, the child of this strictly speaking bigamous marriage, was to prove an outstanding Chief, later fighting loyally for King Charles I, who in return raised him to the peerage as the first Lord Reay and subsequently created him Earl of Strathnaver, though, owing to the Civil War, then at its height, the necessary patent for the latter title was sadly never completed.

Being widely resented by the inhabitants who, despite all attempts to discipline them, remained as turbulent as ever, James IV's decision to transfer responsibility for what happened in the Highlands to Royal Lieutenants was doomed to failure, doing in the long run far more harm than good. After what had appeared to be the final eclipse of the Lordship of the Isles, the Macleans of Duart, for centuries the MacDonalds' most loyal supporters, showed for a time, it is true, serious signs of coming to terms with the Crown and in 1496 their lands, hitherto held under charter from the Lords of the Isles, were erected into a feudal barony by James IV. But, like the other Islesmen, they remained restless at heart so that, when in 1501 the MacDonalds rose again, this time under old John of the Isles' nineteen year old grandson, Donald Dubh, son of the notorious and later legitimized Angus Og, they readily threw in their lot with young Donald. Having, with the help of some loyal MacDonalds from Glencoe, escaped from

the Campbell castle of Innischonnail on Loch Awe, where he was being held in custody by his uncle, Argyll, Donald, at the head of a strong force of MacDonalds, Macleans and other Islesmen, marched in his turn on Inverness, sacked it and burned the Royal Castle to the ground. Realising their role in the rising, the King now personally took the field against the Macleans, who, under their Chief, Hector the Swarthy of Duart, held out manfully until in the end James brought the full force of his Navy and Artillery to bear on them. By 1506 young Donald Dubh had been hunted down and re-imprisoned, this time in Edinburgh Castle, and the rising had collapsed. In anticipation of further trouble, the King now set about establishing a number of strategically placed strongpoints throughout the Highlands, at Tarbert and Loch Kilkerran in Kintyre, at Inverlochy on Loch Linnhe, and at Castle Urquhart on Loch Ness, while at the same time greatly strengthening his fleet.

By this time an alliance, if not an even closer connection with Scotland, was being strenuously sought after by both France and England; and at the Scottish court

Breacachadh Castle, the medieval stronghold of the Macleans of Coll. The oldest part probably dates from the time of Iain Garbh, first chieftain of Coll (15th century). Beyond it is the Georgian House where Coll's eldest son Donald entertained Dr Johnson in 1773.

pro-French and pro-English factions were busily manoeuvring for position. In 1503 James IV had been married at Holyrood amid scenes of great splendour to Margaret Tudor, the fifteen-year-old daughter of King Henry VII of England, at the same time signing with her father a treaty of perpetual peace. This did not, however, mean the end of Scotland's Auld Alliance with France, which was formally renewed in 1512. The following year France, confronted by a powerful coalition which included the Pope, the Emperor, the King of Spain and, last but not least, James's bellicose young brother-in-law, who had recently come to the throne as Henry VIII of England, appealed to James for help. In response to this appeal, James sent Henry an ultimatum and, on being told in reply that Henry regarded himself as "the verie owner of Scotland", which the Scottish King "held of him by homage", invaded England. Scotland's survival as an independent country was at stake.

Like Bruce, two centuries earlier, James carried his country with him, leading into battle a couple of weeks later the flower of Scottish chivalry. On 9 September 1513, the opposing armies met at Flodden, where in a few hours the King's army was annihilated and he with it, leaving his infant son James to succeed him. "O what a noble and triumphant courage was this," wrote an English Chronicler admiringly, "for a kynge to fyghte in a battaye as a meane soldier."

At Flodden, as at Bannockburn two centuries before, not only the great nobles of the South, but a number of Highland Chiefs, some of them not always noted for their loyalty to the Crown, fell fighting for King and Country. Archibald of Argyll, "a man of great action and a valiant captain", who led the right wing of the Royal Army, was amongst those who gave their lives, as were his kinsmen, Campbell of Strachur and Campbell of Glenorchy. The Master of Lovat likewise, Maclean of Duart, who half a dozen years before had been in open rebellion against King James, is usually claimed to have died gloriously in the forefront of the battle.* Ewen Cameron of Lochiel was certainly among the survivors, as was Huntly who, leaving the battlefield early on with his brother Adam Gordon, succeeded in securing a seat on the Council of Regency set up on the King's death, an office of which he was to make the best possible use.

* Such at any rate is the version of the Maclean seanachies. There is, however, some doubt as to which Maclean chief this can have been. If Swarthy Hector had still been alive, he would have been 96 at the time of the battle. On the other hand, whether he fought at Flodden or not, his successor Shaggy Lachlan undoubtedly lived long enough to be murdered in bed by his Campbell brother-in-law in 1527, a dozen years after the battle.

Another survivor of Flodden who, quickly switching loyalties, took full advantage of the Scottish defeat and of the opportunities it clearly offered, was Sir Donald Gallda MacDonald of Lochalsh, eldest son of the murdered Alexander of Lochalsh. Though the King had actually knighted him on Flodden fields, two months later he was in revolt. Proclaiming himself Lord of the Isles on behalf of his kinsman Donald Dubh, once again safely in prison, Donald Gallda, together with the MacDonalds of Dunyveg and Glengarry, now stormed Castle Urquhart which King James had established as a royal stronghold less than ten years before. At the same time Lachlan Cattanach Maclean of Duart seized the Royal Castle of Cairnburgh on its island off Mull and massacred the royal garrison, while Macleod of Harris took Dunskaith in Skye. In this emergency, Albany, recently proclaimed Regent, authorized young Colin Campbell, who had succeeded his father as Earl of Argyll, and who in 1517 was appointed Royal Lieutenant, to handle the Macleans, leaving MacIain of Ardnamurchan, who, as we have seen, had murdered Donald Gallda's father, to deal with Clan Donald, and appointing Lochiel and The Mackintosh temporary Lieutenants in Lochaber. In the north he relied on the Mackenzies to hold their own against the MacDonalds, while in the north-east Huntly, his power still further increased, continued as Royal Lieutenant. Unfortunately for Donald Gallda, he was not universally popular with the Islanders. For a time his insurrection hung fire and a peaceful outcome seemed possible, until emissaries from England eventually persuaded him to persist in his revolt. But Donald had counted without Shaggy Lachlan Maclean of Duart, who, having at first enthusiastically supported him, all at once executed a complete volte-face and made his peace with the Crown. After which, turning against his former ally, he strongly urged the Lords in Council to eliminate him and his two brothers and thus, as he put it, "destroy the wicked blood of the Isles". "For," he added, "as long as that blood reigns, the King shall never have the Isles in peace." For this well timed change of allegiance Lachlan was rewarded by the Crown with a generous grant of lands. In the end Donald Gallda's rising was successfully suppressed, though Donald himself lived long enough to kill his father's murderer MacIain of Ardnamurchan in battle at Craiganairgid, the Silver Crag, in Morvern. Meanwhile Colin of Argyll made prompt and skilful use of the opportunity thus offered still further to increase the power and influence of his clan.

CHAPTER VIII
Clan Wars and the Stuarts

Flodden and its aftermath had plunged Scotland into turmoil. The war with England dragged on. As a child, little James V was in the phrase of a contemporary, "coupit from hand to hand" by embattled factions, while Regents ruled in his stead. After his father's death his Tudor mother, Margaret, had married the Red Douglas Earl of Angus, leader of the so-called English party, who was actively plotting with his brother-in-law Henry VIII to kidnap the little King and carry him off to England. But having in 1528 attained the age of sixteen, James, who hated his stepfather, managed to escape and reach Stirling. "I vow," he declared, "that Scotland will not hold us both." He was as good as his word. Not long after, Angus was driven across the border into England, whence with English Henry's encouragement he continued to plot against his stepson who retaliated by burning Angus's beautiful sister Lady Glamis as a witch.

In the Western Highlands, after six or seven years of uneasy peace, shrewdly used by Colin of Argyll still further to consolidate his position, trouble broke out once more. Not unnaturally, the new Maclean Chief, Hector of Duart, bore a grudge against the Campbells for the assassination of his father Shaggy Lachlan by Argyll's brother John of Cawdor, while Alexander MacDonald of Islay was firmly convinced that Argyll had designs on certain Crown lands which had been granted to him. This gave them something in common. Accordingly, in the summer of 1529 Macleans and MacDonalds joined forces to raid Campbell territory, while the Campbells, for their part, responded by raiding Morvern and Mull.

By this time Colin of Argyll had died and had been succeeded by his son Archibald, who as Fourth Earl assumed most of his father's offices, including his Lieutenancy for the West. Like his father, Archibald was soon pressing at Court for more effective action against the rebellious Western clans. In the end, after various changes of plan, the decision seems to have been reached that the King should himself lead an expedition against the rebels and preparations were made accordingly. It was now that Archibald of Argyll submitted to the Privy Council drastic new plans for what he called the "danting of the Ilis", asking for a fresh Commission of Lieutenancy for himself and offering to destroy the rebels root and branch without any help from the Government. This, he pointed out, was something of which he and his clan were more than capable and of which they had had considerable experience.

Lord Mungo Murray (1688–1700), a younger son of the Marquess of Atholl, painted by John Michael Wright in the mid 1680's. It is the earliest major portrait of Highland dress.

Simultaneously the King's bastard half-brother, the Earl of Moray, eagerly offered to perform a similar service in the North.

On hearing of the preparations that were being made against them, both Alexander of Islay and Hector of Duart thought it advisable to offer their submission to the Crown and were duly pardoned. Disgusted at this setback to his plans, Argyll now deliberately set out to provoke disorders in the West in the hope of thus securing a fresh pretext for intervening there. But James's disturbed childhood had given him some insight into the character and methods of power-hungry nobles. Ignoring the far-reaching but, as it happened, unfounded accusations brought by Argyll against MacDonald of Islay, who had of late been careful not to put himself in the wrong, the King listened not so much to Argyll's charges, but rather to MacDonald's counter-charges, namely that Argyll and his father before him had abused their position as Royal Lieutenants to further their private interests and ambitions. As a result, Argyll was now deprived of his offices and for a time actually imprisoned, while Moray also fell from favour. James did not, however, avail himself of MacDonald's offer to raise a strong force of his own in order, as he put it, "to get reason of the Earl". Instead, he despatched MacDonald to Ireland to make trouble there for Henry of England, while prudently retaining his son James in Edinburgh "to be educated" – in other words, as a hostage. For a time, thanks to direct royal intervention, rather than by the agency of Royal Lieutenants, peace of a kind was brought to the Highlands and a working relationship established between the King and the Western Clans. Indeed, Alexander of Islay was later even entrusted with certain official responsibilities. But this respite was shortlived. Less than ten years later, in 1540, James found it necessary to sail in person with a strong naval force right round Scotland, from the Forth on the east to Dumbarton in the West, inviting on board and carrying off with him as he went, part guests and part prisoners, the Chiefs of a considerable number of clans, notably Mackay of Strathnaver, the MacLeods of Dunvegan and Lewis, Mackenzie of Kintail, MacDonell of Glengarry, the Captain of Clanranald, MacDonald of Islay and Maclean of Duart, later releasing them one by one in return for firm pledges of good behaviour. As .a further precaution, a Royal Governor and garrison were now installed in MacDonald's castle of Dunyveg on the southern coast of Islay.

By the middle of the sixteenth century it had become clearer than ever that for Scotland the choice now lay between a closer connection either with her old ally, France, or else with her southern neighbour and hereditary enemy, England. This was the age of the Reformation. Having himself broken with Rome in 1534, Henry VIII of England was now determined to turn Scotland Protestant too, in the hope of thus winning her away from Catholic France and bringing her under his own domination. But, despite the

English King's persistent attempts to follow up the advantage gained at Flodden, the Scots still somehow managed to retain their independence.

In pursuance of his aims, Henry had first sought to persuade James to marry his daughter (and James's first cousin) Mary, but in 1538 James, whose first wife Madeleine de Valois had died the year before after only a few months of marriage, married instead another Frenchwoman, Marie de Guise-Lorraine, thereby further strengthening Scotland's French and Roman Catholic connection. The English, meanwhile, were growing increasingly aggressive. In 1542 some Irish chiefs gave Henry a convenient pretext for what he already had in mind by offering James the Crown of Ireland. Despatching some troops across the border, the English King simply proclaimed himself Lord-Superior of Scotland. James, by now a sick man and unable to rely on his nobles, replied by invading England. On 24 November 1542 his army, mutinous and badly led by his favourite Oliver Sinclair, was overwhelmed at Solway Moss. Sadly the King rode to Falkland where, two weeks later, he received on his deathbed the far from welcome news that his wife had borne him a daughter. Remembering how the Crown had come to his family through Marjory Bruce, "It came with a lass," he said, "and it will gang with a lass." Then, bitterly, he gave "one little laughtir" and fell back dead. The baby girl, who had been christened Mary, was at once proclaimed Queen.

Mary Queen of Scots was less than a week old when she succeeded to the Scottish throne. For guidance and support, her mother, the staunchly Catholic Marie de Guise Lorraine, turned not unnaturally to her native France and to David Beaton, the powerful, able and intensely political Cardinal Archbishop of St Andrews. After some initial hesitation, the Regent, the Hamilton Earl of Arran, a man of limited intelligence ("half an idiot" one contemporary calls him) likewise lent his support to the ruling French party.

Having attempted, but failed to win the promise of little Mary's hand in marriage for his own son, Henry VIII now invaded Scotland in strength, burning Edinburgh and laying waste the Borders in what was known as the Rough Wooing. "Put all to fyre and sworde", ran the English Privy Council's instruction, "Burne Edinborough towne, so rased and defaced when you have sacked an gotten what ye can of it, as there may remayne forever a perpetual memory of the vengeance of God" – a strange enough prelude to a proposal of union between sovereign states.

At this critical juncture in Scottish history, the English found, not for the first time, ready allies in the Western Highlands and Islands. Managing to escape once more after

Robe of a Knight of the Thistle, 1687, made for one of the first knights of the Thistle. It follows closely the terms of the 1687 statutes, drawn up by James VII, specifying garments of unusual splendour.

nearly forty years in prison, Donald Dubh of the Isles had soon succeeded in raising a force of several thousand Islesmen to fight against the Scottish Crown. "Auld enemys to the realme of Scotland", they proudly styled themselves. The Macleans of Duart, Ardgour and Lochbuie, the Macdonalds of Clanranald and Ardnamurchan, the MacLeods of Dunvegan and Lewis and the MacNeils of Barra all rallied readily to Donald's cause. James MacDonald of Islay seems, for reasons of his own, to have held aloof, leaving his younger brother Angus to serve on the hastily reconstituted Council of the Isles.

From the outset the Islesmen enjoyed the support of the Stewart Earl of Lennox, who, disappointed in his hope of supplanting his rival, Arran, as Regent, had shown his resentment against Cardinal Beaton and the Queen Mother (whom he had hoped to marry) by joining the English Party. He now acted, though not very effectively, as go-between and paymaster for Henry VIII in his often tortuous dealings with Donald Dubh and the Islesmen. While the English laid waste the Borders, the Islesmen readily set

about devastating Argyll's lands, as usual slaughtering such of his vassals as they could catch and carrying off considerable quantities of his cattle. In Ireland, meanwhile, considerable numbers of English troops were assembling with the avowed intention of invading Western Scotland. There they were joined in the summer of 1545 by Donald Dubh himself with a force of no less than one hundred and eighty galleys and four thousand men, "three thousand of them", the English King was informed, "very tall men, clothed, for the most part, in habergeons of mail, armed with long swords and long bows, but with few guns; the other thousand, tall maryners that rowed in the galleys." A further four thousand of Donald's warriors remained in Scotland to keep up the pressure on the Royal Lieutenants Huntly and Argyll, both of them at this stage still loyal to the Crown and to the French connexion. At Knockfergus in Ireland meanwhile, Donald Dubh and his assembled followers had in August taken an oath of allegiance to the King of England, recognized Lennox as Regent of Scotland and, in return for a substantial sum of money, undertaken to join the English in their proposed invasion.

But in the end, as is apt to happen, nothing came of this promising project. As the weeks went by, enthusiasm for it waned. Leadership was lacking. After a time the Islesmen made their way back to Scotland where, having quarrelled among

themselves over the way in which Maclean of Duart had distributed the funds, they finally dispersed. Donald Dubh himself returned to Ireland, where he died the following year of a fever and was accorded a fine funeral which, the records show, cost the King of England four hundred pounds sterling. He is reliably said to have left a bastard son, but as his successor and titular Lord of the Isles the Islesmen now adopted James MacDonald of Islay. When, in his turn, James of Islay offered his services to the English King, the latter, being by then otherwise occupied, seems, however, to have returned no reply. The power of the Isles, it soon became all too clear, had flared up for the last time. The MacDonalds fell out among themselves. The Western Clans split along new lines of cleavage. And the Campbells, for whom a new era was now opening, cleverly exploiting their neighbours' disagreements, continued their own steady ascent to paramount power.

Henry VIII of England died in 1547. Shortly before his death he had offered a reward of a thousand pounds for the elimination of Cardinal Beaton, the leading protagonist of the French connexion and a close associate of the Queen Mother. The Cardinal had in due course been assassinated but, with French help, his assassins had been rounded up and disposed of. After defeating the Scots in battle at Pinkie, the

The Gowrie Conspiracy. In August 1600 James VI visited Gowrie House, residence of the Earl of Gowrie. His courtiers saw him at a turret window shouting "I am murdered, help, help!" Led by a youth named John Ramsay, the nobles rushed into the house. Ramsay stabbed Ruthven and the nobles then slashed him to death. The Lord Gowrie was also killed by Ramsay.

English now withdrew, protesting, a trifle unconvincingly, that their only purpose in invading Scotland had been to "forward the godly purpose of marriage".

The French troops, on the other hand, stayed on and, for the time being, Scotland remained both Roman Catholic and closely linked to France. In 1548 the six year old Mary Queen of Scots was sent to France as the affianced bride of the Dauphin Francois, whom she married ten years later. "France and Scotland," declared the French King, "leaping for blithness, are one country." In 1554 the half-idiot Arran resigned the Regency and the Queen Mother, Marie de Guise-Lorraine, took his place. Meanwhile, under the inspiring leadership of John Knox, the Protestant movement in Scotland had continued to gain ground. In 1557 a number of powerful nobles signed what came to be known as the First Covenant, openly declaring against Rome. Prominent amongst them was Archibald Roy (Red Archibald), Fourth Earl of Argyll. On his death the following year he was succeeded as Fifth Earl by his son Archibald Donn (Brown Archibald), who was likewise to play an active part in the events leading to the Scottish Reformation, which thus from the start enjoyed solid Campbell support.

Then in 1558 came news of the death of Mary Tudor, of the accession to the English throne of her sister Elizabeth and of England's reversion to Protestantism, bringing fresh comfort and encouragement to Protestants in Scotland. In June 1560 the death of Marie de Guise removed the last serious obstacle to a Protestant victory in Scotland. Despite early setbacks, John Knox had triumphed in the end. "Now it is come!" he could cry on his death-bed a dozen years later. In July a Treaty was signed in Edinburgh, formally recognising Elizabeth as Queen of England and providing for the withdrawal from Scotland of all English, but also of all French troops, thus marking in effect the end of the Auld Alliance and opening the way to ultimate union with England.

In the Highlands, meanwhile, things followed their usual turbulent course. With the rest of Clan Chattan, the Mackintoshes continued to play their full part in Highland affairs. Duncan, their 11th Chief, had, it will be recalled, been renowned for his gentleness and prudence as well as for his vigour. Though not all his successors were endowed with his gentleness and prudence, some could certainly match him for vigour.

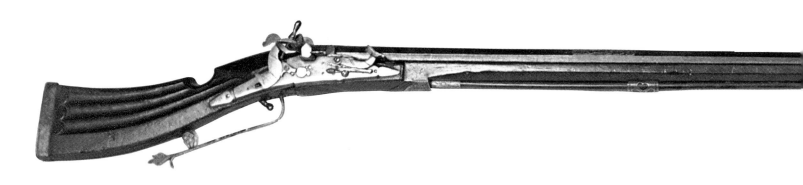

Against his father's wishes, Duncan's son Ferquhard had in 1491 joined Alexander of Lochalsh in his rebellion against the Crown and with him had stormed and burned Inverness Castle. As a result of this, by the time he succeeded his father as twelfth Chief in 1495, he was already in jail, where he was to remain for the next eighteen years. While Ferquhard was a prisoner, his cousin William acted as Chief in his place and, as such, led a series of not unsuccessful forays against the MacGregors, always ready for a fight, and the Camerons, who still occupied large areas claimed by Clan Chattan in Badenoch and Strathnairn and had further incurred the King's wrath by supporting Alexander of Lochalsh in his insurrection of 1491.

Having finally been released from prison after James IV's death at Flodden, Ferquhard MacKintosh had been enthusistically acclaimed as Chief in Inverness by a huge concourse of loyal clansmen, but the following year he had died and been succeeded by his cousin William, who had long led the Clan in his place. In the event, however, William did not enjoy the Chiefship for long, being murdered the very next year by his second cousin, John, who had long been convinced that he would himself have made a better Chief. Instead of which, however, having been caught in the act, he was promptly executed for his cousin's murder.

For the next nine years, from 1515 to 1524, Clan Mackintosh enjoyed a period of comparative calm under the leadership of William's diminutive brother, Lachlan Beg or Little Lachlan, "a verie honest and wise gentleman, of a peace-loving and law-abiding character". Of Lachlan Beg it is said that he ruled his clan with prudence and judgement and kept them to their duties. This did not, however, prevent two of them, Milmoir MacDhaibidh and John Mackintosh of Connage, from lying in wait for him while he was out hunting in the woods round Raigmore on the outskirts of Inverness and treacherously murdering him there.

In 1524 Little Lachlan's only legitimate son, William, succeeded his father as Fifteenth Chief. Being three years old at the time, he was at once taken away to be looked after by his uncle, James Stewart, Earl of Moray. This, not unnaturally, aroused the indignation of big Hector Mackintosh, a bastard son of Ferquhard, the twelfth Chief, whom, as being a man of great courage and physical strength, the Clan had chosen to occupy the post of Captain of Clan Chattan during their little Chief's minority. Disgusted by Moray's high-handed action, Clan Chattan, led by their burly Captain, now invaded and harried his lands. At this an extermination order was issued against them, which, though not immediately carried out, served as a temporary deterrent. The only lives to be spared, the Order specified, were those of priests, women and children, who instead were to be deported to the Shetland Islands and to Norway.

Threatened with extermination, the Mackintoshes, having once withdrawn, did not

The Breadalbane Gun (Dundee 1599) is believed to be the earliest complete Scottish gun. It bears the arms and initials of Sir Duncan Campbell of Glenorchy from whom the Earls of Breadalbane were descended. Made by Patrick Ramsay of Dundee, one of the main centres for gunmaking in the late 16th and early 17th centuries.

Stirling Castle (above and right) occupies a vital strategic position between Highlands and Lowlands. There has undoubtedly been a fortress there from prehistoric times. It was in order to prevent the Castle from falling into Scottish hands that in 1314 the English King Edward II met the army of Robert the Bruce at Bannockburn.

again invade Moray's territory until 1531. This time Moray was waiting for them. In the course of the ensuing engagement, he took three hundred of them prisoner, many of whom he executed, including Big Hector's brother William, whom he hanged. Hector himself managed to escape and was later granted a royal Pardon, but was eventually assassinated by, it was believed, a monk from St Andrews.

Such was the background of sustained violence that young William Mackintosh, by now nineteen and described as "a gentleman of fine qualities, much distinguished for his spirit and politeness, a perfect pattern of virtue", took up his duties as fifteenth Chief in 1540.

On Moray's death four years later, Huntly became Lieutenant of the North. Losing no time in asserting his authority, he immediately called on young William Mackintosh to join him and Fraser of Lovat (the third Lord Lovat) in supporting the latter's nephew, Ranald Macdonald, as Chief of Clanranald against the claims of his illegitimate, but infinitely more effective kinsman, Iain Moydertach or Iain of Moidart, famous throughout the Highlands for his "many foul and monstrous pranks". It was in itself unusual for a Fraser to marry into a West Highland clan, a course which was only too likely to lead to trouble. And now, as a result of his sister's marriage to a MacDonald, Lovat found himself deeply involved in a thoroughly unsavoury West Highland imbroglio.

Final stanzas of Cathal
MacMhuirich's poem
"Do isligh onior
Ghaoidheal", 1649.
MacMhuirich is
considered to have been
one of the finest Gaelic
poets of his period.

Having been brought up by the Frasers, Ranald was known to his own people as Gallda, the Stranger. Worse still, the great majority of Ranald's clansmen much preferred the bastard Iain Moydertach, whom they knew, to Ranald, the rightful heir, who was unknown to them. It was thus that in July 1544 Huntly and Lovat, at the head of a mixed force of four thousand Frasers, Gordons, Grants and Mackintoshes, including as many as 1500 of the latter clan, marched southwards together along the Great Glen to Inverlochy with the object of reinstating Ranald. At the approach of this formidable force, Iain Moydertach and his MacDonalds wisely took to the hills and Huntly and Lovat, having to all appearances attained their purpose, set out for home.

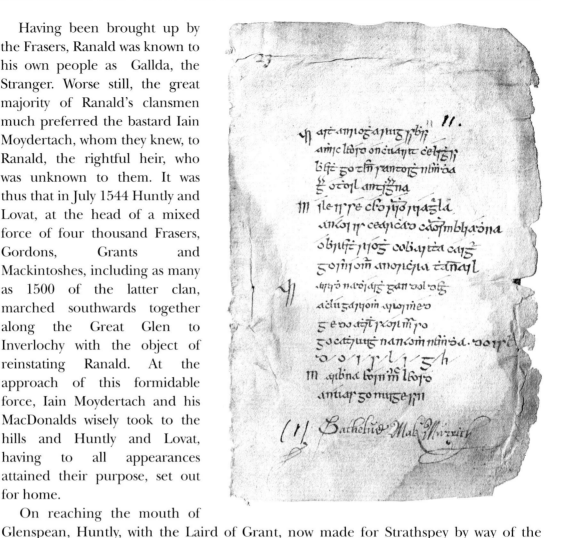

On reaching the mouth of Glenspean, Huntly, with the Laird of Grant, now made for Strathspey by way of the Braes of Lochaber and Badenoch, while Lovat, accompanied by Ranald Gallda, set out northwards for home along Glen Spean with some three hundred of his clansmen. But on 15 July at Kinlochlochy, at the eastern end of Loch Lochy, he was suddenly set upon by five or six hundred MacDonalds and Camerons who, resenting his attempted interference in their affairs, gleefully seized this opportunity of redressing the balance. To Lovat's dismay he was at this juncture joined by his nineteen year old son and heir, the Master of Lovat, lately returned from the University of Paris, whom he had been particularly anxious to leave at home but who, owing to the taunts of his stepmother, who possibly wished him dead, had hastened to join him. In the savage hand-to-hand fighting that followed, both Lovat and his son were killed, as was Ranald Gallda, the original cause of the dispute. Of the three hundred Frasers engaged, including most of the gentlemen of the clan, barely half a dozen survived and their allies and opponents suffered almost equally heavy losses. Because in the summer heat the contestants stripped to their shirts, the battle went down in history as *Blar na Leine*, the Field of the Shirts. Fortunately for their clan, the wives of most of the Frasers killed were pregnant at the time, with the result that within a matter of months the losses they had suffered in battle were made good. From their base in the West, Clan Mackenzie had throughout the sixteenth century continued their steady progress to ever greater influence and power. By one means or another their clan lands had been further extended, while a number of well planned marriages appreciably increased their standing and prestige. Kenneth of the Battle had married Agnes Fraser of Lovat, his son John, Elizabeth of Grant, and John's son Kenneth, Lady Elizabeth Stewart of Atholl, who in her turn possessed valuable Campbell connections. Nor was it long before Clan Kenneth's newly acquired standing was put triumphantly to the test. In 1544 Huntly, on becoming Lieutenant for the North, had directed young Kenneth Mackenzie of Kintail to attack the rebellious and newly victorious Iain Moydertach MacDonald and, when he refused, had ordered the other clans under his authority, Rosses, Grants and Mackintoshes, to join forces against him. But this the clans concerned, disliking Huntly and preferring to avoid a clash with so formidable an adversary, declined to do, with the result that, despite the best efforts of the Queen's Lieutenant, Mackenzie's disobedience went unpunished. Worse still, when, not long after, Huntly himself visited the neighbourhood, Kenneth, not wishing to see him settle there, chased him unceremoniously away.

Following the Battle of the Shirts, Iain Moydertach had in defiance of the Royal Lieutenant, successfully established himself as Chief of Clan Ranald. His accession to the Chiefship happened to coincide with Donald Dubh's final rising in the West in which Iain Moydertach joined enthusiastically. In the aftermath of the rising, The Mackintosh managed, as Huntly's Deputy and Steward of Lochaber, to capture two of his own hereditary enemies, both of whom had joined the rising, Cameron of Lochiel and MacDonald of Keppoch. These were duly handed over to Huntly, who beheaded them both. As for Iain Moydertach himself, who had taken a no less active part in the rising, he was in due course pardoned and went down in history as one of the great chiefs of Clan Ranald. He died in 1584 at his family's ancestral stronghold Castle Tioram on Loch Moidart.

In 1548 Huntly, in addition to his other honours, was created Earl of

Sir Alexander MacDonald of Sleat, by Copley. It shows him in full Highland dress in about 1775, in green tartan, later chosen as the tartan of the Chief of Clan MacDonald.

DESCENT OF JAMES I.
ENGLISH 17TH CENTURY

Moray and as such became William Mackintosh's immediate feudal superior. This was unlucky for William, for, in spite of his politeness and other sterling qualities, Huntly had a strong dislike for him, resenting in particular his close connection with the previous Earl of Moray, of whom his successor was still obsessively jealous. William, moreover, had an enemy in his own clan, Lachlan, the son of one of the men who had murdered his father and later been beheaded for their crime. Set on revenge, Lachlan Mackintosh now went to Huntly with a story that William was conspiring to assassinate him. This was enough for Huntly who, seizing William, carried him off to Aberdeen, tried him with himself as judge and condemned him to death.

After this the Fifteenth Chief of Clan Mackintosh was never seen again. Just how he met his end is uncertain. It is believed, however, that, having managed to escape from his captors, he made his way to Bog of Gight, now Gordon Castle, where Huntly resided, a score of miles to the north of Aberdeen, and there threw himself on the mercy of Lady Huntly, dramatically declaring that, to save his Clan, he was prepared to lay his own head on the block. Lady Huntly had, as it happened, received him in the kitchen and, the better to illustrate his point, William imprudently laid his neck on a rough wooden block which the cook used for chopping up meat. At this Lady Huntly, who disliked him as much as did her husband, quickly made a sign to the cook, whereupon the latter, seizing a heavy cleaver, promptly severed William's head from his body. Not long after which Huntly seized all William's lands and made them over to his own eldest son, Alexander Lord Gordon.

The story was, however, to have a happier ending for the Mackintoshes than might have been expected. In due course, Huntly himself, having fallen into disfavour, was deprived of the Earldom of Moray, which was bestowed instead on James V's natural son, Lord James Stewart. William's lands were then restored to his seven year old son, Lachlan, while the sentence of death that had been passed on him by Huntly and so promptly carried out by his wife was declared in retrospect to be null and void.

Genealogy of James VI of Scotland, illustrating his descendants' claim to the English throne. The tree reads from the bottom, with James IV on the 2nd row from the bottom on the left. (English School, 17th century.)

CHAPTER IX
Mary, Queen of Scots and James VI

In 1559 the Dauphin François, husband of Mary Queen of Scots, succeeded his father as King of France and briefly the crowns of the two countries were linked. But the following year François died and in 1561 Mary, a widow at eighteen and by birth as well as by conviction a Roman Catholic, returned to the austerely Protestant Scotland of John Knox to begin her short and turbulent reign. While declaring that she did not intend to abandon her own faith, Mary made it clear that she would equally not seek to impose it on her subjects. Indeed, she deliberately surrounded herself with Protestant advisers, amongst them her bastard half-brother, Lord James Stewart. But, for all that, the Protestant divines were shocked to hear that Mass was being celebrated in Holyroodhouse and scandalized, too, by what they regarded as the frivolous conduct of the pretty young Queen and her Court.

Not long after Mary's arrival from France her advisers began to feel increasing concern at the excessive power wielded in the north and north-east by that leading Roman Catholic nobleman, the Earl of Huntly. During the first half of the sixteenth century the strength and influence of Clan Gordon in the East had, like that of Clan Campbell in the West, continued to increase. Indeed, it was to a tendency to go too far in whatever they undertook, rather than to any natural gaiety or other such trends, that they owed their sobriquet, the Gay (or more properly Gey) Gordons. Having successfully, if not very gallantly, survived the slaughter of Flodden, their chief, the Third Earl of Huntly, had in 1517 become Vice-Regent for the young King James V. Meanwhile Huntly's younger brother had married and so given his name to the daughter and heiress of the Eighth Earl of Sutherland, thereby establishing a mutually useful connection between the two families and also helping to extend his clan's influence northwards. Huntly's grandson, who in 1523 succeeded him as Fourth Earl, had in his turn become a Privy Councillor and later Lord Chancellor as well as a member of the Council of Government during the childhood of Mary Queen of Scots. In 1549 he had, as we have seen, been rewarded for his services with the lands and Earldom of Moray. But now, a dozen years later, both lands and earldom had, greatly to his disgust, been taken away from him and given instead to the Queen's bastard half-brother, Lord James Stewart. At this the Gordons broke into open rebellion and it was accordingly now decided that the Queen and Moray should together set out for the north at the head of a strong military force on a royal progress designed to overawe Huntly and bring him to heel. "Finding the Earl Fractious", Mary and her brother

Mary, Queen of Scots, at the age of seventeen as Queen of France. For nearly a decade she outshone all her contemporaries with her beauty and style.

began by storming Inverness Castle, which was in Gordon hands, and hanging its Governor. From Inverness they next marched southwards to confront Huntly himself at Corrichie on Deeside some fifteen miles west of Aberdeen, where the Gordons were soundly defeated. Being "gross, corpulent and short of breath", Huntly himself died on the field of battle shortly after being taken prisoner. Which, in all the circumstances, was probably the best thing that could have happened to him, for seven months later his embalmed body was taken and propped up at the bar of Parliament to receive on his behalf a sentence of treason and forfeiture.

It has been suggested that Mary's troubles began with Huntly's fall. But by all accounts the young Queen thoroughly enjoyed the expedition and attendant blood-letting, only regretting that she was not a man who could ride forth "in jack and knapskull". Moreover, in 1563 Mary, whose thoughts were already firmly focussed on the English succession, took a further step to show her lack of bigotry and conciliate the Protestant establishment in both countries by causing no less than forty-eight Catholic priests to be arrested and prosecuted for saying Mass, among them Cardinal Beaton's successor, Archbishop John Hamilton.

Cameo pendant (above) from the Penicuick Jewels, and necklace, pendant and earrings (right), all part of Mary, Queen of Scots' collection of jewellery. These are of contemporary workmanship.

The question now arose of finding a new husband for the young Queen. This was fraught with every possible personal, dynastic, religious and international complication. Numerous more or less suitable names were put forward, but in 1565 Mary fell in love with, or at any rate married, her cousin Lennox's son, Henry Stewart, Lord Darnley, a teenaged Roman Catholic of notoriously bad character, their marriage, so Mary's watchful cousin Elizabeth of England was informed, being celebrated "with all the solemnities of the Popish time". Barely a year later, in March 1566, Darnley, having apparently become jealous of Mary's Secretary, Rizzio, "a stranger Italian called Davie", had him murdered in her presence with the ready help of some of his friends. This not unnaturally distressed the Queen, who was pregnant at the time. It also turned her against her young husband. For almost a year nothing happened. Then, eleven months later, in February 1567, came the news that the house at Kirk O'Field in which Darnley was staying at the time had been blown up and his body found among the wreckage. On closer inspection, it turned out that he had previously been strangled.

Just who murdered Darnley remains a mystery to this day, but it seems certain that James Hepburn, Earl of Bothwell, a reckless adventurer of undoubted charm but deplorable character, was heavily implicated, not to mention the Queen herself. Eight weeks later, on 15 May 1567 Mary, wearing an old black dress trimmed with braid, married Bothwell, this time according to the Protestant rite, thereby alienating Catholics as well as Protestants. "One cannot expect much from persons who are the slaves of their passions," was the shrewd comment of the Cardinal Secretary of State from his vantage point in the Vatican.

Mary, Queen of Scots, forces the surrender of the Castle of Inverness. Drawing by David Allan.

Events now succeeded one another with frightening rapidity. A month after Mary's marriage the Protestant Lords of the Congregation of Jesus Christ, as they called themselves, raised an army and, on the pretext that they were rescuing her from Bothwell, seized the Queen, most of whose supporters had by now deserted her, and took her as a prisoner to Edinburgh where, while Bothwell made his escape to Norway, they paraded her through the streets in a short red petticoat amid the jeers of the crowd. After which, having been removed from Edinburgh to Loch Leven Castle, she was forced to abdicate in favour of her infant son, who was now crowned King as James VI. At the same time her bastard Protestant half-brother, Moray, was declared Regent.

In 1568, after less than a year's imprisonment, Mary managed to escape from Loch Leven and, with the help of the Hamiltons, who had ambitions of their own, and of the Gordons under the Fifth Earl of Huntly, to raise another army. But she did not remain at liberty for long. At Langside, then a mile or two south of Glasgow, she and her supporters were defeated in battle by Moray, after which, crossing the Solway with a handful of followers, she imprudently threw herself on the mercy of Elizabeth of England who, remembering her cousin's undoubted designs on the English throne, promptly imprisoned her and, in 1587 found cause to cut off her head – an action which drew only a formal protest from Mary's son James, who had his eyes firmly set on succeeding Queen Elizabeth on the English throne.

While little King James VI was growing up, Scotland was again governed by a succession of Regents. Not until 1583, after twenty years of turmoil, was a measure of stability established, when King James, by now seventeen, succeeded in escaping from a group of Protestant nobles who had kidnapped him, and in making his way to St Andrews where he publicly proclaimed himself King in fact as well as in name. Despite this promising start, James was, like his predecessors, to have difficulty in controlling

Execution of Mary Queen of Scots, 8 February 1587, after seventeen years of confinement. Contemporary drawing by an unknown artist.

the great nobles. Possessed of considerable natural shrewdness and subtlety, his praiseworthy purpose was to make himself, not the leader of a faction within his own Kingdom, but "universal King". While some Protestants thought him too lenient in his treatment of the Catholic Earls of Huntly, Erroll and Angus, whose rebellions at this time kept the north in a state of constant turmoil, others felt

Prayer book and rosary belonging to Mary, Queen of Scots. She took the rosary to her execution. When the Dean of Peterborough began to pray in English, Mary knelt and prayed loudly in Latin.

differently. In fact, the King's firm intention was to keep some sort of a balance between conflicting factions.

In the north, Huntly's neighbours, the Mackintoshes, were once more a force to be reckoned with. Having succeeded his unfortunate father William as 16th Chief in 1550, Lachlan Mackintosh was to lead his clan for more than half a century. Though an early convert to Protestantism, he had, when it suited him, shown himself an active supporter of the unfortunate Queen Mary, helping her to win back Inverness Castle from Huntly and fighting for her with his clan against Huntly at Corrichie and probably also at Langside. Indeed it was only when Mary fled to England that The Mackintosh finally deserted what by then was clearly a lost cause. In 1568, after years of bickering with his neighbours the Grants, Lachlan, an able and ambitious man, removed a continuing source of resentment by surrendering to them the lands of Rothiemurchus, which have remained in Grant hands ever since. "*Came the Grants of Rothiemurchus,*" ran the jingle

"Ilka ane as proud as Turk is,

Every man a sword and dirk has."

For the next fifty years or so, Lachlan Mackintosh continued to play an active part in the affairs of the region, protecting the now friendly Grants against the new Earl of Huntly, raiding Strathbogie, laying waste Huntly's lands, fighting off the attacks of the Camerons and calling out his Clan to help discipline the ever turbulent MacGregors. Finally, having made a bond with Argyll against the three Catholic Earls, he was, as we have seen, defeated by them at Glenlivet in 1594, though without in the long run suffering any serious consequences for himself.

Of Clan Grant, now at long last on good terms with The Mackintosh, it has been said that throughout their history they acted with greater prudence than any other Highland clan. In general this cautious attitude stood them in good stead. As early as 1263 Sir Laurence le Grand or le Grant had held the important appointment of Sheriff of Inverness, probably in succession to his father, Gregory the Great, and not long after there are tales of Laurence's son John and other Grants fighting manfully against the English invaders. This, with other evidence, all points to an Anglo-Norman origin for the Grants, by then clearly well established in north-eastern Scotland. One Grant married Bigla or Matilda, heiress of Gilbert Lord of Glencharnie, who brought with her as her

Memorial of James Stewart, 2nd Earl of Moray, showing every wound in detail. As Gordon of Gight slashed his face he exclaimed "You have spoilt a better face than your own." This life-size painting was commissioned by Moray's mother as a strident call for revenge, in the long-standing feud between the Huntlys and the Morays.

dowry Glencharnie (now Duthie) and half the Barony of Freuchie in Strathspey, both being in due course inherited by her son, Sir Duncan, who now assumed the style of Grant of Freuchie. In 1509 James IV bestowed Glenurquhart on John, the second Laird of Freuchie, while his two sons were given Glenmoriston and Coriemoney. A "Clan of Grantes" is first mentioned in 1537 and by the end of the century the Laird of Freuchie was already being styled Grant of Grant, with full feudal rights of jurisdiction. Other lands followed, and before long the Grants had by one means or another built up "ane great hudge estait" in Strathspey, where the Grant *duthaich* or heartland roughly covers the thirty miles between the source of the Spey in the uplands of Badenoch and the point where it enters the coastal plain ofMorayshire. Of the cadet branches the most important were Glenmoriston and Rothiemurchus, descended respectively from the second and fourth lairds of Freuchie. While the Grant earldom of Seafield, formerly held by the Grant Chiefs, has passed through the female line to the present Lord Seafield, the present Grant of Grant and Chief of the name is his kinsman Lord Strathspey.

Lying between the respective spheres of influence of the Earls of Moray and Huntly, the Grants, prudent as ever, were throughout the 16th century careful to keep on good terms with Huntly without becoming embroiled with his rival Moray or indeed with their other neighbours, the Mackintoshes. By 1594, however, their relations with Huntly had considerably deteriorated and at the Battle of Glenlivet they fought as good Protestants on Argyll's side against Huntly and his fellow Catholic Earls.

In the West meanwhile, the Campbells, acting under successive Chiefs with the sustained singleness of purpose for which they are already famous, had lost no time in taking advantage of the disarray in which the once mighty MacDonalds now found themselves, their immediate aim being to appropriate as much MacDonald territory as they could lay hands on.

In 1569 Angus MacDonald of Islay, whose mother had been a Campbell of Argyll, while his wife was the sister of Lachlan Maclean of Duart, had succeeded his brother as Chief of the MacDonalds of the South, namely of Islay and the neighbouring islands, as well as of Kintyre and of Antrim, across the sea in Northern Ireland. But in the event these particular connections were to bring him but little advantage.

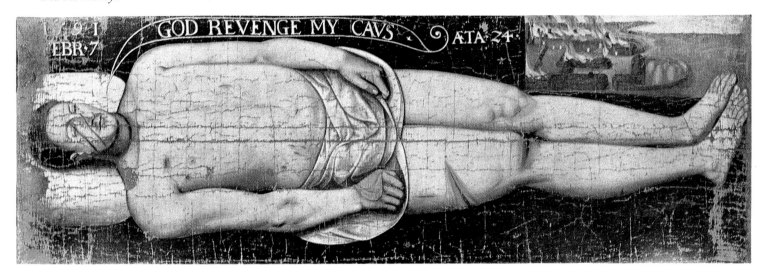

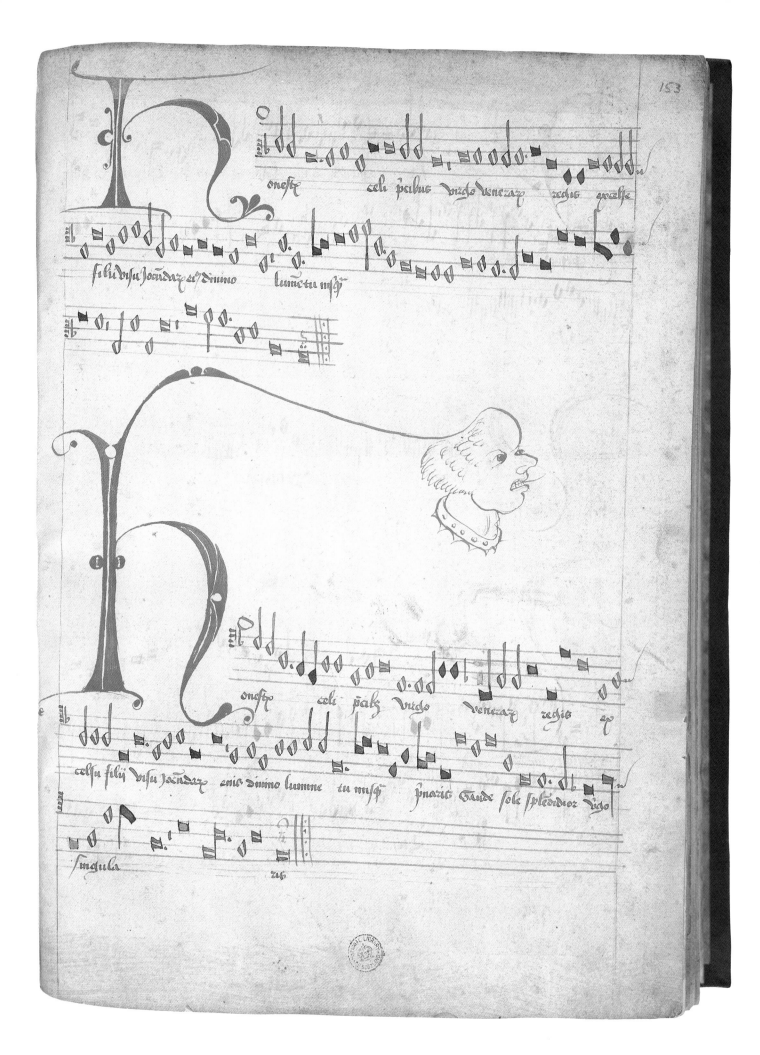

CHAPTER X

The Irish Connection

Over the years, the permanently disturbed situation in Ireland provided abundant scope for diversionary activities of one kind or another on the part of the Western Clans, notably the MacDonalds, who had kept in close touch with their kinsmen across the Irish Sea. Outstanding amongst these was the famous Somhairle Buidhe, Golden-haired Somerled MacDonnell, ancestor of the future MacDonnell Earls of Antrim and commonly known as Sorley Boy. For the greater part of the sixteenth century Sorley Boy played a lively part in Irish affairs, siding now with the native insurgents and now with the English and generally fishing in troubled waters for all he was worth. For years now Queen Elizabeth of England had been trying to put down an Irish national uprising led by Red Hugh O'Neill, Earl of Tyrone and last native King of Ulster, and supported by more than one chieftain of Clan Donald. Acutely conscious of the threat from Catholic Spain, Elizabeth's main concern was to keep the Spaniards out of Ireland where, as Roman Catholics and as enemies of the hated English, they could at any time have counted on ready support. From the first, the English Queen's prolonged struggle with the Irish offered promising opportunities for enterprising West Highlanders, "who", in the words of her envoy, Sir Henry Sidney, "from that region, and namely, the outer Isles, dayly swarm hither, to the great annoyance of the north part of this realme". Or, to quote another of Elizabeth's advisers who saw the advantages of playing one West Highland tribe off against another, "the people which most annoy Ulster from Scotland are the Clan Donells, who are ever in continual wars with another sept of the people of the Isles, named MacAlanes (Macleans), and if on MacAlane Her Majesty would bestow some convenient pension, he will, I think, undertake to keep the Clan Donells continually engaged as they shall be able to send none of their people to disturb Her Majesty's subjects in Ulster".

Like the MacDonalds, the Macleans had links of their own with Northern Ireland. A good example of this is Hector Mor Maclean of Duart's daughter, Catherine, who, as her first husband, had married Archibald Earl of Argyll. Catherine is described as "a high spirited woman, distinguished for her beauty and culture" – "not unlernyd" adds the chronicler, "in the Latin tong, speakyth good French and, it is sayd, some lytell Italyone". Soon after Argyll's death she crossed to Ireland where she had cousins and there married The O'Donnell, ruler of Tirconnel. But not long after this she was carried off, some say not unwillingly, by a rival Irish dynast, The O'Neill, ruler of

Carver's choir book (1500-60). Much of it consists of Carver's compositions, written in his own hand. Carver is probably Scotland's greatest composer. It is possible that he was the natural son of Bishop Arnot.

Painted ceiling with musicians from the long Gallery at Crathes Castle, begun in 1553 (below). Opposite is a detail of a harpist.

Tyrone, whose mistress she became and who, it is said, kept her "chained by day to a little boy and only released to amuse her master's drunken leisure". According to another version O'Neill in fact married her. However this may be, Catherine had sons by both Calvagh O'Donnell and Shane O'Neill, sons who in the next generation remained on the best of terms with their Maclean cousins across the North Channel, lending them when necessary their active support.

In 1567 Shane O'Neill, of whom we learn on the authority of one "Phettiplace the pirate" that "his personal bravery was not conspicuous", met a violent death, not in battle, but in the course of a drunken brawl during "a sumptuous banquet ... prepared to inaugurate the reunion of the O'Neills and the Macdonnells". On this occasion the Macdonnells, the chronicler tells us, "assembled together in a throng and thrust into the tent, where the said Oneile was, and there with theire slaughter-swords hewed him to pieces, slew his secretorie and all those that were with him, except a few which escaped by their horses". These, it appears, included the fair Catherine who, setting spurs to her mount, very sensibly sought safety in flight. She happened to be a cousin of Gillespeck MacDonnell who "began the melee in which Shane, her last husband, was slain". This involved her in one of those embarrassing conflicts of loyalty which seem to be an inescapable feature of tribal society. That the "sumptuous banquet" did not

fulfil its original purpose is obvious. And it is scarcely surprising that Catherine, finding herself, through no fault of her own, in a difficult situation, should in the end have preferred to make her way back to her native island of Mull.

The story had a rather squalid sequel. It so happened that Sidney, Queen Elizabeth's Lord Deputy, had publicly offered a substantial sum, no less than 1000, for Shane O'Neill's body, which had been carelessly flung into a pit, and "1000 marks for his head". What was left of the body was accordingly now exhumed by an enterprising Yorkshireman, Captain William Piers, (forebear of Sir John Piers, ninth of Tristernagh Abbey in the County of Westmeath) the head cut off and "pickled in a pipkin". After which it was delivered to Sidney in Dublin and the reward duly claimed by Captain Piers, who, leaving Yorkshire, became the progenitor of a long line of Anglo-Irish baronets.

In the confused situation prevailing in Ireland it was not long before the Chiefs of the Western Clans, the Macleans in particular, had discovered that Elizabeth and her Secretary, Sir Robert Cecil, were prepared to pay them good money to fight for her there or even to refrain from fighting against her. No one benefited more from the English Queen's reluctant generosity than Hector Mor's son, Sir Lachlan Mor Maclean of Duart, an early and enthusiastic convert to Protestantism and an

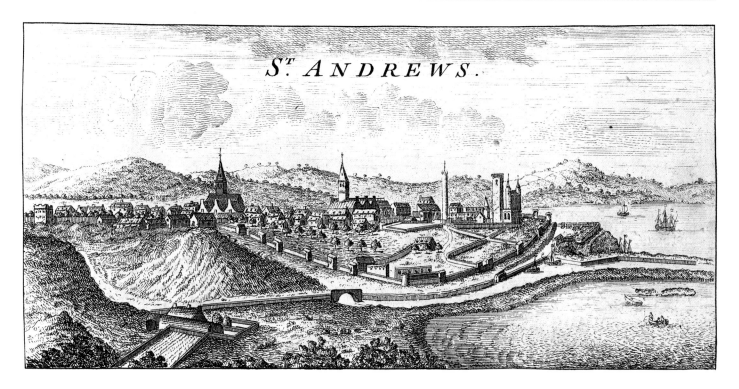

ST ANDREWS.

St Andrews University in 1600, when Scotland had four universities and England had no more than two.

outstandingly able and enterprising Chief, who constantly declared his readiness to further the English cause in Ireland, always provided the necessary funds were forthcoming. For what has been described as "a bauld onset and prattie feit of weir", namely, neatly intercepting in the summer of 1595 a force of several hundred MacDonalds who, while on their way to Ireland to fight for Red Hugh against the English, had imprudently anchored in Tobermory Bay, for seizing their ships and putting their leaders, including the Captain of Clanranald and his three uncles, in irons, Lachlan Mor received from Elizabeth no less than a thousand crowns as "an honouyrable token of her favour", with, on top of this, the promise of a pension.

Just what else Lachlan did or did not do in return for these favours is less clear, though there was talk of at least one projected expedition to Ireland. "If I were once landed in Ireland with this company," he wrote, "I hope in God the earl (Tyrone) shoud lose that name ere our return". In their modest way Sir Lachlan and his Confidential Secretary John Auchinross, accurately described by Tytler as "a shrewd Celt", seem to have been more than adequate match for Elizabeth and Secretary Cecil. Indeed one eminent authority has actually suggested that Duart's "prattie feit of weir", was in fact a put up job, that he and Clanranald were throughout in collusion and that in the event they did little or nothing and simply divided the proceeds between them. Certainly by 1598 the two were once again on the best of terms.

There was another aspect to the situation. For a number of reasons, sea communications between Scotland and Ireland were at this time of considerable importance. From the entrance to Loch Foyle in Northern Ireland to the mouth of Loch Indaal in Islay is a distance of some thirty miles of relatively sheltered waters, providing a safer and more easily navigable route than the shorter but often considerably more dangerous direct passage from Northern Ireland to the nearest point on the Mull of Kintyre. So long as the MacDonalds held Islay, it was they who controlled this vital route. In the course of the sixteenth century, however, the Macleans had managed to gain a foothold in both Jura and Islay, thus threatening the MacDonalds' hold on the main trade route to the West. For this reason the strategically sited Rhinns of Islay, forming an oddly shaped peninsula on the western side of the island, were over the years to become a constant bone of contention between MacDonalds and Macleans.

The Lamont harp, crafted in the 15th or early 16th century. This was the Scottish national instrument before the bagpipes. A small portable harp was used by Celtic bards, to provide an instrumental background to an essentially vocal lyric tradition.

Piper
To The Laird of Grant.

CHAPTER XI

James VI and
the Power of the Clans

Having in the end regained control of Islay, Sir James MacDonald of Dunyveg now sought to ingratiate himself with the King or at any rate to keep the ever-encroaching Campbells at bay by suggesting that a royal garrison should occupy his castle of Dunyveg and that he should surrender the Mull of Kintyre to the Crown. But, this was not to be. For some time ill-feeling had persisted between James, who in the meantime had married a daughter of Campbell of Cawdor, and his old father Angus, who, though later released, still resented the episode of the burning house and had since been led to suppose that his son was again plotting against him. In the end old Angus was, without too much difficulty, persuaded in his turn to arrest his son and hand him over to Campbell of Auchinbreck, who immediately delivered him to his Chief, Grim Archibald of Argyll. In 1603 still further charges were brought against the unfortunate Sir James and he was imprisoned by the Crown in Blackness Castle. In this manner Argyll succeeded in securing for himself the Crown tenancy of Kintyre as well as of the adjoining island of Jura and at once set about hunting down and evicting any MacDonalds who still remained there.

As for James of Dunyveg, though he made several attempts to escape, he was kept a prisoner at Blackness until 1609, when he was taken to Edinburgh, tried for treason, condemned to death and all his possessions forfeited. Meanwhile he remained in prison under sentence of death. Then, in 1614, old Angus, his father, finally died and James, still in jail under sentence of death, at long last became Chief of the Southern MacDonalds.

Despite their numerous misfortunes and the lamentations of their bards, events were soon to show that there was still plenty of fight left in Clan Donald. During the next few years the Castle of Dunyveg, long the principal stronghold of the MacDonalds of the South, was to change hands a number of times. Sir James MacDonald was, as we have seen, in jail in Edinburgh under sentence of death. Acting as Chief in his absence was his younger brother Angus Og, who had long stubbornly resisted the King's demands that he should surrender Dunyveg to the Earl of Argyll. But on the arrival in Islay in August 1608 of a Royal expedition, Angus had in the end agreed to hand it over to Lord Ochiltree, the newly appointed Lieutenant of the Isles, who, installing a small Royal garrison there, had in 1610 appointed Bishop Andrew Knox of the Isles as its Constable.

The Piper to the Laird of Grant, painted by Richard Waitt in 1714. The picture typifies a leading chieftain's piper, with the inclusion of the banner, the coat of arms, the livery worn by the piper, and the stronghold in the background.

For the next three or four years the Western Highlands and Isles were, in Gregory's words, "almost entirely free from disorders or rebellions". But this, as can be imagined, was no more than a passing phase. In the spring of 1614 Dunyveg, "carelessly guarded" by its little garrison, was suddenly surprised and seized by Ranald Oig, a bastard son of Old Angus of Dunyveg, described by the chronicler as "a vagabound fellow without any residence" who, with three or four hangers-on, managed to chase out the Royal garrison and take possession of the Castle.

At this, Angus Og, who lived only five or six miles away, at once sent out the fiery cross, calling on his clansmen to recover the Castle, ostensibly for the King, and at the same time enlisting the help of his kinsman Coll MacGillespick, or Col Kitto, a formidable warrior with abundant experience of such operations. The response to Angus Og's summons was immediate, and within a few days Ranald Oig and his companions had duly been driven out. After making their escape by sea, they were quickly hunted down by Angus Og and for the most part put to death. After which, Angus Og, having himself occupied the castle, immediately prepared for a siege.

For the Privy Council Angus Og's preparations for a siege were proof enough that he had been behind his bastard half-brother's seizure of the Castle, the more so since he had so quickly eliminated most of those responsible before they could give evidence. Indeed it was even suggested that from his prison cell in Edinburgh, Sir James had himself somehow inspired the attack.

Whatever the truth, Angus Og, with his older brother James's apparent approval, now offered to restore the castle to Bishop Knox, always provided that he was granted full remission for any previous misdemeanours. To this the Privy Council responded by ordering Angus to surrender the castle without delay to the Bishop, whom they furnished with a commission of fire and sword in the event of a refusal. But Angus in the meanwhile had been in correspondence with the Earl of Argyll, who, it is alleged, privately urged him to resist the Privy Council's demands, in the hope that he would thereby do himself irreparable damage. Following his correspondence with Argyll, Angus now became ever more suspicious of the Privy Council's intentions and ever more difficult to deal with. And when, in September, Bishop Knox landed in Islay without adequate military backing, and bringing with him no more than a conditional pardon for Angus Og, Angus not only refused to hand over the Castle to him but actually forced the Bishop to guarantee him a seven year lease for the Crown lands of Islay and possession of Dunyveg as well as a free pardon for any offences he might have committed. He further obliged the Bishop, greatly against the latter's better judgement, to hand over to him his own son Thomas Knox and his nephew John Knox of Ranfurly "as sureties for the due discharge of the agreement", in other words, as hostages. What is more, he let it be known that he was taking this action at the instance of none other than the Earl of Argyll.

Disappointed by the Bishop's handling of the matter, the Privy Council now turned to Sir John Campbell of Cawdor, who at once declared that "in return for a grant of the lands of Islay" at a rental to be agreed and if provided with cannon and men expert in the "battering of housis", he was himself prepared to undertake a commission for the reduction of the island at his own expense. Realising that such action, if taken, would make the MacDonalds more rebellious than ever, as well as seriously endangering the lives of the unfortunate hostages, namely his own son and nephew, Bishop Knox raised the strongest objections to the action proposed, adding sagaciously that no one familiar with conditions in the Isles would "think it either good or profitable to His Majesty to make that name (Campbell) greater in the isles than they are already; nor yet to root out one pestiferous clan, and plant in another little better". The situation in the Southern Isles, he suggested, could best be resolved by bringing in "honest men" under the protection of an armed force from the West of Scotland and "old soldiers out of Ireland" in much the same way as King James had recently done in Ulster.

On learning in his prison what was being proposed, Sir James MacDonald now decided that he must make a last attempt to save what was left of his inheritance from the Campbells. In a petition to the Privy Council in October he declared himself ready to take over the Crown lands in Islay at a suitable rent. Or, if this offer were to be refused, he offered, in return for a free pardon, to transport himself, his brother Angus and all his clan out of the King's dominions to Holland. In the event, however, no consideration seems to have been given either to his proposals or to those put forward by Bishop Knox.

It is at this stage that a new, rather equivocal character appears on the scene, described as "a Ross-shire man named George Graham of Eryne, familiar with the Gaelic language". Privately employed by the Chancellor of Scotland, Lord Dunfermline (who had not bothered to inform his fellow Privy Councillors of this initiative), George Graham landed in Islay in November 1614 and, representing himself as an emissary of

the Privy Council (which he was not), prevailed on Angus Og (whom he already knew) first of all to release the hostages he had taken and then, having initially surrendered the Castle of Dunyveg, to re-occupy it and hold it as its Constable against all comers, including the King's Lieutenant. In return for which, said Graham, all proceedings against him would be suspended. While securing the release of the hostages, remarks the historian of Clan Donald, Graham thus "enclosed Angus in a trap ingeniously designed for his destruction". Having duly released the hostages, Angus Og now stubbornly refused to surrender Dunyveg and, on Graham's advice, went out of his

17th-century dirk (far left).

James VI and I by J. de Critz, 1610. In 1603, James VI of Scotland became James I of England, uniting the two kingdoms for the first time. The Highland clans, who were devoted to the House of Stuart, were well pleased by this. Under the Stuart Kings they had enjoyed a certain degree of freedom and understanding. James VI and I tried hard to bring peace to the Highlands and Islands

A Child of the Mist, from the drama "Montrose" (or "Children of the Mist"), 1822. The MacGregor chieftain was father to the Children of the Mist.

way to ill-treat the properly accredited herald who called upon him to do so.

Cawdor, meanwhile, had been pressing on with the preparations for his expedition and at the end of October received formal authority to proceed against Angus Og. Accordingly, early in January 1615, he landed on Islay with a force of over three hundred men. These were followed by a number of cannon, with which he proceeded to bombard Dunyveg, producing, we learn, "a perceptible effect" on the garrison, who quickly declared themselves ready for a parley.

In the course of the ensuing parley it was explained to Angus Og that he had been deliberately misled by George Graham. At this he at first undertook to surrender. But, after returning to the Castle and talking things over with the invariably bellicose Colkitto, he withdrew his undertaking and the siege continued.

Cawdor now resumed his bombardment with the result that, early in February, the garrison were forced to surrender unconditionally. Only Colkitto and a few of his followers managed to escape by sea but these, with the exception of Colkitto, were captured when their boat sprang a leak. On 3 February Cawdor took possession of Dunyveg which, we are told, was found to contain "a number of images connected with the Catholic form of worship" which were promptly destroyed "by the zeal of Archibald Campbell, a son of the Prior of Ardchattan". Once in possession, he held a justice court at which fourteen of the garrison were tried, found guilty and executed, Angus Og himself and one or two others being kept back for examination by the Privy Council, who, after prolonged deliberations were in the end to condemn them to death for high treason.

But, towards the end of May, long before the Privy Council had reached a verdict, came the astonishing news that Sir James MacDonald himself had somehow managed to escape from Edinburgh Castle and was already on his way to the Isles to join the insurrection and put himself at the head of his clan. Immediately, a reward of two thousand pounds was offered for his capture, dead or alive. But, having crossed the

Forth by boat from Newhaven to Burntisland with help from the MacDonalds of Keppoch and Moidart, James had by this time already reached the Perthshire highlands. More than once he came very near to being captured and was on one occasion, greatly to his distress, obliged to abandon the little library of books which, being a man of considerable cultivation, he invariably carried with him. But he slipped through notwithstanding and, with the help of Keppoch's clansmen was soon heading by way of Rannoch, Lochaber, Moidart, Morar and Knoydart for Sleat in Skye. Here he was greeted with the greatest enthusiasm by Colkitto and his piratical crew who, we are told, marched round him for a full half hour, discharging their small arms in the air before coming forward each in his turn to shake his Chief by the hand. And now, as more and more MacDonalds joined Sir James, the rebellion in Gregory's words "assumed every day a more formidable appearance". By this time the Privy Council, though lacking precise information of what was afoot, were quite rightly becoming seriously disturbed, substantially increasing the rewards offered for Sir James's capture and issuing commissions to all and sundry for the defence of the West against the rebels. To these the various chieftains and chiefs to whom they were addressed responded with varying degrees of enthusiasm. Only a few made any effective response. Some were inclined to side with the MacDonalds. Most bided their time till the probable outcome of the insurrection became clearer. In this emergency it now became known that, instead of being at Inveraray, the Earl of Argyll, whom the King had appointed Royal Lieutenant for the West, was in London, where he had gone to escape his creditors, while more than one Campbell chieftain was so involved in his Chief's "embarrassments" that he dared not show himself in Argyllshire. Indeed Campbell of Auchinbreck was actually in prison in Edinburgh.

By 23 June Sir James MacDonald, for whose capture the Privy Council were by now offering a reward of five thousand pounds, had to the Privy Council's utter dismay landed in Islay and without much difficulty seized Dunyveg, driving what remained of Cawdor's garrison right off the island.

At this, the Privy Council wrote in despair to the King strongly urging him to send the Earl of Argyll home with all haste, to play his part as Royal Lieutenant against the rebels. But, though in the meantime different Campbell Chieftains assumed different responsibilities it was not until September that Argyll himself in the end came back and took command.

Meanwhile, Sir James MacDonald, after first fortifying Islay to his satisfaction and leaving his bastard son Donald Gorme in charge of Dunyveg, had landed in Kintyre with a force of four hundred men and boldly sent out the fiery cross calling on Argyll's vassals there to receive new charters of their lands from him. A detachment of twenty four men having already taken possession of the Royal Castle of Kinloch or Kilkerran (now Campbeltown), Sir James next moved northwards towards the end of July to Tarbert pitching his camp on the West Coast of Kintyre near the Isle of Cara. Early in September, Argyll, having at long last arrived, assembled his forces at Duntroon on Loch Crinan, keeping some of his ships on the east coast of Kintyre and some on the west. After being reinforced by some English ships of war, he then attacked MacDonald in strength from both east and west. In the ensuing confusion Sir James managed to

A 17th-century dirk.

Sir Duncan Campbell of Glenorchy (1554–1561).

escape to Rathlin, while Colkitto, making for Islay, promptly took possession of Dunyveg. On Argyll now crossing to Jura, Sir James made next in his turn for Islay, intending to make a stand there. He was at once followed there by Argyll, supported by a number of English warships and by a strong force under Cawdor.

Finding himself confronted by forces greatly superior to his own and unable, as he had hoped, to escape with his galleys to the northern isles, Sir James now sent a messenger to Argyll seeking a truce. To this Argyll agreed, providing Dunyveg and the other MacDonald stronghold of Loch Gorm were both surrendered within twenty four hours. But when Sir James called on Colkitto, who was now in command of the two fortresses, to surrender them, the latter flatly refused to do so.

At this, Argyll, who, as it happened, was himself privately in touch with Colkitto and had received from him an assurance of his readiness to hand over both forts when the time was ripe, now despatched Cawdor with a force of a thousand men to take Sir James by surprise and seize his galleys. But Sir James, who, thanks to an efficient system of fire signals, had received advance warning of the intended attack, had time to make his escape together with Keppoch and some forty others. As Sir James was embarking, some of the principal men of Islay came down to the shore and pleaded with him to stay, reminding him that they had risked everything for him and now faced certain death. But Sir James refused to let himself be dissuaded and embarked notwithstanding, followed by Keppoch and some others "desperate to save their heads".

Next day, Colkitto, in accordance with the private bargain he had made with Argyll, surrendered Dunyveg and Lochgorm in return for an undertaking from the Earl to spare his life and the lives of some of his followers. What is more, "in order to testify his abhorence of his former behaviour, he became an active partisan against his former associates", even going so far as to seize and hand over to Argyll Macfie of Colonsay and eighteen other leaders of the rebellion. Colkitto's conduct, says Gregory, "had many imitators", notably Macfie who, finding himself in a thoroughly unenviable position, lost no time in shifting loyalties and in his turn "doing His Majesty's service against the remaining rebels".

But not all those who had joined the insurrection were so adaptable or so lucky. Argyll was taking no chances. Handing over Dunyveg and Loch Gorm to Cawdor, he seized another nineteen leading islanders who had given Sir James their support and had them tried and executed without delay. Then, moving to Kintyre at the end of October, he spent a couple of weeks methodically hunting down a good many more

Panorama of Taymouth Castle and Loch Tay by James Norie, 1733, who was paid nine pounds by John Campbell, Lord Glenorchy, for painting this view of his property.

former rebels, of whom he executed enough to make any fresh outbreak of trouble unlikely. Meanwhile, Sir James MacDonald had with his son Donald Gorme and a couple of followers managed to escape to Ireland. There he was kept hidden for a time in Galway by some Jesuits, who in the end helped him escape to the Spanish Netherlands. MacDonald of Keppoch, having first returned to Lochaber, likewise escaped to Spanish territory. Colkitto, having made a deal with Argyll, had been pardoned. To both Lord Binning, the Secretary of State, and to the Privy Council it was a matter of concern that so many ring-leaders of the insurrection should by one means or another have survived. Argyll, for his part, was well aware how dangerous the situation had been. "I thank God," he wrote to Binning on 7 November, "that the suppression of the rebellion was in time; for, on my credits, if it had been twenty days longer protracted, few of my countrymen, betwixt Tarbert and Inveraray, had proven good subjects: much less could there have been any good expected of further remote places, where there was no obedience to His Majesty at all." But, however great the danger had been, for the time being at any rate the "great rebellion" of Clan Donald, as it came to be known, had been effectively crushed.

Sir James MacDonald and Keppoch had not been long in the Spanish Netherlands when they were joined there by their former adversary, the Earl of Argyll, whose history, as Gregory is quick to point out, provides a striking instance of the mutability of human affairs. In 1616 Argyll had gone to Court to make a personal report on the rebellion of Clan Donald and on his own success in suppressing it. That he was at this time in favour at Court is shown clearly enough by an act of Parliament settling on his younger son, James, the Lordship of Kintyre. Two years later, in 1618, he had asked for and obtained permission to go abroad to Spa for reasons of health. But, after he had

117

left the country, it became known that, rather than going to Spa, he had in fact gone to the Spanish Netherlands. Moreover, once there, the Earl, who some years before had married a Roman Catholic, had now himself publicly declared his adherence to Rome. What is more, it was reported to the King that, while in the Spanish Netherlands, he had made contact with his former foes Sir James MacDonald and Alistair MacRanald of Keppoch.

On learning of this the King at once withdrew Argyll's licence to be abroad, ordered him to appear before the Privy Council at the beginning of February 1619 and, when he failed to return, declared him a traitor by an act expressly denouncing his hypocrisy and dissimulation. Meanwhile, steps were taken by the Privy Council to make a score or more of the "barons and gentlemen" of Argyllshire answerable for the maintenance of law and order there, while Argyll's able and ambitious son, Lord Lorne, another Archibald, took over his father's duties as Chief. While in the Spanish Netherlands, Argyll is said to have served with distinction in the army of King Philip III and his campaigns against the Dutch. He did not return to Britain until the next reign, by when his misdemeanours had doubtless been conveniently forgotten. He died in London soon after his arrival there in 1638. Following Argyll's disgrace and downfall it was perhaps only natural that the MacDonalds should for a time at any rate have returned to favour. In due course Sir James MacDonald and Keppoch were recalled from the Spanish Netherlands by King James and each awarded a pension on his arrival in London. But, though granted remission for his offences, Sir James was perhaps wisely debarred from visiting Scotland and died five years later in London, the last of his line. Keppoch, on the other hand, was allowed to return to Lochaber, where for the rest of his life he did nothing to disturb the peace of the realm.

The Campbells had in the long run yet again managed to extend their dominions. Argyll was now Crown Tenant of most of Kintyre, Sir John Campbell of Cawdor had gained the superiority of Islay directly from the Crown and just before his death old Angus of Islay had sold him what remained of Kintyre. "You stole green, pleasant Islay from us by trickery," sang the MacDonald bard, Iain Lom, "and Kintyre with its fertile plains." Throughout his reign, King James VI had continued to keep one object firmly in view: he was utterly determined to succeed his cousin Elizabeth on the throne of England. This, with the assiduous help of the astute Sir Robert Cecil, he in the end achieved on Elizabeth's death in 1603, when he immediately left Scotland for London, returning to his native land only once in the remaining twenty-two years of his reign. Thereafter he ruled his northern kingdom by remote control. "This I must say for Scotland," he remarked appreciatively. "Here I sit and govern it with my pen. I write and it is done, and by a clerk of the Council I govern Scotland now, which others could not do with the sword."

With the Union of the Crowns an accomplished feat, the perennial problem of the Highlands took on a new aspect. Beyond the Highland Line the old Celtic way of life still persisted, while the Clans pursued their ancestral feuds with little regard for what happened further south. But, now that the seat of power had effectively shifted from Edinburgh to London, the Highlands had in one sense become remoter and of less immediate importance. In another it had become more desirable than ever for the central government to solve once and for all a problem which many people, and no one more than the King, regarded as a squalid and alien nuisance. "As for the Highlands," wrote James to his son, "I shortly comprehend them all in two sorts of people: the one, that dwelleth in our mainland that are barbarous and yet mixed with some show of civility: the other that dwelleth in the Isles and are utterly barbarous." And again: "all utterly barbarous, without any sort of show of civility ... think no more of them all than of wolves and wild boars."

As often as not, James approached the problem by the rough and ready method of issuing what were known as Letters of Fire and Sword, authorising one or more Clans to deal with their erring neighbours by whatever means they thought best, usually a violent one. As a long term solution, however, this method left much to be desired, old feuds being perpetuated by it and yet greater bitterness engendered.

Of all the Highland clans none had a worse reputation as trouble-makers than the

Gordon clansman, print by McIan, 19th century.

119

MacGregors. For this there were various reasons, not necessarily all attributable to their own natural unruliness, though this certainly played its part. Among the titles proudly borne to this day by Sir Gregor MacGregor of MacGregor, the present Chief of Clan Gregor, is that of Father of the Children of the Mist and it is true to say that, like those of most Highland clans, the origins of the MacGregors are shrouded in the mists of antiquity. Gregor of the Golden Bridles, Chief and seemingly name-father of the Clan, is believed to have been living in Glenorchy in Argyll around the middle of the 14th century. Gregor's son, One-eyed Iain of Glenorchy, died in 1390. Before that, their forebears seem to have held sway in the Three Glens, Glen Orchy, Glen Strae and Glen Lochy, to which are sometimes added Glen Lyon and Glendochart. These were their clan lands. Thence they later expanded to Glengyll and Roro. But, before many years were out, their main clan territory of Glenorchy had passed, like so much else, into Campbell hands, and as early as 1432 Sir Duncan Campbell of Lochawe had been able to install his son Colin as the first Campbell Chieftain of that region, conveniently adjacent to Inveraray and the other Campbell lands in north Argyll. After which, the MacGregor chiefs continued in Glenstrae as tenants of the Campbells. But, with the loss of Glenorchy, what remained of their clan lands no longer sufficed as a base for the bulk of their clansmen, who, by the end of the fifteenth century, found themselves dispersed and living as best they could under the jurisdiction of alien chiefs.

Early in the 16th century, however, after all these misfortunes, came the cheering news that the origins of Clan Gregor were royal. For Highlanders genealogy has always been an important pastime and here, clearly, was a major breakthrough. With the help of his younger brother Duncan, Sir James MacGregor, Dean of Lismore, published in the year 1512 a work said to be taken "from the books of the genealogies of the kings". This proved to the satisfaction at any rate of the author that the MacGregor chiefs were in fact descended from Alpin, father of Kenneth, High King of Scotland, by way of Alpin's third son, whose name, it now conveniently emerged, had been Gregor. A disturbing gap of some three hundred years, to which someone unkindly drew attention, was neatly bridged and the MacGregors finally set the seal on their achievement by adopting as their clan motto the words *S Rioghal Mo Dhream*, Royal is my Race. The Dean's happy discovery also brought the MacGregors a multitude of new and no less distinguished kith and kin. In 1591 we find Alasdair MacGregor of Glenstrae and Aulay MacAulay of Ardincaple boldly concluding, in the light of their respective researches, a far-reaching offensive and defensive alliance, "understanding ourselfs and our name to be M'Calppins of auld and to be our just and trew surname, whereof we are all cumin", while in the Mackinnons of Strathardill in Skye the MacGregors were equally happy to discover kinsmen "of auld descent". Meanwhile, long after the regions in question had passed into Campbell keeping, the MacGregors cheerfully continued to style themselves Chiefs of Glenorchy and Glenlyon.

But by this time the MacGregors were in serious trouble. Whether the lack of a firm base had an unsettling effect on them or whether, as a clan, they were more than usually turbulent, their story, from the middle years of the sixteenth century is one of unceasing strife. With time it became harder than ever for the Chief to control his scattered clansmen or "broken men", as they were called. Again and again there was

trouble in Rannoch, trouble in Glenlyon, trouble in Breadalbane, all caused, or so it was claimed, by lawless and rootless MacGregors, who at one time or another had settled or possibly chosen to remain in the areas in question.

Like so many other clans, the MacGregors suffered from the close proximity of the Campbells, who as early as the 15th century had relieved them of Glenorchy. For most of the sixteenth century we find them involved in acts of mayhem for which the blame rests sometimes on them and sometimes on their neighbours, but which almost invariably ended in punitive action being taken against them by the Crown or its agents, usually the Campbells, who in 1519 even put up a puppet MacGregor chief of their own in order further to confuse an already confused issue, at the same time murdering any rival claimants who might have made difficulties. At the turn of the sixteenth century came a crisis in the affairs of Clan Gregor. For ten years Colin Glas, Grey Colin Campbell 6th of Glenorchy, had conducted a private vendetta against Gregor Roy MacGregor of Glenstrae, seeking to deprive him of the allegiance of his clansmen and of his long-standing superiority over Glenstrae and even bringing in Camerons and MacDonalds from Keppoch to drive the MacGregors out of Rannoch. In the end Grey Colin achieved his object. Forced into acts of increasing violence, Gregor Roy was first outlawed and then captured and killed at Kenmore in Perthshire. In retaliation for which the MacGregors at once laid waste Glenorchy as far as Kilchurn and for a time Grey Colin felt it wiser to leave Glenstrae in peace.

In 1588, however, when Gregor Roy's eldest son Alasdair, having come of age, applied in his turn to be invested in Glenstrae, he, like his father before him, was frustrated in this by Grey Colin's successor, Black Duncan of Glenorchy. But even now the MacGregors were not easily discouraged. The following year a number of them, having murdered the King's Forester, Drummond of Drummond-Ernoch, an old enemy of their clan who in his time had clipped the ears of numerous MacGregor poachers, fled to the Kirk of Balquhidder. There, Alasdair of Glenstrae joined them and, having mustered his clan, himself formally assumed the blood-guilt on their behalf by laying his hand on the dead man's severed head, which his clansmen had conveniently brought with them to Balquhidder. For this misdemeanour they were in due course outlawed, but later, as it happened, pardoned owing to the timely intervention of the Earl of Atholl and, strangely enough, of Campbell of Cawdor, who, for no doubt quite valid reasons of their own, were at this period in time both glad to afford them a measure of protection.

For the next ten years Alasdair managed to keep his scattered clan under some kind of control, punctually furnishing hostages for the good behaviour of his clansmen, against whom for a time no serious charges of bloodshed were made, despite much provocation, it was claimed, from both Camerons and Macleans. But then, for one reason or another, there came a time when Alasdair failed to furnish fresh hostages. This gave his enemies the opportunity they had been waiting for. In one, comprehensive gesture the Privy Council simply handed over control of Clan MacGregor to Archibald, 7th Earl of Argyll, at that time Justice-General of Scotland, and Alasdair had no choice but to surrender to him.

What happened next is not entirely clear. According to Alasdair's own account, Argyll now deliberately encouraged Alasdair's brother, Iain Dubh, to pillage the lands of Colquhoun of Luss on Loch Lomondside. As Iain's brother, Alasdair felt himself quite naturally bound to give him his support; the MacGregors accordingly now raided the Lennox; and in the process a number of Colquhouns were killed.

King James had, as it happened, long been unusually well disposed towards the Colquhouns, a little clan whose Chiefs claimed descent through the female line from Maelduin of Luss, Dean of Lennox in the 13th century and hereditary custodian of the Crozier of St Kessog, an early saint said to have dwelt at one time on an island in Loch Lomond. Maelduin's inheritance had later passed through an heiress to Sir Robert Colquhoun, who had fought for Bruce in the War of Independence and had been rewarded accordingly. Thereafter his successors loyally supported the Stewart Kings, who continued to regard them with favour, making them Constables of the Royal Castle of Dumbarton, occupying an important strategic position on the River Clyde at no great distance from Luss.

On learning what had happened, the King at once gave Colquhoun authority to proceed against the MacGregors. Whereupon Alasdair MacGregor, without waiting to be attacked by Colquhoun, advanced south from Rannoch to meet him at the head of three hundred of his own clansmen, together with some Camerons and the notoriously rapacious MacDonalds of Glencoe. At this, Luss hastily assembled a rather larger body of Colquhouns and Buchanans, backed up by the burgesses of nearby Dumbarton, and on 7th February 1603 the two forces met in neighbouring Glen Fruin, running westwards from Loch Lomond. In the ensuing battle, though Alasdair's brother Iain

Scroll butt pistols, about 1670.

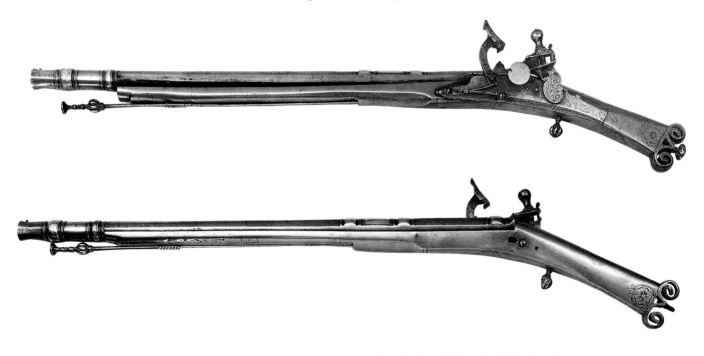

Dubh, who had started all the trouble, was killed, the more warlike MacGregors in the end soundly defeated the Colquhouns and their allies and once more utterly devastated their lands.

The Macgregors' victory was, however, to cost them dear. Luss, who represented the Crown, had been defeated no more than a dozen miles from the Royal Castle of Dumbarton of which he was Constable. For King James, who had never liked Highlanders, least of all MacGregors, this was the last straw. After some sixty wailing Colquhoun widows, carrying their husbands' bloody shirts on poles and clamouring for revenge, had descended on him at Stirling, he gave immediate orders for "that unhappie and detestable race", meaning the MacGregors, to be "exptirpat and ruttit out". Henceforth the MacGregors became outlaws whom anyone who felt so inclined could with impunity hunt down and kill. Their very name was by law abolished, all who bore it being obliged, under pain of death, to take another. "Make winter as autumn," ran a contemporary MacGregor lament, "the wolf-days as summer; thy bed be the bare rock, and light be thy slumber." For almost a year Alasdair MacGregor of Glenstrae, being a man of considerable agility, managed to escape capture. Then, hoping "to saif my lyfe and landis", he gave himself up to Argyll who, having promised a safe conduct to England to see the King, first took him across the border to Berwick and then sent him to Edinburgh to be tried by a jury packed with his worst enemies. But there was still some fight left in Alasdair. In his defence he pleaded, possibly with some justification, that it was Argyll who had in the first place instigated the slaughter of Glen Fruin and the plundering of Luss. "I confess here before God," he declared "that I have been persuaded, moved and enticed, as I am now presently accused and troubled for." "Also," he went on, "if I had used Counsel or Command of the Man that has enticed me, I would have done and committed sundry high murders more. For truly, since I was first His Majesty's man, I could never be at any ease by my Lord

Detail of stock of a Long Highland sporting gun of the Lairds of Grant. This type of decorated lock and carved stock was characteristic of these Highland weapons.

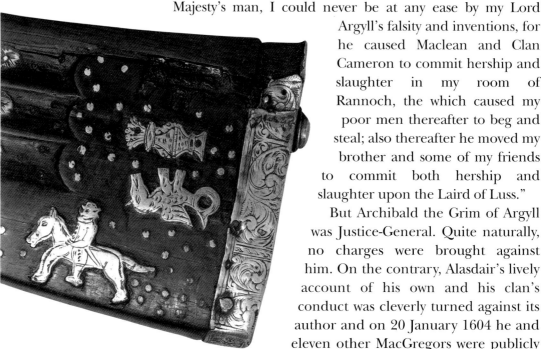

Argyll's falsity and inventions, for he caused Maclean and Clan Cameron to commit hership and slaughter in my room of Rannoch, the which caused my poor men thereafter to beg and steal; also thereafter he moved my brother and some of my friends to commit both hership and slaughter upon the Laird of Luss."

But Archibald the Grim of Argyll was Justice-General. Quite naturally, no charges were brought against him. On the contrary, Alasdair's lively account of his own and his clan's conduct was cleverly turned against its author and on 20 January 1604 he and eleven other MacGregors were publicly hanged at the Mercat Cross in Edinburgh. After which the Government pressed on urgently with their efforts to extirpate what was left of their clan. For more than four of them to meet together became a capital offence. The clergy were forbidden to baptise their children. They were denied the right to own for any purpose whatsoever a knife possessing a point. Women of the clan who failed to take another name were branded on the face and deported. Surviving MacGregor children were sent to Ireland or to the Lowlands. Blood money was offered for a MacGregor's head, while any MacGregor could gain a free pardon by killing one of his fellow clansmen.

In the event there were not many more executions, probably because so few MacGregors let themselves be taken alive. Of the thirty-six MacGregors actually brought to trial, almost all were executed, as were six more who had served as hostages. Yet when in 1611 the King again gave Argyll fresh orders "to lay mercie aside and by justice and the sword to ruit out and extirpate all of that race", Alasdair's cousin Duncan, as Tutor for Iain Dubh's young son Gregor, who had succeeded his uncle Alasdair as Chief, could still manage to rally close on a hundred and fifty clansmen for an extended raid which from Loch Katrine took them eastwards to Fortingall and Comrie and westwards as far as the Campbell heartland round Loch Awe.

Two years later, however, this was no longer so. The measures against them had their full effect. Ten years after Glen Fruin, the only MacGregors still alive and at large were "bot unworthie poore miserable bodyis", while the young Chief and his two brothers, now safely in Government hands, had been forced to change their name to Murray. Thereafter there were only spasmodic bouts of trouble from the Griogaraich, though even this was enough to cause the Government to re-enact the original laws against them.

CHAPTER XII

The Northwest

From London, King James had, for his part, continued to follow Scottish affairs with interest and on occasion himself directed the measures taken to establish more effective control over the Western Highlands and Islands, a process which with time had come to be known as the Danting or Daunting of the Isles. A notable example of this was the treatment meted out to the MacLeods of Lewis and Harris.

In the northern isles the MacLeods of Lewis had for some years been engaged in internecine strife which, shrewdly exploited by their neighbours, the Mackenzies of Kintail, was in the end to prove their downfall. To the King's reforming zeal and keen business sense they thus offered a tempting target, "exerceing sic beistlie and monstrous cruelteis upoun utheris as hes not bene hard of amangis Turkis or Infidellis, and with that thay ar plantit and possest with the maist fertile and commodious part of the haill realme, quhilk, being enrichit with a incredible fertlitie of cornes and plenty of fischeis, wald render maist inestemable commoditeis of the haill realme, gif the barbaritie of the vyld and savage inhabitantis thairof wald suffer and permit a peceable and trafficque amangis thame." Such at any rate was the view of the Scottish Privy Council.

Under an Act of Parliament passed in 1597, deploring "the barbarous inhumanity" of both Highlanders and Islanders, the Macleod islands of Lewis and Harris as well as the lands of Dunvegan and Glenelg were now simply declared to be at the King's disposal. The three latter estates belonged, as it happened, to the exceptionally able Rory Mor MacLeod of Dunvegan, who, though officially outlawed, had somehow managed to hold on to them. The MacLeods of Lewis were less fortunate.

In 1598 a dozen so-called Fife Adventurers, provided with a contract from the King and actively backed by James's cousin, the Duke of Lennox, attempted at the head of a force of five or six hundred mercenaries to seize the Isle of Lewis by force and eradicate its inhabitants with a view to the commercial exploitation of its natural resources. Much to the King's disappointment, however, the Adventurers were, when it came to the point, successfully repulsed by the embattled islanders, whom they described as "barbarous, bludie and wiket Hielandmen", armed with "bows, darlochs, hackbuts, pistols and other weapons". These, it should be added, were most effectively led by Neil MacLeod, the surviving bastard brother of their late Chief, Torquil Dubh, recently

Eilean Donan Castle, Loch Duich. This great western stronghold of the Mackenzie Chiefs was originally built in the Middle Ages. It was destroyed by the Royal Navy after the Rising of 1715, but rebuilt in the early part of 20th century by the MacRaes who had been hereditary Keepers for the Mackenzie Chiefs.

'Speckled pipes', owned by the legendary MacCrimmons School of Piping, Skye. The school was founded by the 8th Chief of MacLeod, about 1500.

beheaded "without doom or law" on the instructions of Mackenzie of Kintail, who was watching the situation closely and grasping the advantages to be gained by such a course and had by this time very shrewdly managed to get possession of most of the MacLeod charters.

The Adventurers, meanwhile, had suffered yet another setback. One of their number, the unfortunate James Learmonth of Balcomie, described as "the Frenchiest, Italianest jolly gentleman", had without regard to the season been carried off in midwinter by the "wiket Hielandmen" in question to one of the Summer Isles and there exorbitantly held to ransom, only to die shortly after his eventual release. The Adventurers having after this withdrawn discomfited, a fresh expedition was now planned with the enthusiastic support of the ever watchful Mackenzie of Kintail, who, in return for his readily proffered help to the Crown, was in due course admitted to membership of the Privy Council. But once again Neil and his islanders succeeded in repelling the invaders.

The task of clearing and re-settling the northern isles was proving a good deal harder than had been anticipated. Disgusted, James next offered it to the Cock of the North, Huntly, promising him as his reward "the whole North Isles, except Skye and Lewis, in feu" and specifying "that he should end the service, not by agreement with the country people, but by extirpating them". While naturally endeavouring to secure rather better financial terms, Huntly readily accepted the offer, replying in 1607 that "his Lordship offers to take in hand the service of settling the North Isles ... and to put an end to that service by extirpation of the barbrous people of the Isles within a year". Fortunately for the Islanders, however, this particular proposal was in the end dropped, owing to the objections raised by a number of intransigent Presbyterians at the idea of such an important, agreeable and lucrative task being entrusted to a notorious Roman Catholic. So that King James's ill-conceived project had in the end to be abandoned, though in Northern Ireland a similar scheme enforced by comparable methods was to prove considerably more rewarding. As for the Adventurers, "some", we are told, "died; others had greater occasions and business elsewhere to abstract them; all of them began to declyne apace in their riches and meanes, and so, being continuallie vexed by Neill Macloyd, they forsook the island and returned into Fyff". It was at this stage that MacKenzie of Kintail, who from the start had played a clever double game, shrewdly moved in to buy up the rights of the disheartened and disgruntled Adventurers. After which, having by methods of his own devising reduced the islanders to obedience, he successfully "catched his long wished and expected prey", greatly extending his own clan's territory and influence at the expense of the MacLeods. For a time after this Neil

MacLeod tried his hand at piracy, but a couple of years later was caught, condemned to death in April 1613 and died "very Christianlie" on the scaffold. Such, says the chronicler, a trifle sanctimoniously, was "the lamentable historie and decay of Macloyd of the Lewis ... which punishment was justlie inflicted upon them, for killing and destroying one another wiht intestin and civill warrs". The Mackenzies, meanwhile, went on from strength to strength.

Not many years later a bitter feud with the Macdonells of Glengarry over certain lands in Wester Ross ended in further substantial territorial gains for Clan Kenneth, though not before the MacDonells had managed to burn alive a whole congregation of Mackenzies in the parish church at Kilchrist while Glengarry's pipes drowned the screams of the dying with a specially devised pibroch which thereafter became famous under the name of Kilchrist and remains to this day Glengarry's traditional family lilt.

Following the abandonment of King James's plans for the re-settlement of Lewis and after further discussion between the King and his advisers, a new approach to the problem of the Western Highlands and Islands was now planned, this time to be carried out without widespread confiscation of lands or even the mass eradication of the inhabitants. In 1608, Andrew Stewart, Lord Ochiltree, a nobleman highly regarded, we are told, for his "fidelity, courage and magnanimity", and Andrew Knox, famous, when Minister of Paisley, for his timely discovery of the "Spanish Blanks" and now Bishop of the Isles, were appointed Royal Commissioners for the purpose of pacifying the Western Highlands and Islands and restoring order there with the support of a

17th-century powder horn, depicting a hunter and gillie coursing deer.

number of other notables, constituting a Council and backed by a sizeable military and naval force.

As a first step, a number of the Western chiefs and their kin, notably Hector Maclean of Duart, his brother Lachlan, Allan Maclean of Lochbuidhe, Allan Maclean younger of Ardgour, Donald Gorm MacDonald of Sleat, Donald MacDonald of Clanranald and MacLeod of Dunvegan's brother Alexander, were invited, or perhaps it would be more accurate to say lured on board one of His Majesty's ships, *The Moon*, for the purpose of hearing a sermon to be preached on board by the Bishop of the Isles, to be followed, it was implied, by a banquet. Once HMS Moon had sailed, however, it became apparent to her passengers that they were simply being kidnapped. From Ayr, where they were in the end safely put ashore, they were next taken directly to Edinburgh and there brought before the Privy Council, on whose orders they were then variously consigned to the royal castles of Dumbarton, Stirling and Blackness and only released once they had accepted all the conditions proposed to them, made due submission to the Crown and given adequate guarantees for their future good behaviour.

The principles which it was hoped would govern their future conduct were now embodied in what were to be known as the Statues of Iona, being a series of measures designed to put relations between chiefs and Crown on a more satisfactory footing. These were solemnly drawn up by a special episcopal court and countersigned by the chiefs concerned at a kind of peace conference held the following year in Iona and presided over by Bishop Knox in person. In addition to discouraging begging, heavy drinking and the use of firearms, the Statutes also committed the signatories to reduce the numbers of their own entourage and dispense as far as possible with the services of clan bards. Significantly the Sixth Statute, which blamed the "continuance of barbarity, impiety and incivility" in the Highlands on the natives' ignorance of the English language, laid down that the chiefs must in future send their eldest sons to the Lowlands to learn "to speik, reid and write Englische", and looked forward to the time when the "Irishe language, which is one of the chief and principal causes of the continewance of barbarities and incivilitie amongst the inhabitants of the isles and Heylandis", would duly be "abolisheit and removeit".

The Macleans, as it happened, were to bear the full brunt of the government's measures of pacification. Under Lachlan Mor, who, as we have seen, had in 1598 met his death in Islay at the hands of the MacDonalds, Clan Gillean had reached the peak of their power. Under his son, the twenty-year-old *Euchan Og*, Young Hector, who succeeded him, they began to encounter the series of difficulties and misfortunes which were to dog them through the centuries that followed. Already in 1604 Hector Og's great stronghold of Duart had been seized by the King's Commissioner (it having been decided that "strong steps be taken with such houses"), and only given back to him in return for an undertaking to surrender it again whenever called upon to do so. In 1608, with Lachlan Maclean of Coll, Hector Maclean of Lochbuidhe and Allan, Younger of Ardgour, Hector Og had been among the chiefs who had been lured on board ship by Lord Ochiltree and then held as prisoners, Hector himself being relegated together with Coll and Lochbuie to Dumbarton Castle and the others to Stirling and Blackness. After which they had all been forced to subscribe to the nine

The Right Honble
JAMES, FIFTH EARL OF WEMYSS
CAPTAIN GENERAL, R.C.A.
1743–1756
Painted by Allan Ramsay.
PRESENTED BY SIR HENRY COOK, SECRETARY, R.C.A.

Statutes of Iona. As befitted a chief of his standing, Hector Og had, however, been granted the right to a somewhat greater retinue than the others and a special allowance of four tuns of wine a year. Likewise, in 1616, after he and a number of other Chiefs had duly bound themselves to appear each year before the Privy Council, he was granted the right to be accompanied on such occasions by four followers, while Coll, Ardgour and Lochbuie had to content themselves with no more than three.

In 1617, however, the fortunes of Clan Gillean took a sharp turn for the worse. In that year Hector Og was arrested and his castle of Duart seized for debt, apparently in respect of a sum of a thousand merks he had borrowed nine years earlier while a prisoner in Dumbarton Castle. But, as he was by that time already in jail, the chief sufferer turned out to be the castle's new occupant, Sir Rory Mackenzie of Coigeach, who, as soon as he had taken possession of the Castle, found himself being dunned for Duart's debts by William Stewart, son of the Keeper of Dumbarton Castle, who had made the mistake of lending Young Hector the money in the first place.

For a time now things were quieter in the north-west. Since 1545 no more had been heard of the long sustained claims of the Lords of the Isles to be independent sovereigns and, with the Union of the Crowns of Scotland and England, the days when the MacDonalds could look to Westminster for support were past. Cleverly, King James

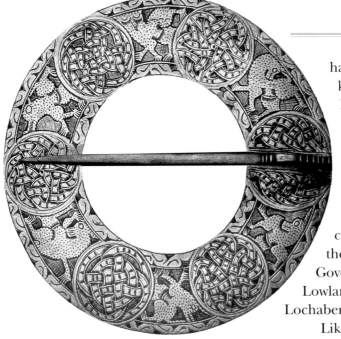

had played them off against their kinsmen and former allies, the Macleans, and they now took their place among the other western clans as equals rather than overlords, suffering, as did their neighbours, from the continuing encroachments of the Campbells of Argyll, already confirmed by long practice in their role of agents of the central Government and protectors of the Lowlands against the warlike clans of Lochaber and the west.

Like his predecessors, Grim Archibald 7th of Argyll, who had succeeded his

Circular brass brooch, Tomintoul, Banffshire, 17th century, used to fasten a woman's plaid or "earasaid".

The HEN WIFE
Castle GRANT
A, D, 1706

"The Hen Wife", at Castle Grant, by Richard Waitt. She is wearing the kertch, or breid, commonly worn by countrywomen of the 17th and 18th centuries.

133

father Colin as a child in 1584 and ten years later had, at the King's behest, sought to subdue the Catholic Earls at Glenlivet, played his full part in suppressing disorder in the Western Highlands and Islands. It was he who in 1603 had lured Alasdair MacGregor to his destruction. In 1607 King James VI had made him a grant of the lands of Kintyre, forfeited by the MacDonalds, in return for which he had built on Loch Kilkerran a new burgh to which he gave the name of Campbeltown. Later, having married a Catholic wife, he himself became, ironically enough, a Roman Catholic, taking service with the King of Spain and leaving his able and ambitious son, Lord Lorne, another Archibald, to take over his duties as Chief.

For Clan MacLeod, against others, the sixteenth century had been a period of perpetual conflict with one neighbour or another. A long-standing feud with the Frasers concerned the ownership of part of Glenelg. In 1513 the MacKenzies had attacked Gairloch and Coigach, both of which were claimed, indeed held, by the MacLeods of Lewis. Both branches of the clan had taken an active part in two of the three attempts which had been made to restore the Lordship of the Isles. But in the running battle between the Macleans and MacDonalds in the second half of the sixteenth century the two MacLeod septs of Siol Tormod and Siol Torquil actually found themselves fighting on opposing sides. With the MacDonalds the MacLeods continued to dispute the lands taken from them in the past by the Lords of the Isles, which had either remained in MacDonald hands or were at any rate still claimed by the MacDonalds. As early as 1480 MacDonald of Clanranald had raided Skye, while in 1493 MacDonald of Sleat had seized most of

Trotternish. A concentrated attack by Sleat and Clanranald on MacLeod territory in 1528 had culminated two years later in the bloody battle of Glendale, when the enemy's onslaught was only checked by the unfurling of the Fairy Flag. Fifty years after that, in 1580, Clanranald had attacked again, this time burning down the Church of Trumpan in Waternish, with its congregation of MacLeods inside it, but in return had themselves suffered heavy casualties thanks yet again to the MacLeods' timely tactical use of their Fairy Flag. In 1599 came further savage fighting between Sleat and the MacLeods, a last pitched battle between the two clans being fought in 1601, this time in the Cuillin.

At such periods in its history, a clan is fortunate to possess a capable Chief. When Alasdair Crotach MacLeod, 8th of Dunvegan, well versed in the arts of both peace and war, died in 1547 he had presided over the fortunes of his clan for more than half a century. It was he who added the Fairy Tower to Dunvegan and built St Clement's Church at Rodel in Harris, where he himself lies buried in an exceptionally handsome tomb. It was he, too, according to tradition, who first brought the MacCrimmons to Skye and founded their famous school of piping at Borreraig, which his successors were to maintain through several centuries. It was not long after this and very largely thanks to him that the pipes effectively took the place of the *clarsach* or Celtic harp as Scotland's national instrument.

Another outstanding MacLeod Chief was Rory Mor, 15th of Dunvegan, who was Chief during King James VI's attempts to impose

Lochranza Bay, Isle of Arran, with basking shark. Engraving by Thomas Pennant.

order on the Western Highlands and Islands. Though clever enough to avoid being kidnapped with his fellow chiefs by Lord Ochiltree and Bishop Knox in 1608 by sending his son in his place, he duly signed the Statutes of Iona the following year, committing himself with the others to changing his way of life, reducing the numbers of his household, discouraging drunkenness, abandoning the use of two-handed swords, having his children taught English and appearing once a year before the Privy Council. In the end Rory Mor came to terms with the King and in 1613 actually visited London, where James was gracious enough to bestow a knighthood upon him.

Like Alasdair Crotach, Rory Mor was a compulsive builder and added a massive new wing to Dunvegan, linking the keep with the Fairy Tower. Despite the restrictions imposed by the Statues of Iona, he actively encouraged piping and the bardic arts, both of which reached their zenith in his day, and continued to maintain a lavish way of life at Dunvegan, vividly celebrated in the verse of his famous kinswoman, Mairi Nighean Alasdair MacLeod. "With Roderick Mor Macleod of the Banners in this great house," she wrote, "I have been joyful, dancing merrily on a wide floor." He also seems to have done something to restore his family's severely strained finances. Though no doubt used by him (in defiance of the Statutes of Iona), the mighty, cross-hilted, two-handed weapon, known as Rory Mor's Sword, seems from its workmanship and design to have been made more probably for his predecessor, the great warrior Alasdair Crotach. Meanwhile, the less fortunate MacLeods of Lewis had, as we have seen, been effectively deprived of their birthright.

Of the other Western clans, the Mackenzies had successfully used the concluding years of the sixteenth century to strengthen their position, rising, it has been aptly said, on the ruins of the MacDonalds. Their skilfully conducted feud with MacDonell of Glengarry left them in possession of much former MacDonell territory round Lochalsh and Loch Carron, including MacDonell's own castle of Strome. By much clever manoeuvring and by successfully playing each side off against the other, they also managed to acquire a large part of Coigach which had formerly belonged to the MacLeods, and established themselves on Lewis by similar means. Shortly after this, in 1609, Mackenzie of Kintail, already a Privy Councillor, was created Lord Mackenzie of Kintail by King James VI who, still intent on developing the economic resources of the Western Highlands, had authorised him to deal with the MacLeods on his behalf, "by force or policy, as he may best have it".

Nor were the Mackenzies' territorial gains confined to the West coast. As early as the fifteenth century their Chiefs, backed by skilful lawyers, had moved eastwards across Scotland, first to Kinellan near Strathpeffer and thence to Brahan near Dingwall, where early in the seventeenth century they built themselves a magnificent castle. Meanwhile one of the first Lord Mackenzie's younger brothers, Roderick, from whom are descended the Earls of Cromartie, had installed himself as Mackenzie of Coigach in Wester Ross in place of the MacLeods. Closely linked with the Mackenzies over the centuries were the MacRaes, who later assumed on their behalf the Captaincy of their strategically situated stronghold of Eilean Donan on Loch Duich. In 1623 the second Lord Mackenzie was created Earl of Seaforth. There could now no longer be any doubt of Clan Kenneth's power or importance. It was not until a couple of centuries later that the fearful doom foretold for them by the famous Brahan Seer was finally to overtake them.

In a commission issued from Holyrood House in January 1578 ordering his apprehension, the Brahan Seer, *Coinneach Odhar* or Sallow Kenneth, is described as "principal or leader in the art of magic". While Mackenzie of Seaforth, the Mackenzie Chief of the day was away in France Kenneth's gift of the second sight enabled him to recount to Mackenzie's wife Lady Seaforth just how her husband was conducting himself there. Infuriated by these revelations, she rather unfairly and, as it turned out, unwisely vented her wrath on the unfortunate Seer, causing him to be rolled down hill in a blazing tar-barrel lined with sharp spikes. With his dying breath Kenneth cursed the Mackenzies of Seaforth in a detailed and remarkably accurate prophecy foretelling the terrible doom which would in due course overtake them. Many of his other prophecies including those concerning, for example, both World Wars, have over the years proved no less accurate.

Jockies Lamentation,

Whose Seditious Work,   Was the loss of his Country and his Kirk.
To a Stately New Scottish Tune.

When first the Scottish wars began
The English-man did lead the Uan
with Musket & Pike,
The bonny blith & cunning Scot
Had laid a Plot, but we could not
smell out the like.
Although he could neither write no2 Read
Yet General Lashly past the Tweed
With his gay gang of Blew-caps tall
Along we marcht with our General
New-castle we took all in a trice
And thought fo2 to make it our Paradice
And then we were gallant and gay
Fo2 why we took their Pillage away.

Then straight to Plundering we did fall
Of great & small, fo2 we were all
most valiant that day
And Jenny in her silken Gown
The best in town from foot to Crown
was bonny & gay.
Our suits & our silks did make such a smother
That hardly next day we knew one another
Fo2 Jockey he was wond2ous fine
And Jenny in her silks did shine
Fo2 there ise did get me a Beaver then
But now it is beat to a Cap agen
Fo2 a Red-coat got every rag
That Jockey now & Jenny must bag.

The English rais'd an Army straight
With mickle state, & we did wait
to charge them all.
Then every valiant musket-man
Put fire in pan that we began
apace to fall   (coal
Fo2 when that the Powder was toucht by the
Then every man did pay fo2 his pole
Fo2 the Red-Coat the battel won
And Jockey fast to Scotland did run.
And at Dunbar fight a weel & a neer
Fo2 there we were put to a mickle fear
They took our Guns & silver all
And hung up our silks in Westminster-hall.

Full well I wot in Lancashire
Our b2ethren dear, did plunder there
both Rich and Poo2.
Which caus'd the fury of the No2th
When we set fo2th to be in w2oth
and vex us so2e,   (down
Fo2 when that the Red-Coats had knockt us
The country people in every Town
Did beat Jockey over the face
And was not this a pittiful case ?
They bid us remember our Plundering tricks
And thumpt us & beat us, with cudgels & sticks
But the deel burst my body & wem
I ever ise gang to England agen.

CHAPTER XIII

The Covenanters and the Civil War

King Charles I, who succeeded to the thrones of Scotland and England on James's death in 1625, possessed none of his father's natural caution, shrewdness or statecraft, being deeply and unquestioningly convinced of the divine right of Kings. Though Scottish-born, he had but little understanding for Scotland or Scottish affairs. Neither the Highlands nor the Lowlands, with their diverse and individual traditions, meant much to him. A devout Episcopalian, his chief duty towards Scotland, as he conceived it, was to bring the Scottish Kirk into line with the Church of England, bishops and all. It was not long before, by his efforts to do so, he had managed to antagonize most sections of Scottish opinion.

In 1633 Charles was crowned King in Edinburgh with full Anglican rites. At the same time a Commission was appointed to draw up a revised Prayer Book for Scotland to replace extempore prayer. Moreover, to the dismay of all those whose forebears had profited from the confiscation and re-distribution of Church lands at the time of the Reformation, he decreed that these should now be returned to the Church, thus alienating for a start a large number of powerful nobles. Opposition to the new prayer book, which was published in July 1637, and to the other measures which accompanied it, was noisy and widespread. From London Charles simply sent orders that those who protested against his prayer book should be punished and its use enforced.

Towards the end of February 1638 a formidable gathering of several hundred representatives of the nobles, the gentry, the clergy and the burghs flocked to the Greyfriars Kirk in Edinburgh to sign a National Covenant protesting against the latest "innovations" and pledging its signatories to uphold "the true religion". In the east of Scotland those who supported the Covenant were led by James Graham, Earl of Montrose, a handsome, gifted and adventurous young man who was soon to show that he possessed the makings of a considerable military commander. He was also a poet who accurately summed up his philosophy of life in four lines:

He either fears his fate too much
Or his deserts are small
Who dares not put it to the touch
To win or lose it all.

In the west the Covenanters' leader was to be the exceptionally able Archibald Campbell, Eighth Earl of Argyll, soft spoken, red-haired, ill-favoured with crooked

"Jockies Lamentation",
broadsheet on the
defeat of the Scots at
Dunbar in 1650.

features and a squint which led him to be called "The Gleyed Argyll". Of him his contemporary Clarendon wrote that "he wanted nothing but honesty and courage to be a very extraordinary man, having all other good talents in a very high degree". Each of the two was in his own way a force to be reckoned with.

Soon thousands more signatures had been collected. The significance of the Covenant was not merely religious but to a high degree political. By many of those who signed it, it was regarded as a defence "against our poor country being made an English province". In November 1638 things came to a crisis. At a meeting in Glasgow of the General Assembly of the Church of Scotland, all the bishops appointed by Charles or his father were summarily deposed and the new prayer-book abolished. To this the King simply replied from London that the Assembly's decisions were not valid.

Early in the summer of 1639, Charles, who had by this time decided to impose his will on Scotland by force, but who possessed no standing army with which to do so, assembled some twenty thousand poorly trained men in the north of England and with them advanced to the Border. At Berwick he encountered a rather better trained Scottish force commanded by Alexander Leslie, an able soldier of fortune who had already made a considerable reputation for himself on the continent of Europe. But when it came to the point, it emerged that neither side really wanted a fight and in the end it was agreed that all disputed questions should be referred to another General Assembly or to Parliament.

The new General Assembly's first move was simply to re-enact the measures passed by its predecessor. Parliament went further still, expressly doing away with bishops and freeing itself from royal control. Again both sides stood to arms. This time Alexander Leslie, with the support of Montrose, carried the war into England, scattering Charles's forces and actually seizing Newcastle and Durham.

Forced once more to negotiate and needing further funds, Charles now summoned the English Parliament. It was to prove a fateful decision. From the first things went badly between them. Soon civil war threatened. In the autumn of 1641 Charles came to Scotland, this time in search of badly needed support. In the hope of winning them over to his side, he made Argyll a marquess and created Leslie Earl of Leven. The demands of the General Assembly and Scottish Parliament he accepted as they stood.

Archibald Campbell, 1st Marquess of Argyll, by Scougal. Campbell was a leading presbyterian statesman: a poor soldier but a shrewd politician.

140

"The Covenanters' Preaching", by George Harvey, 1830.

In August 1642 came the news that in England civil war had broken out between the King's forces and those of Parliament. At first the Scots held aloof. But in the autumn of 1643 an agreement, known as the Solemn League and Covenant, was signed between the Scottish Covenanters and representatives of the English Parliament, under which the former undertook to attack the Royalist forces from the north in return for the sum of £30,000 a month. At the same time they were given an undertaking by Parliament that the Church of England would in due course be brought into line with the Church of Scotland in matters of doctrine. The following summer the Parliamentary forces, under the formidable leadership of Oliver Cromwell, managed, with Scottish help, to inflict a heavy defeat on the Royalists under Prince Rupert on Marston Moor in Yorkshire.

It was at this stage that the King, now in Oxford, gained a new ally. For some time Montrose had felt himself more in sympathy with the Royalists and less with his fellow Covenanters, least of all with Argyll, against whom the latter's own father, Archibald Gruamach, had shortly before his death warned the King from his retirement, writing "he is a man of craft, subtilty and falsehood and can love no man; and if ever he finds it in his power to do you a mischief, he will be sure to do it". In the spring of 1644 Montrose made his choice, riding north from Oxford "to raise Scotland for the King", who in return made him a marquess and appointed him his Lieutenant-General for Scotland.

The General Assembly of the Kirk of Scotland 1787.

How was the new Lieutenant-General to raise Scotland for the King and where was he to find the troops with which to do it? The outlook was not promising. There was certainly little prospect of help from the Lowlands, already for the most part strongly committed to the Covenant. In Perth and Angus Montrose had a number of kinsmen and friends. But his best hope by far lay in the Highlands, where, in the West at any rate, a deep-seated hatred of Clan Campbell might, with luck, prove to outweigh Argyll's widespread influence and power. So far, however, almost the only firm promise of help had come from Ireland, from the strongly Royalist Macdonell Earl of Antrim, who had offered to send over to Scotland a thousand or more Irish levies to fight for the King.

In the summer of 1644 Montrose, who had made his way north secretly in several stages disguised as a groom, entered the Braes of Atholl on foot in Highland garb with two companions and a couple of pack horses. There, greatly to his relief, he found Antrim's Irish levies under the command of the latter's kinsman, Alasdair MacColla MacDonald, a dark-haired giant of a man, son of old left-handed Coll MacDonald of Colonsay, of the ancient stock of Dunyveg in Islay, commonly known as ColKitto. These had landed in Ardnamurchan some weeks before. Since then, having established their base in Mingaray Castle and in the old keep of Lochaline, at the point where the River Aline enters the sound of Mull, they had been happily employed, in company with a number of other MacDonalds who had joined them, hunting down any Campbells or Covenanters they could find in Ardnamurchan and Lochaber and ravaging their lands.

Alasdair's sixteen hundred Scots-Irish were to form the nucleus of Montrose's army, being in due course joined by still more MacDonalds and by contingents from other clans who had old scores to settle with the Covenanting Campbells – Camerons,

Macleans, MacGregors, Mackintoshes, Stewarts of Appin and, despite Huntly's lingering distrust of Montrose as a former Covenanter, some Gordons under his son Lord Gordon. As far as these clansmen were concerned, the mere fact that the Covenanters were led by Argyll quickly determined their alignment. Here for most of them was a heaven-sent opportunity to settle old scores, while at the same time effectively demonstrating any loyalty as they might feel for the Crown.

The sudden arrival in Atholl of Alasdair MacColla's force and their ferocious appearance at first dismayed the more orderly Athollmen. Indeed the garrison of Blair Atholl fled at the mere sight of them, leaving the castle to fall into their hands without a fight. But with Montrose came his kinsman Black Pate Graeme of Inchbrakie, whose sister was young Robertson of Struan's mother, and, when next morning Montrose raised King Charles's standard at Lude on a green knoll by the waters of the Tilt, the Robertsons, reassured by Black Pate's presence and captivated by Montrose's charm, rallied readily enough to the Royal cause. With them came the Murrays of Atholl. At this time Alexander Robertson, Twelfth of Struan, was no more than a child, but the men of Clan

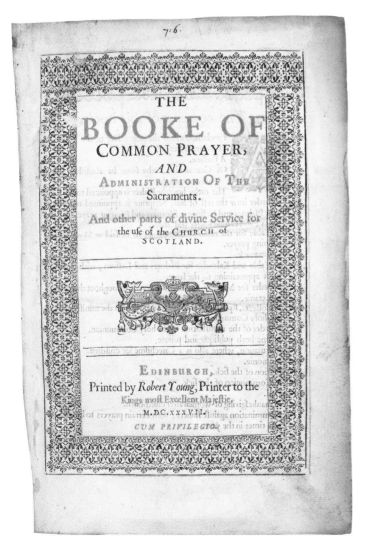

Donnachaidh gladly accepted as their leaders his uncles Black Pate and Donald Robertson. Though the Earl of Atholl had married a Campbell of Glenorchy, the Campbells were hated in Atholl, and not without cause. Four years earlier, in 1640, a strong Campbell force under Argyll had invaded Atholl in the name of the Covenant and treacherously made prisoner Atholl himself, who later died as a result of the treatment he had received at their hands, leaving a young boy to succeed him. Altogether, eight hundred Athollmen now joined Montrose, as did the strongly Royalist Lord Ogilvy, whose "bonny House of Airlie" had been "despitefully" burned down four years earlier by marauding Campbells. Again Argyll invaded and ravaged Atholl. But this time the Athollmen did not have to wait long for their revenge.

In seeking support for King Charles against the Campbells, Montrose found no readier volunteers than the Macleans. For this there was good reason. Their

An extremely rare copy of Laud's prayerbook, 1637. The enforcement of this prayer book on the Scots caused the famous incident of Jenny Geddes throwing her stool at the preacher in St Giles' Cathedral, Edinburgh, and ultimately led to the Bishop's War.

chief at this time was Sir Lachlan of Duart, a personal friend of King Charles, who had recently created him a baronet of Nova Scotia. Lachlan had never been a rich man. A compulsive builder and a man of expensive tastes he was by now heavily in debt. To satisfy his creditors, he had even been obliged to surrender to the Campbells the sacred Isle of Iona, of which the Macleans, as staunch Protestants, had taken possession at the time of the Reformation. Worse still, Lachlan had unhappily become involved with the rich and wily Argyll himself who, he had discovered, was only too glad to lend him considerable sums of money. Not long after this Argyll had "bought Maclean's debts", taking over, in addition to the sums he had already lent him, all Lachlan's debts to the Crown and his other creditors. Then, having become his sole creditor, he had promptly had him imprisoned for debt in Carrick Castle in Cowal, releasing him two years later in return for a formal acknowledgement that he now owed him no less than £30,000 Scots. It was thus that few had better reason to wish Argyll out of the way than Lachlan, whose personal interests neatly coincided with his natural inclinations. The consequences of his action in siding with Montrose were predictable. As soon as the Macleans joined Montrose, Argyll started to lay waste their lands with a vengeance, while the Macleans immediately retaliated by pillaging the Campbell lands at Muckart and Dollar and burning down Castle Campbell in the Ochil Hills.

Forgetting their former sufferings at the hands of the House of Stewart, the MacGregors under their Chief Patrick Roy now also joined Montrose, in return, it may

Battle of Dunbar, 1650. Here, Cromwell routed the Scottish army under David Leslie, so ending Charles II's hope of ruling effectively. An 18th-century engraving by Peter Stent.

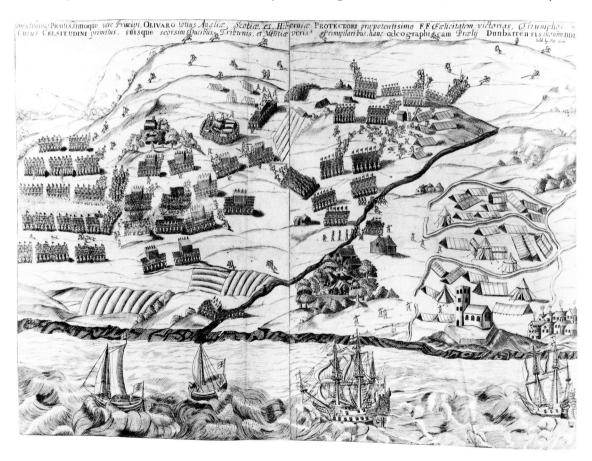

be said, for an easily given undertaking that "whatsoever lands and possessions belonged justlie to the Laird of MacGregor and his predecessors in Glenlyon, Rannoch or Glenorchy" should be restored to him "when it will please God to put an end to thes present troubles", in other words after the greatly longed for overthrow of the Campbells, who for the past two hundred years had been firmly in possession of the lands in question.

Opposing Montrose, in addition to the Campbells and the strong Lowland forces mobilized by the Committee of Estates, were the Covenanting clans of the North under the leadership of the Earls of Sutherland and Seaforth – Frasers, MacKays, Forbeses, Monroes, Rosses, MacLeods, Mackenzies and, though cautious as ever, lacking somewhat in conviction and far from united, the Grants.

Advancing on Perth in September at the head of his oddly assorted force, Montrose soundly defeated a much larger army of Covenanters under Lord Elcho at Tippermuir and captured the city. A couple of weeks later, moving northwards, he entered Aberdeen, a rich prey for the hungry Highlanders, who on this occasion conducted themselves with less than their usual chivalry, while the Irish contingent murdered and looted with characteristic gusto, thereby alienating a large number of potential allies. Next he turned westwards through the hills into Campbell country and, at the head of Alasdair MacCollal MacDonald's Highlanders, for the most part Macleans and MacDonalds, all ready to sink their former differences in so good a cause, swooped down on Argyll's great stronghold of Inverary and burned it to the ground and, causing its noble occupant who, whatever his other qualities, was no soldier, to rise abruptly from his dinner table and take refuge in a boat in the middle of Loch Fyne.

In the cold clear dawn of 2 February, 1645, once more against overwhelming odds, Montrose won yet another important victory at Inverlochy, where, after an arduous and strategically brilliant march through the snowy hills, he yet again surprised and routed the Campbells and their Covenanting allies. While the Campbells' Chief once more made off by boat, their commander in the field, Sir Duncan Campbell of Auchinbreck, together with no less than forty other Campbell barons and some fifteen hundred clansmen, were slaughtered and their lands utterly laid waste. Hemmed in, with their backs to the loch and the river, they tried fighting in small, disparate groups.

Duncan of Auchinbreck's sister Finuloa was, as it happened, the wife of Maclean of Coll, but there could be no doubt where her loyalties lay. "Red-haired Hector of that wicked clan," she wrote in savage Gaelic couplets, bitterly cursing her own eldest son, "I care not if you come to harm or if your line be unfruitful.... Had I been at Inverary with a two-edged sword in my hands and the strength and skill to match my desire, I would

James Graham, 5th Earl and 1st Marquess of Montrose. Covenanter and Royalist, he emerged as the greatest general after Cromwell, a key supporter of Charles I in Scotland during the Civil War. A painting by Honthorst.

Montrose's sword, given to him by Charles I. From the collection of Walter Scott.

The Battle of Bothwell Brig, an important event in the countless wars of the 17th century. Here, the Covenanters were heavily defeated and 1200 men were taken prisoner.

have shed much blood there and I would myself have mown down the Macleans and MacDonalds."

Continuing this triumphant progress through Scotland, Montrose, moving eastwards, went on in March to storm and sack the rich city of Dundee; in May he defeated the Covenanters at Auldearn by the Moray Firth where the Highland charge once again proved its worth; in July he routed them at Alford, outside Aberdeen, where Huntly's son, Lord Gordon, was killed; and in August, having defeated them decisively at Kilsyth in Stirlingshire, where the Macleans under Lachlan of Duart and Allan of Ardgour, and the MacDonalds of Clanranald under Donald of Moidart, carried all before them, occupied Glasgow. Of the six thousand Covenanters who took the field at Kilsyth barely a hundred managed to escape, while their leaders, who had better horses than the rank and file, were quick to seek safety in flight. After galloping twenty miles to Queensferry, Argyll himself was once again lucky enough to find a friendly fishing boat to carry him out of harm's way.

Militarily, Montrose and his Highland allies were by now to all intents and purposes the masters of Scotland. But they had so far failed to win support in the Lowlands – "subdued but not converted" – or for that matter to relieve, as they had intended, the pressure on the King's forces in England, whence had come in June the news of Cromwell's overwhelming victory at Naseby. Meanwhile, as so often happened with Highlanders, with harvest time coming on, Montrose's army had begun to melt away. Disappointed by his refusal to allow them to plunder Glasgow, as they had plundered Aberdeen and Dundee, most of his Highland contingent simply made their way home to Mull, to Morvern, to Moidart and to Ardnamurchan, using the occasion, it is true, to inflict such damage as they could on any enemies they met en route, the Macleans in particular putting to flight a large force of Campbells they encountered in Mamore. Some five hundred of Antrim's Irish fought on in Scotland under Colonel O'Kean, but, though promising to return, Alasdair MacDonald, who had given Montrose good service as his brigadier and on whom Montrose had bestowed the honour of knighthood, now took the remainder back with him to Ireland, where he himself was later killed in battle. No less damaging than Alasdair's defection was Huntley's decision, taken after much prevarication, to withdraw the bulk of the Gordon horse and foot, leaving Montrose with scarcely any cavalry and grave doubts as to the future attitude of the Gordons.

Towards the middle of September, after seeking unsuccessfully to win allies in the south of Scotland, Montrose, with severely depleted numbers, reached the flats of Philipshaugh near Selkirk in the Borders and there pitched camp with the six hundred men who remained to him. It was here that on the following morning, before he had had time to seek out a more favourable position, he was surprised by David Leslie, an experienced commander newly arrived from England with a force of six thousand men. Digging themselves in as best they could, the five hundred Irish fought back stubbornly. With a handful of troopers, Montrose himself charged the enemy again and again. But his little force was outnumbered tenfold. Soon more than four hundred of his five hundred Irish lay dead. In return for a promise of quarter from the Covenanters the remainder surrendered, but were promptly massacred to a man along with the three hundred women and children who accompanied them. With only a few surviving companions, Montrose left the stricken field, his year of victories at an end.

Philipshaugh was Montrose's first defeat. But it was to prove decisive. From the Borders he turned north and in a week was back in Atholl. During the months that followed he still had hopes of restoring the King's fortunes in Scotland, waging desultory guerilla warfare in the valley of the Spey. For a time his nephew Lord Napier bravely defended the Graham castle of Kincardine, and early in 1646, at Callander, seven hundred Athollmen under Black Pate of Inchbrakie fell upon and routed twelve hundred Campbells under Campbell of Ardkinglas. These, it seems, had "fled like madmen, divers of them being slain in the fight and more drowned in the river of Goodie, their haste being such that they staid not to seek the fords". But, from allies, Huntly's two thousand Gordons had by this time come close to being enemies, and with now no more than a thousand men under his command there was not much Montrose could do and few friends who would join him.

Then, on the last day of May 1646 came the shattering news that King Charles had surrendered to the Scottish army at Newark in England and that it had been made a condition of his surrender that Montrose should disband his followers and leave Scotland. Disillusioned and depressed, he took ship to Norway.

Of Montrose's allies, the Macleans, who under Lachlan of Duart and Allan of Ardgour had been in the forefront of the battle at Inverlochy and Kilsyth and whose guiding motive had, as usual, been to revenge themselves on Clan Diarmid, were to pay dearly for their part in the campaign. After Montrose's defeat David Leslie occupied their stronghold of Duart, which was then quickly taken over by the Campbells. Three years later the debt-ridden Sir Lachlan died and was buried on Iona, by now also in Campbell hands. He was succeeded by his son Eachunn Ruadh, Hector the Red.

Clan Donald fared no better. After Montrose's defeat the remaining MacDonald castles of Dunaverty in Kintyre and Dunyveg in Islay were quickly captured. By now Alasdair MacDonald had been killed in battle in Ireland,

Covenanters' Banner probably carried at the Battle of Bothwell Brig, 1679.

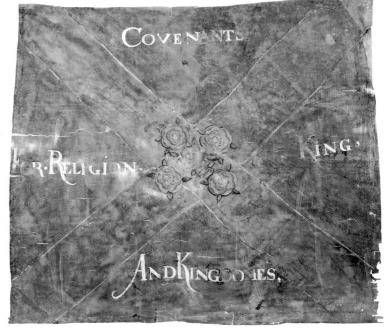

William Alexander was the driving force in the attempt to establish a "New Scotland" – Nova Scotia – across the Atlantic. He was given Nova Scotia in 1621 by James VI, but it had been handed over to the French by 1632.

while his old father, Coll Macgillespick, who had been left in charge at Dunyveg, had been handed over to the Campbells and hanged from the mast of his own galley. As for Argyll, he was awarded by Parliament the sum of £15,000 for the not inconsiderable damage done to his property by all concerned.

In Cowal, the Lamonts, who had sided with Montrose and, together with Col Kitto and his Irish, boldly invaded and laid waste the Campbell lands adjoining theirs, were now set upon by the infuriated Campbells and having, as they thought, surrendered, were massacred in their hundreds in Dunoon churchyard, "by Shotts, by durks, by cutting their throats, as they doe with beasts.... And lastly they hanged on one tree thirty and six at one tyme of the chiefs and speciall gentlemen of that name, and before they were half hanged they cutt them downe and threw them in by dozens in pits prepared for the same; and many of them, striving to ryse upon their feet, were violently holden doune untill that by throwing the earth in great quantity upon them they were stifled to death". Meanwhile the Lamonts' houses and lands had been laid waste and burnt and three thousand head of their cattle carried off. Thereafter Clan Lamont were to play a relatively small part in Highland history.

Justly famed for their prudence, the Grants had during these difficult times tried, though without much success, to keep out of trouble. Their Chief, although hardly an enthusiastic Covenanter, had suffered severely when Montrose occupied Strathspey and, having, in order to avoid further unpleasantness, duly made submission to him, had suffered no less severely when the Covenanters returned to take a savage revenge on all who had opposed them even nominally.

With the King's surrender to them at Newark, the Scots in England now found themselves in something of a dilemma. Being only indirectly concerned with the quarrel between King and Parliament, their primary purpose in signing the Solemn League and Covenant with the English Parliament had been to secure England's conversion to the Presbyterian faith. But, despite the undertakings he had given, neither Cromwell nor his Army seemed much interested in turning England Presbyterian. Nor, despite the valuable service they had rendered, had the Scots received the substantial monthly payments promised them under the agreement. Had the King now declared his readiness to establish Presbyterianism in England, they would at this stage have been prepared to change sides and fight for him. But this was something that Charles could even now not bring himself to do. And so, in return for a promise of £400,000, they simply handed him over to the English and made their way back to Scotland.

Having once done this, they almost immediately began to have doubts about the wisdom, let alone the morality, of their action and again sought contact with Charles. Under an agreement secretly arrived at towards the end of 1647 between the King and representatives of the Scottish Parliament at Carisbrooke Castle on the Isle of Wight and known as the Engagement, the latter now undertook to send an army to England to support the King in return for a belated and doubtless half-hearted promise from him to give Presbyterianism a three years' trial in England. Thus it was that, in the summer of 1648, a Scottish army actually set out for England for the purpose of restoring the King's position. At Preston in Lancashire it was heavily defeated by Cromwell; after which the survivors surrendered.

The Engagement had from the first been strongly opposed by the more extreme Covenanters. Taking the disaster of Preston as their cue, these now marched on Edinburgh from the south-west, where their strength lay, and overthrew the Government. This left their leader Argyll in effect master of Scotland. Under his auspices, Cromwell now came to Edinburgh, where he received a hero's welcome. A few days later came the news that King Charles had been executed in Whitehall.

The news of the King's execution by the English filled the Scots with dismay. Even to those of them most strongly opposed to Charles's policies it seemed unbecoming that, as a result of English action, Scotland should be left

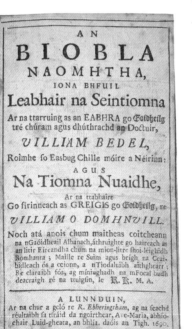

without a king. Accordingly, Argyll now made contact with the dead King's eighteen-year-old son Charles and had him proclaimed King in Edinburgh.

Montrose, too, had offered the new monarch his services and had been encouraged by him to invade the north of Scotland. Landing at Thurso, which he reached by way of the Orkneys in April 1650, he assembled a mixed force of foreign mercenaries, native Orcadians and a few local recruits. These were, however, easily dispersed by the Covenanters at

Bible, 1690. This edition of the Irish Bible was printed in Roman type for use in Scottish churches. "Formal register" Irish Gaelic was used in both Ireland and Scotland, but there were differences in the local vernacular. The New Testament was published in Scots Gaelic for the first time in 1767, with the complete Bible appearing in 1807.

Members of the 43rd Highlanders. Print by Muller.

Carbisdale, and in the end Montrose, a wanderer once more, was betrayed to his enemies by "ane of his auld acquentance", Macleod of Assynt, for, it was said, four hundred bolls of meal. At the instance of Argyll he was then taken to Edinburgh, put on trial and hanged and quartered as a traitor to the King he had served so loyally. It is said that, as the cart carrying Montrose came in sight of the balcony on which Argyll was standing, the latter turned away and went inside. Another supporter of King Charles I who suffered the same fate was Huntly. "You may," he declared eloquently, "take my head from my shoulders, but not my heart from my Sovereign." Whereupon his brother-in-law Argyll, taking him at his word, caused him to be beheaded less than two months after King Charles's death.

With Montrose gone, Charles II was entirely dependent on Argyll and bound to comply with his wishes. In the summer of 1650, having formally accepted both Covenants, he came to Scotland to claim his kingdom. He could now count on the support both of the Covenanters and of their former enemies. In addition to the clans who had fought for Montrose many of those who had opposed him now rallied to the Royal Standard, Frasers, Mackenzies, and Macleods and, last but by no manner of means least, Campbells.

Cromwell's answer was to invade Scotland. At Dunbar he outmanoeuvred and utterly routed a Scottish army under his former ally, David Leslie. But Cromwell's failure to fulfil the terms of the Solemn League and Covenant rankled with the Covenanters, who were still reluctant to deal with him. Even now they would not admit defeat. On New Year's Day 1651 Argyll himself solemnly crowned Charles King at Scone. By the summer David Leslie had assembled a sizeable army with which to guard the approaches to Stirling.

And now once again disaster overtook the Scots. At Inverkeithing, near North Queensferry on the Firth of Forth, a Scottish force composed of both Highlanders and Lowlanders, hurriedly thrown in to check Cromwell's progress northwards, found themselves heavily outnumbered by an English army under General Lambert, an outstanding military leader. Under Holborn of Menstrie the bulk of the Lowland cavalry turned and fled. The Highlanders, mainly Macleans, stood and fought, bearing the brunt of the English onslaught. Of eight hundred Maclean clansmen who took the field under Red Hector of Duart, seven hundred and sixty were killed, as was Duart himself and two of the sons of Maclean of Ardgour. "*Fear eile airson Eachuinn*", "Another for Hector", the clansmen cried as they fell beside their Chief. It was rumoured afterwards that Argyll, for reasons of his own, had ensured that no reinforcements reached them. However this may be, the way was now open for Cromwell who, quickly marching on Perth, soon controlled the country both to the north and to the south of the Forth.

Outmanoeuvred in Scotland, Leslie and his main force crossed into England, where on 3 September 1651 they were heavily defeated at Worcester and finally forced to surrender. Amongst those who eluded capture was Charles himself, who, as he put it, now "went on his travels", leaving Cromwell master of both England and Scotland.

Ensign of the 43rd Highlanders

Officer of the 43rd Highlanders

151

DVKE OF YORK

CHAPTER XIV

The Revolution

In Scotland, soon for a time to be formally united with England, Cromwell now set up an unusually efficient system of military government, backed by an army of 20,000 men, with English garrisons in all the principal cities and strong-points at Perth, Inverlochy and Inverness. In General George Monk he possessed a shrewd and exceptionally able Commander in Chief. In 1654 a Royalist rising was attempted in the Highlands under the Earl of Glencairn and General John Middleton. But although in theory it had the support of the Mackenzies, Frasers, MacNaughtons, Camerons, Macleans, MacDonalds of Keppoch, Macdonells of Glengarry and, surprisingly enough, of Argyll's own son Lorne, in the end nothing came of it and for a time even the Highlands were relatively quiet.

After holding out for as long as he reasonably could, even that astute warrior Ewen Cameron of Lochiel, who from the first had fought valiantly against the English, reached in the end an honourable accommodation with General Monk, allowing him to retain his arms and rule undisturbed over his own clan territories. Most other chiefs did likewise and it could be said that thereafter Monk gathered the Highlands through the Chiefs. Prominent among these who had come to terms with Cromwell from the start was Argyll himself, "that political lord", as a contemporary called him. His luck was however to change abruptly after Cromwell's death, when, largely through General Monk's prompt shift of allegiance, the Monarchy was restored in both England and Scotland.

On Charles II's restoration in 1660 Argyll duly made his way to London to offer his services, but instead was at once sent back to Edinburgh, charged with high treason, found guilty and executed. Ironically enough, much of the evidence against him was furnished by General Monk, now high in Charles's favour; this showed that Argyll had offered his services to Monk when Monk was Cromwell's representative. Which was enough for his enemies' purpose. Argyll met his end with dignity. "I set the crown on the King's head," he said. "He hastens me now to a better crown than his." After his execution his severed head was impaled on the same spike which had formerly borne the head of his rival Montrose. "I charge you forget," Argyll wrote to his son, "and not harbour any animosity or particular anger against any man concerning me. Such heart-burnings have been the destruction of many a Noble person in this kingdom. I know not of any person so given, but the very same measure has been meted to him again. The Cup has gone round, and therefore content yourself."

James VII and II, the last of the Stuart kings. Painted here, by Sir Peter Lely, as the Duke of York, when he acted as Royal Commissioner in Scotland.

153

As for General Monk, Charles created him Duke of Albermarle.

Charles, who back in 1649 had only signed the two Covenants in order to secure his own coronation, had no intention of carrying out his obligations under them. When the Scottish Parliament reassembled in 1661, it was packed with reliable royalists, Bishops were brought back, parish ministers who refused to accept the new dispensation were "outed" and troops sent to deal with those who persisted in their covenanting ways. But the Covenanters stubbornly continued to resist, while Government repression became increasingly severe. More troops were now raised for this purpose under Sir Thomas Dalziel of the Binns, until recently in the Russian Service, who, according to that shrewd observer Bishop Gilbert Burnet, could, even by the standards of the day, be said to have "acted the Muscovite too grossly". He is credited with having brought back with him from Russia amongst other things, the thumbscrew, a useful little device until then unknown in Scotland.

In 1677, alarmed by the scale of the disturbances in the south-west, where the Covenanters were strongest, the Government hit on a novel and ingenious expedient. Lacking a standing army, they despatched to Ayrshire to keep order there what became known as the Highland Host, a force of some eight thousand Highlanders, led by Atholl and Perth and not, it must be said, seriously concerned with church matters. Dismayed by the ferocious appearance and alien tongue of the Highlanders, "a host of savages ... more terrible than Turks or Tartars", the good people of Ayrshire lay low; no lives were lost; for a time peace was restored and not many months later the clansmen returned home, laden, as usual, with loot, but having from the Government's point of view, performed a useful and necessary service. Later, Graham of Claverhouse, a distant kinsman of the great Montrose, was to restore order by more drastic means, earning from his opponents the well-deserved name of Bloody Clavers.

By actively supporting Montrose, Clan

Sir Ewen Cameron of Lochiel, 1629–1719. The 17th Chief of Clan Cameron, he was known as the Great Lochiel. He fought with Montrose and later with Claverhouse. He was a striking man about whom a contemporary wrote "His very look so fierce might fright the boldest foe".

Gregor had for their part also deserved well of the House of Stewart. Some two hundred MacGregors had taken part in Glencairn's abortive rising, when an island in Loch Rannoch served as a gathering place for the loyal clans. It was thus only to be expected that after the Restoration in April 1661 King Charles II would, as a reward for their clan's services, erase all memories of their "former miscarriages", restoring to them their name and the other rights due to them as loyal subjects of the Crown. To their bitter disappointment, however, he did not restore to them the clan lands which their bards assured them were their heritage. These continued, as before, in Campbell hands, with the result that, apart from the Menzies lands they held illegally at the Western end of Loch Rannoch, Clan Gregor remained landless, later chiefs moving further south to the neighbourhood of Loch Lomond, where from their previous exploits they were already all too well known.

In 1685 Charles II died and was succeeded by his in some ways less gifted brother James VII and II, who towards the end of Charles's reign had, as Duke of York, briefly acted as Royal Commissioner in Scotland and who, in 1671, had publicly declared himself a Roman Catholic. For the first time for nearly a hundred and twenty years Scotland and England now had a Roman Catholic monarch and one whom his Protestant subjects, in Scotland, as in England, strongly suspected of wanting to impose on them his own religion. Nor, for allied reasons, did they approve of the close connection which James was known to have with the French court.

With the restoration of Charles II the fortunes of the Catholic Gordons were not unnaturally once more in the ascendant. Their estates, which had been forfeited, were now restored to the Fourth Marquess of Huntly, who in 1684 was created Duke of Gordon. Like others of his family he had been educated in France and served in the French Army. Under James VII and II this, as well as his family's continued adherence to the Church of Rome, was anything but a disadvantage and he was accordingly appointed Governor of Edinburgh Castle.

It would be wrong to suppose that these troublous times left the clans and their chiefs, whatever their sympathies, with no leisure for their private concerns. On the contrary, these quite naturally continued to be their principal preoccupation. The Mackintoshes were no exception. Since the fourteenth century or earlier, they and the Camerons had continued to dispute the lands of Glenloy, Loch Arkaig and Brae Lochaber, which the Mackintoshes had claimed since 1291, but which the Camerons had actually held for almost as long.

Now, in 1665, after three and a half centuries of bickering, Lachlan Mackintosh, Nineteenth of that Ilk, finally agreed, with the encouragement of the wily Lord

Claymore, crafted in 1588. This two-handed sword belonged to Allan Cameron, 16th Chief of Clan Cameron, who led his clan in support of Huntly and Errol against Argyll at the Battle of Glenlivet, in 1594. The sword was captured by the Aberdeen Wrights and Cupars Guild around 1800, but was later returned to the Clan Chief.

155

Breadalbane, first cousin to both disputants, to sell the lands in question to Sir Ewen Cameron of Lochiel, in whose possession they already were, for 72,000 merks, using this substantial sum to pay off part of the burdens on his estate.

Having settled his dispute with the Camerons, Lachlan Mackintosh, who was by now approaching the age of fifty, deliberately revived another old feud by demanding arrears of rent from the MacDonalds of Keppoch in respect of lands allegedly held by them from him in Glenroy and Glenspean. Though The Mackintosh possessed unimpeachable sheepskin titles to these lands, the MacDonalds had in fact held them by simple right of occupation since time immemorial. After failing to secure satisfaction from Keppoch, Lachlan in the end obtained in 1688 a Commission of Fire and Sword against him from the Privy Council. Armed with this and supported by a company of regular troops, making up their numbers to over a thousand men, the Mackintoshes advanced on Mulroy to the north-east of Glenspean, where they found that the MacDonalds had taken up a strong position on top of Meall Ruadh, the Round Red Hill which gives Mulroy its name. Unfortunately for the Mackintoshes, the MacDonalds were commanded on this occasion by young Coll MacDonald of Keppoch, a resourceful and remarkably effective leader. Coll had been summoned from the University of St Andrews five or six years earlier to assume the Chiefship of his Clan and had by his skill as a small scale raider already earned the significant title of Coll of the Cows. "Of low stature, but full of craft and enterprise", is how a contemporary described him.

As the Mackintoshes started to climb Meall Rudh, Coll and the men of Keppoch, swinging their Lochaber axes, swooped down on them from above with a terrible yell and devastating effect. At the start of the battle that followed The Mackintosh himself, feeling that he would be more comfortable there, had installed himself in Keppoch's house, temporarily vacated by its owner.

A lively account of the engagement comes from Donald McBean, a tobacco-spinner from Inverness and one of The Mackintosh's less enthusiastic clansmen. "For my part," wrote Donald, "I repeated my former wish that I had been spinning tobacco in Inverness. The MacDonalds came down the hill upon us without either shoes or

17th-century Lochaber axe, with its original yew shaft. This axe was a popular weapon during the Covenant wars, useful for unhorsing and dispatching your enemy.

17th-century thumbscrew.

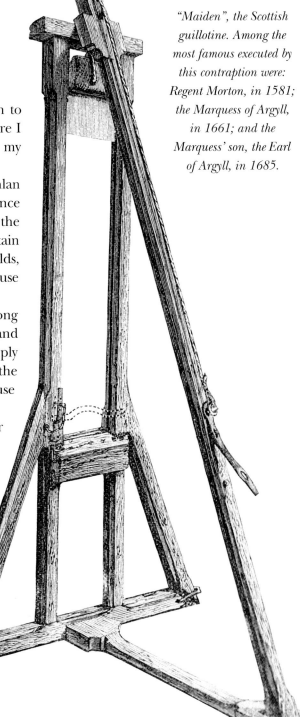

"Maiden", the Scottish guillotine. Among the most famous executed by this contraption were: Regent Morton, in 1581; the Marquess of Argyll, in 1661; and the Marquess' son, the Earl of Argyll, in 1685.

stockings or bonnets on their heads.... Seeing the Highlandmen to come fast upon me, I took to my heels and ran thirty miles before I looked behind me. Every person I saw or met, I took him for my enemy."

It was, in the circumstances, only fortunate that Lachlan Mackintosh's nominal clansmen the Macphersons, who had once more demonstrated their independence by not taking part in the actual battle, arrived on the scene just in time to rescue the Captain of Clan Chattan from the clutches of the triumphant Macdonalds, who had to their delight come on him in their own Chief's house where he had been quietly awaiting the outcome of the battle.

Following the battle of Mulroy, the Privy Council sent a strong force to deal with the MacDonalds, laying waste their land and burning their houses and crops, while Coll and his clansmen simply withdrew into the hills. None of which, strangely enough, was in the long term to affect the Keppoch MacDonalds' loyalty to the House of Stewart.

As supporters of the Covenant, the Mackenzies had, for their part, fought against Montrose, but after the execution of Charles I Seaforth, their Chief, realising that the monarchy itself was now in danger, had joined Charles II in Holland, where he died two years later. When in 1650 Charles landed in Scotland, Seaforth's eldest son and successor left Aberdeen University to call out his clan, which he led against Cromwell at the disastrous battle of Worcester. In 1653 and 1654, after the establishment of the Commonwealth, he likewise took a leading part in Glencairn's rising, finally capitulating on honourable terms in January 1655. For the Mackenzies the Restoration brought happier times and in 1685 George, grandson of Roderick Mackenzie of Coigach, was created Viscount Tarbat by James VII and II.* Clan Kenneth was now by any standards a considerable power in the northern Highlands.

Over the years, Clan Cameron had, as we have seen, suffered severely from the proximity, not only of the Mackintoshes, but on the one hand of Huntly and his Gordons and on the other of Argyll and his Campbells. Nor were their relations much better with the MacDonalds of Keppoch and Glengarry. At one time or another all these clans had sought to acquire the superiorities of Cameron lands, thereby openly challenging the authority of successive Cameron chiefs and provoking endless disputes.

During the second half of the 17th century and the early years of the eighteenth, a period of almost continuous strife, the Camerons were, however, fortunate enough to possess an altogether outstanding Chief. Sir Ewen Cameron 17th of Lochiel, deservedly known as the Great Lochiel, did much to give his clan the standing and influence it has rightly enjoyed ever since. Born in 1629 of a Campbell mother in the Campbell castle of Kilchurn, Ewen had grown up at the time of Montrose's campaign, during which his grandfather and predecessor had sent some three hundred Cameron clansmen to support Montrose against Argyll at Inverlochy. As a boy of sixteen he had later been taken by Argyll, who was his legal guardian, to witness the execution of a number of Royalist prisoners. Whatever Argyll's intention, this and a conversation which the young Ewen managed to have with some of the condemned men before they were put to death, had made of him a loyal supporter of the King.

In 1647, "in his eighteenth year, healthful and full of spirit and grown up to the height of a man, though somewhat slender", Ewen had become Chief of Clan Cameron and already under the Commonwealth had fought valiantly against the English army of occupation. In 1654, at the time of Glencairn's rising, General Monk, landing with a strong force at nearby Inverlochy, had built a fort there and for the next twelve months Lochiel and his clan had waged a successful guerrilla war against the English garrison before finally coming to terms.

It was during this fighting that Ewen won fame by tearing an English officer's throat out with his teeth. "It was," he said long afterwards to his son-in-law, "the sweetest bite I ever had in my life-time." Some years later, it is said, after the Restoration, Lochiel happened to visit a London barber to be shaved before going to Court. "You are from the North, Sir?" said the barber, passing the razor over his throat. "Yes," said Sir Ewen. "Do you know people from the North?" "No," came the answer, "nor do I wish to. They are savages there. Would you believe it? One of them tore the throat out of my father with his teeth. I only wish I had that fellow's throat near me, as I have yours." Lochiel was glad when, having finished shaving him, the Englishman put his razor away.

A paragon of manliness, Ewen Dubh, as he was called, was a splendid figure, black-avised with piratical good looks and blazing black eyes. "His very look," wrote a contemporary, "so fierce might fright the boldest foe. His savage glance and the swarthy hue of his Spanish countenance, his flashing eyes, his beard and moustache, curled as the moon's horns." As a young man he had killed the last wolf in Scotland

John Graham of Claverhouse, 1648–1689, created 1st Viscount Dundee by James VII. He earned the name Bloody Clavers for his part against the Covenanters.

* The Earldom of Cromartie followed some seventeen years later.

and the story was told that one night in the hills, finding his son resting his head on a lump of frozen snow, he angrily kicked it away, asking if the boy was really so soft that he could not sleep without a pillow. What is more, his physical toughness and resilience were more than matched by an equally tough and resilient view of life. He could on occasion show himself a subtle and resourceful politician. In politics as in guerrilla warfare, flexibility and an eye to the main chance never come amiss. For all his avowed hatred of the English, he had found it to his advantage to reach an accommodation with Monk which allowed him to retain his arms and indeed use them when it suited him against certain of his neighbours. It is related that for the signing of this agreement he marched to Inverlochy at the head of his clan with the pipes playing and every clansman armed to the teeth and afterwards dined at the fort with the English governor, Major Hill. For the next five years, Lochiel found Monk a useful friend. At the Restoration, when Monk proclaimed Charles II King, Lochiel was present and, like Monk, had no difficulty in winning Charles's friendship.

Captain Robert Campbell, 5th Laird of Glenlyon.

When the King's brother, James Duke of York, came to Edinburgh as Lord Commissioner, Lochiel was amongst those upon whom, as loyal supporters of his family, he bestowed the honour of knighthood. James seems to have had a good idea of the kind of man he was dealing with. When James asked for Lochiel's sword to perform the ceremony, he found he could not draw it. Taking it from him, Lochiel drew it without difficulty and handed it back to James. "You see, my lords," said the Duke to the attendant courtiers, "Lochiel's sword gives obedience to no hand save his own." On a later occasion, when walking through St James's Palace with Lochiel in his train, he remarked, this time less flatteringly: "My Lords and Gentlemen, I advise you to have a guard of your purses, for the King of Thieves is at my back." He is an ancestor from whom the present author is proud to claim direct descent.

For the Highland clans, as for the rest of his subjects, the short reign of King James VII and II after he had succeeded his brother as King, was a period of uncertainty and strife. From the first, opposition to the new monarch was actively encouraged by his Dutch son-in-law, William of Orange, a cold, ruthless, devious man with barely disguised designs on his father-in-law's throne. Attempted insurrections against James led by Archibald of Argyll in Scotland and by Charles I's bastard son Monmouth in England were both unsuccessful. Having set out from Holland with three ships and three hundred men, Argyll landed in Kintyre in mid-May 1685. Collecting a couple of thousand of his clansmen, he soon managed to seize the Campbell castle of Ardkinglas on the eastern shore of Loch Fyne. Thence he headed southwards by way of the Gareloch in an attempt to reach the Lowlands. But in anticipation of his landing the

Privy Council had already despatched a body of MacDonalds, Macleans and Athollmen, led by Argyll's bitter enemy the Earl of Atholl, with the title of Lord Lieutenant of Argyll, to occupy as much Campbell territory as they could, including Inveraray. Confronted with this formidable force, Argyll's Campbells soon dispersed and, while seeking to escape in disguise, their Chief himself was taken prisoner. Being already under sentence of death from his previous conviction of 1681, he was carried off to Edinburgh and executed there on 30 June, his head being afterwards placed on the very same spike in the Tolbooth as that of his father twenty-five years earlier.

Having disposed of Argyll, Atholl now led his willing Highlanders on a punitive expedition deep into Campbell territory, where, burning and looting, they exacted a terrible revenge for the wrongs they had suffered in the past at Campbell hands. From

William III, who was intent on quelling the clans. Portrait after Kneller.

Campbell clansmen transported at this time to the American plantations are descended many families of Campbells now living in the United States. In all this a particularly active part was played by old MacIain, Chief of the Macdonalds of Glencoe, and his notoriously turbulent tribe.

Monmouth, meanwhile, had landed in Dorset in June and, after being defeated at Sedgemoor, had likewise been taken prisoner and executed. But King James's troubles were only beginning. Nor was he, either temperamentally or intellectually, as well equipped to deal with them as his brother had been. As Buckingham wittily remarked, Charles "could see things if he would and the Duke would see things if he could".

In Scotland, particularly in the Highlands, James was not unpopular. ("In this country," Argyll said disconsolately, as he awaited execution, "I see no great party that desire to be relieved".) In England, however, the King's Roman Catholicism and his autocratic methods had made him powerful enemies. In June 1688, the birth of his son, James Edward, assuring the Catholic succession, precipitated what was to be known as the Glorious Revolution. In November of that year, William of Orange, at the invitation of the Whig leaders, landed in England with an army; James fled to France; and in February 1689 his son-in-law William and daughter Mary were proclaimed King and Queen of England and Ireland. Not long after Scotland followed England's example.

Once James was gone, there were however those, particularly in the Highlands, where for traditional reasons the monarchic principle was still greatly prized, who remained loyal to their legitimate monarch. They were known as Jacobites, from Jacobus, the Latin for James. As Duke of York and his brother's Commissioner for Scotland, James had not been unpopular with the Highland chiefs, working through them much as Monk had done in his time, with the result that many of them were now ready to rise on his behalf. Accordingly, on William being proclaimed King, Graham of Claverhouse, in other words

Glencoe, site of the massacre of the Macdonalds of Glencoe in 1692. Painting by Horatio McCullogh.

James Dalrymple, 1st
Viscount Stair,
1619–1695. He served
in the Covenanting
army, was a
Cromwellian
commissioner, and was
Lord President under
William II.

Sir John Dalrymple, Master
of Stair,
1648–1707. As Secretary of
State to William III, he
started the process of events
that led to the Glencoe
massacre.

John Maitland
(1616–82), 1st Duke
of Lauderdale, by Peter
Lely. He was Charles II's
Secretary of State, and
governed Scotland for
nearly twenty years.

John Campbell, 1st Earl of Breadalbane
(1635–1717), was one of Scotland's notorious
double-dealers. "As cunning as a fox, wise as a
serpent and as slippery as an eel." Portrait by
De Medina.

Bloody Clavers, whom James had created Viscount of Dundee, rode north with a troop of fifty horsemen to call out the loyal clans for King James. James, meanwhile, had landed in Ireland, where, as a Roman Catholic, he could count on strong local support.

In Scotland, a strong body of Government troops under General Hugh Mackay had been sent by William to put down the Highland Jacobites. General Mackay, a talented soldier of fortune belonging to the Scourie branch of his clan, had of recent years risen to command the Scots Brigade in Holland and had accompanied William of Orange to Great Britain. William had appointed him his Commander in Chief for Scotland and charged him with the pacification of the Highlands. With him served many of his clan. The Grants, too, for the most part supported William. In 1689 the Eighth Chief of Clan Grant had been a member of the Parliament which offered him the Crown and he and most of his clan took his side in the present conflict. Grant of Glenmoriston, on the other hand, joined Bonny Dundee, as the Bloody Clavers was now known.

At sundown on 27 July 1689, at the head of the narrow gorge of Killiecrankie in Perthshire, Dundee's Highland Army including a thousand Camerons led in battle by the Great Lochiel, by now a man of sixty, the Macleans under the command of Sir John Maclean of Duart, the MacDonalds of Clanranald, Keppoch, Glengarry, Sleat and Glencoe, the Stewarts of Appin and Grants of Glenmoriston, MacLeods, MacNeils, MacGregors, Robertsons and Farquharsons, fell "like madmen" upon Mackay's men and almost annihilated them. But at the moment of victory Dundee himself was killed and his troops left without a leader, with the result that, after another savage encounter with the Government forces in the churchyard at Dunkeld, the Highlanders simply faded back into their hills and glens. In the spring of 1690 a fresh Jacobite attempt ended in utter disaster at the Haughs of Cromdale, and six weeks later the Battle of the Boyne put paid to James's Irish campaign and made him withdraw to France for good.

After a difficult start in life as the son and grandson of condemned traitors, Archibald, Tenth Earl of Argyll had finally come into his own with the departure of James VII and the arrival of William of Orange. Having played a part in bringing Dutch William to the throne and later raised a regiment in his own name to serve in Flanders, Archibald was rewarded with a dukedom. The age of Campbell ascendancy had begun.

The attitude of Clan Mackintosh during these troubled years had been anything but clear cut. At the behest of the Western Chiefs, Coll MacDonald of Keppoch had escorted Bonny Dundee into Lochaber at the head of some eight hundred men and had later laid siege to Inverness. Finding The Mackintosh, with whom his setback at Mulroy continued to rankle, completely unresponsive to his overtures and still deeply hostile to the MacDonalds, Dundee had later encouraged Coll to drive off some more Mackintosh cattle. True to his nickname, Coll of the Cows, he had responded enthusiastically and for good measure had later burned to the ground Mackintosh's fine new house at Dunachton, as a result of which that worthy had held aloof from the rising and only a few of his clan had fought at Killiecrankie.

Despite his clan's long-standing attachment to the House of Stewart, things went rather better for Lachlan Mackintosh under William of Orange. In 1698 the Privy Council of the day, who had no great love for Clan Donald, renewed at the King's personal behest The Mackintosh's Commission of Fire and Sword and mobilised a considerable force to

Loch Eil from the foot of Ben Nevis, showing the lands of the Cameron clan. Many times in the past, other clans fought over and tried to acquire the superiorities of the Cameron lands. Watercolour by Thomas Miles Richardson.

deal with Coll of Keppoch. The latter, who lived barely a dozen miles from the newly strengthened garrison at Fort William, did not for once allow his daring to outweigh his common sense, but entered into negotiation with The Mackintosh, with whom he arrived at a mutually acceptable and enduring arrangement in respect of the lands in dispute.

Lachlan Mackintosh died not long after. Though full of incident, his career had in some ways been less distinguished than that of many of his predecessors. But even by Highland standards his funeral was on a truly magnificent scale, his body lying in state for no less than a month, during the whole of which period the funeral feasting was kept up by relays of cooks and confectioners specially imported from Edinburgh. The funeral itself was attended by two thousand armed men together with all the neighbouring chiefs and their followers. The procession reached for four miles. "The extravagance of the arrangement," we are told by the clan historian, not without a touch of pride, "embarrassed the family finances for many years to come."

Among the Jacobite clans the House of Stewart had no more faithful supporters than the Macleans. Having early in life lost all his lands, Sir John Maclean of Duart had followed King James to France, returning just in time to lead his clan at Killiecrankie. As many as two hundred Macleans had also fought for James at the Haughs of Cromdale, of whom no more than a handful survived the battle; Sir John himself now withdrew to Mull, whence he subsequently fell back on the island fortress of Cairnburgh in the Treshnish Islands. There he managed to hold out until March 1692, when, having finally been authorised by James to surrender, he again joined the exiled King in France. Meanwhile, after being heavily bombarded from the sea by English warships, the great Maclean castle of Duart had been seized and occupied by a well-equipped expeditionary force of no less than 2,500 Campbells.

Another Jacobite Chief who joined King James in France was the Mackenzie Earl of Seaforth. The Revolution of 1688 had found the Fourth Earl as loyal to the Stewart cause as his father and grandfather had been. Having left the country with King James in 1688 and fought at the Battle of the Boyne, he did not return to Scotland until after Killiecrankie, when he was imprisoned and his lands sequestrated. On his release seven years later, he once more joined King James in France, dying there not long after.

The MacGregors were by now totally committed to the Stewart cause. Though they arrived too late for Killiecrankie, they had fought for King James at Dunkeld, with the result that in 1693, under William, the penal statutes against them were reimposed and they again became nameless as well as landless. With the death of the last MacGregor of Glenstrae, they also found themselves without a Chief. This they sought to remedy by adopting as Chief Alexander Drummond, alias MacGregor of Glencarnaig.

As a loyal Jacobite, the Duke of Gordon had, after James's departure held out as long as he could in Edinburgh Castle of which he remained Governor and which had at once been besieged by Government forces. Indeed, in order to apprise him of his plans for a rising, Dundee had been obliged to clamber secretly up that stronghold's precipitous rock-face and seek admittance through a conveniently placed postern. After holding out in the Castle for nearly a year, the Duke was in the end compelled by lack of provisions to capitulate and was therefore not able to fight at Killiecrankie. In due course, like other Jacobite leaders, he came to terms with William of Orange though, as a Roman Catholic, he was debarred from holding high office of any kind. It was largely as a result of this prohibition that in the seventeenth and eighteenth centuries many leading members of Clan Gordon went abroad, taking service in the armies and navies of the Emperor and the Tsar as well as in those of the Kings of France and Poland.

Despite the Jacobites' seemingly decisive defeat, Dutch William's Government and in particular his Secretary of State, Sir John Dalrymple, Master of Stair, remained uneasy about the Highlands and sought assiduously for a means of enforcing their will there. As a first step, they had despatched General Mackay to build and garrison a strongpoint near Inverlochy, to be named Fort William as a compliment to the new King. At the same time the sum of £12,000 was entrusted to Iain Glas, the Campbell Earl of Breadalbane, to be distributed among the Western chiefs in the hope of winning their loyalty. Some chiefs accepted the bribe; others refused it. Few became any more loyal to William.

Indeed, even Breadalbane's own loyalty was open to question. Though two years earlier he had denied King James his support, he had equally sent no one to fight for King William. "It is odds, if he lives long enough," wrote the government agent John Mackay, "but he is a Duke. He is of fair complexion and has the gravity of a Spaniard, is as cunning as a fox, wise as a serpent and as slippery as an eel." To the Jacobites he represented himself as a Jacobite, while General Hugh Mackay described him as "one of the chiefest and cuningest fomentors of the trouble of that Kingdom, not for love of King James, but to make himself necessary to the government". Later, when asked by Lord Nottingham how the money entrusted to him had been distributed, "My Lord," Breadalbane replied, "the Highlands are quiet, the money has been spent and that is the only way of accounting between friends."

Still unconvinced that the problem had been solved, the Government now decided to adopt other tactics. "I think," wrote Stair to Breadalbane, "the clan Donnell must be rooted out and Lochiel. Leave the Macleans to Argyll ... God knows whether the £12,000 sterling had been better employed to settle the Highlands or to ravage them: but since we make them desperate, I think we should root them out before they can get the help they depend upon." "Look on," he wrote next day to the same correspondent, "and you shall be gratified of your revenge." Seldom has the traditional hatred of the Lowlander for the Highlander – *mi-run mor nan Gall* – found more vigorous expression.

The Government now issued a proclamation ordering the chiefs of the various clans to take the oath of allegiance to King William not later than 1 January 1692. Failing this, recourse, it was made clear, would be had to fire and sword. The time of year was carefully chosen. "The winter time," wrote Stair, "is the only season in which we are sure the Highlanders cannot escape and carry their wives, bairns and cattle to the hills.... This is the properr time to maul them in the long dark nights."

But at the last moment, James, from his exile in France, authorised the Jacobite chiefs to swear allegiance to his son-in-law. Stair was sadly disappointed at this. By the appointed date only two chiefs had failed to take the oath, the relatively powerful MacDonell of Glengarry and the elderly chieftain of a minor, but notoriously turbulent, sept of the MacDonalds, MacIan MacDonald of Glencoe. The latter, partly no doubt from natural dilatoriness and partly through the inclemency of the weather, arrived three days late in Inveraray, the seat of the Sheriff-depute, where, owing to the absence of that officer, he was only able to take the oath on 6 January.

This gave William the opportunity he needed. Allowing Glengarry another chance, he picked on MacIan as his victim. "If MacIan of Glencoe and that tribe," he wrote to the general commanding his troops in the Highlands, "can be well separated from the rest, it will be a proper vindication of public justice to extirpate that sect of thieves."

And so a company of the Earl of Argyll's Regiment of Foot, commanded, as it happened, by a relative by marriage of MacIan's, Captain Robert Campbell of Glenlyon, was sent to Glencoe and billeted in the clansmen's cottages. The MacDonalds received them hospitably. Captain Campbell spent a couple of weeks drinking and playing cards with MacIan and his sons, while his soldiers fraternized with the clansmen. Then, on 12 February, he received from his immediate superior, Major Duncanson, the following instructions: "You are hereby ordered to fall upon the MacDonalds of Glencoe and put all to the sword under seventy; you are to have a special care that the old fox and his sons do on no account escape your hands."

That night Robert Campbell and two of his officers accepted an invitation to dine with MacIan. Meanwhile a force of four hundred Government troops moved to block the northern approach to the glen and four hundred more to close the southern. At five in the morning of 13 February Glenlyon and his troops started to carry out their instructions. Parties of soldiers went from cottage to cottage, slaughtering the sleeping MacDonalds and setting light to their houses. MacIan himself was shot by one of his guests of the night before. A Campbell soldier gnawed the rings from Lady Glencoe's fingers with his teeth. A child of six, who clung, begging for mercy, to Glenlyon's knees, was promptly despatched. As the massacre proceeded, snow began to fall. Some of the inhabitants of the glen managed to escape in the confusion; others died in the snow.

It could be said that King William and Stair had succeeded in their object, which was to make an example of a Jacobite clan and establish a measure of control over the Highlands. But the affair gave rise to unfavourable comment, not only in the Highlands, but in the Lowlands and even in England. It had above all been a particularly gross violation of the, to Highlanders, sacred precept of hospitality. Glenlyon's men had in cold blood massacred those whose guests they had been. It was this that inspired revulsion in many who had no special love for Glencoe and his unruly brood. In the end William was forced to dispense with the services of his Secretary of State, though in due course Stair was rewarded with an earldom, while Campbell of Glenlyon was promoted to colonel. As for King William, despite irrefutable evidence to the contrary, he loftily disclaimed any previous knowledge of the affair.

Queen Mary's sister Anne, who on William's death in 1702 succeeded to the thrones of both Scotland and England, left no direct heir, her numerous progeny having all died young. Unlike his half-sisters Mary and Anne, who were Protestants, one young James Edward, the son of James VII and II, who since his father's death in 1701 had in Jacobite eyes legally been King, was, like his father, a staunch Roman Catholic. The Whig Statesmen then in power in England were strongly opposed not only to the idea of a Catholic King, but also to the whole Stewart concept of monarchy. Accordingly in 1701 an Act of Settlement had been passed by the English Parliament to ensure that on Anne's death the English Crown should go, not to the Catholic James Edward, but to the Protestant Electress Sophia of Hanover, likewise a grand-daughter of James VI and I and mother of the Elector George of Hanover.

It remained to bring Scotland into line. This was easier said than done. Relations between the two countries were already strained. By an Act of Security passed in 1704 the Scottish Parliament now assumed the right to name the successor to the Scottish throne who should not be the occupant of the English throne, unless Scotland were given equal trading rights and liberty in government and religion. In March 1705 the English Parliament retaliated with an Aliens Act under which all Scotsmen were to be treated as aliens, unless they accepted the Hanoverian succession by Christmas.

Tension between the two countries heightened and in the summer of 1705 John, the young second Duke of Argyll, who had fought with distinction under Marlborough in the Low Countries and was well regarded in London, was despatched to Edinburgh as the Queen's Commissioner to secure from the Scottish Parliament authority to open negotiations for a treaty of union. In this he proved successful. Negotiations were opened in April 1706. In October a draft Treaty was submitted to the Scottish Parliament. In return for trading and financial benefits this committed the Scots to acceptance of the Hanoverian succession and of a combined Parliament. It met with strong opposition, especially from the Jacobites, to many of whom Queen Anne, as a Stewart, had been acceptable, but an unknown German princeling was less so. In the end, however, it was passed through both Parliaments and in March 1707 became law. The union had been accomplished. "We are bought and sold," sang the Jacobites disgustedly, "for English gold."

CHAPTER XV

Life in the Highlands

During the four hundred years which elapsed between the battle of Bannockburn and the Treaty of Union, the character of the clans changed very little. In the year 1707 they still retained to a remarkable extent the characteristics and way of life they had brought with them from Ireland a dozen centuries before. Despite all the Government's efforts to root it out, the Gaelic tongue was still almost universally spoken in the Highlands, serving as a barrier against anglicization and a guardian of the old values. Only recently had the insidious influence of a money economy begun here and there to make itself felt. Between Highlands and Lowlands, let alone the remainder of the now United Kingdom, the division was as deep as it had ever been, in some ways, perhaps, even deeper, and clearly reflected in their mutual relationship. "To an Englishman of the eighteenth century and to the most Lowland Scots," writes a leading authority on the period, "the Highlands of Scotland were a remote and unpleasant region peopled by barbarians who spoke an obscure tongue, who dressed in skins or bolts of parti-coloured cloth and who equated honour with cattle-stealing and murder." He was in effect doing no more than reproduce a view widely held at the time.

"What is properly called the Highlands of Scotland," wrote Lord President Duncan Forbes of Culloden in the mid-eighteenth century, "is the large tract of mountainous ground to the Northwest of the Tay, where the natives speak the Irish language. The inhabitants stick close to their ancient and idle way of life; retain their barbarous customs and maxims; depend generally on their Chiefs as their sovereign Lords and masters; and, being accustomed to the use of Arms and inured to hard living, are dangerous to the public peace; and must continue to be so until, being deprived of Arms for some years, they forget the use of them." And again: "A Highland Clan is a set of men all bearing the same surname and believing themselves to be related the one to the other and to be descended from the same common stock. In each clan there are several subaltern tribes, who owe their dependence on their own immediate chiefs, but all agree in owing allegiance to the Supreme Chief of the Clan or Kindred and look upon it to be their duty to support him at all adventures."

In their essence, the clans remained military units or formations, ready to take arms against their enemies or, for that matter, their neighbours, at a word from their chief. "Here," wrote the author of the Great Lochiel's *Memoirs*, "are so many heretable

"Highland Dance", 1780 (above) and "Dance in a Barn – illustration for Muirland Willie" (below), both by David Allan. The "ceilidh" is the popular and traditional form of entertainment in the Highlands: an assembly of songs, stories, scenes, talks and music, with dancing. In the west, it has preserved the Gaelic culture of language, literature, songs and manners.

Types of early sporrans. Drawing by James Drummond.

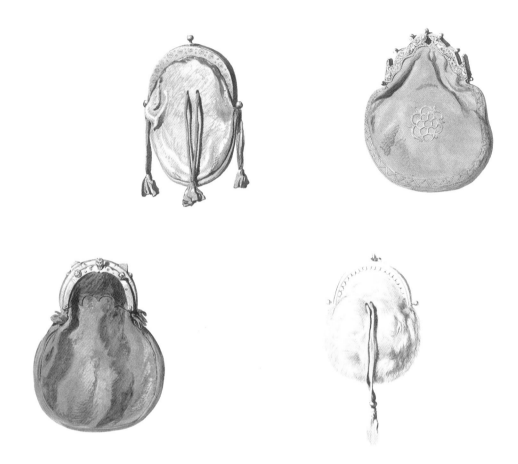

Highlander demonstrating the use of the belted plaid (18th-century French engraving). The belted plaid was the common form of the kilt before the introduction of the pleated version in the 19th century. It had great versatility and could act as a cloak or a blanket. The belted plaid comprised a cloth 16 feet long by 5 feet wide. To don the plaid, it was laid out on the ground on top of the belt. The cloth was pleated over the belt and the wearer laid on top. He then belted the plaid to his waist, leaving the wider half to fall behind. He put on his coat waistcoat and sporran, looping the tail over his left shoulder and tucked in, or as a cloak.

James Moray of Abercairney wearing a belted plaid, circa 1739, by Jeremiah Davison. One of the finest paintings of this type of Highland dress.

collonells and yea severalls of them brigadeers, who have their brigads, their whole officers and souldiers listed by contract not only to themselves but their heirs, can bring them together at their pleasure, and commonly are served and followed by them in all mischievous expeditions, without their asking any questions."

Some of the smaller clans could muster no more than a couple of hundred fighting men; others, the Campbells, for example, several thousand. Without a standing army and with no other ready means of enforcing their will, no government in Edinburgh or indeed in London could afford to ignore such a concentration of military and indeed political strength. Little wonder then that successive Kings chose to make use of this clan or that for their own purposes – Clan Campbell, for example, in the West, and the Gordons, as often as not, in the North and East; or that, in general, they left the clan chiefs to enforce the law themselves, as they themselves saw and interpreted it. There was, when it came to the point, little else they could do. Certainly, for the officers of the law, in so far as there were any, to attempt to penetrate into clan territory in pursuance of their duty was, in most instances, not a practical proposition.

Lace woman with a Distaff, by David Allan, 1784.

A Scotch Maid, by David Allan, circa 1782 (above right).

No one knew this better than Lord President Duncan Forbes of Culloden who, dwelling as he did near Inverness and consorting freely with the chiefs of the neighbouring clans, had a thorough understanding of the Highlands. "It has," he wrote, "been for a great many years impracticable (and hardly thought safe to try it) to give the law its course among the mountains. It required no small degree of courage and a greater degree of power than men are generally possessed of to arrest an offender or debtor in the midst of his Clan. And for this reason it was that the Crown in former times was obliged to put Sheriffships and other jurisdictions in the hands of powerful families in the Highlands, who by their respective Clans and following could give execution to the Laws within their several territories and frequently did so at the expense of considerable bloodshed."

A Fishwife, by David Allan, circa 1780.

Always ready to fulfil their primary, military purpose, the men of a clan were traditionally called out by means of the *crois taraidh* or fiery cross, made from two pieces of burnt or burning wood roughly tied together with a rag soaked in blood and carried from glen to glen with surprising speed by relays of runners.

Not unnaturally, a clan's basic military character and discipline were clearly reflected in its structure and organisation. As in any well-ordered tribal society, the greater part of the work was done by the women and older children, leaving the men free to fight, to hunt, to guard their own lands and cattle and, when the opportunity offered, raid those of their neighbours. For most clans a ready and welcome source of income was the "blackmail" or protection-money paid by their harassed Lowland or other neighbours to buy off the raiders.

In time of war, the Chief himself, assuming that he was adequately fitted for the task, led his men into battle. In peacetime he ruled over them with the authority of an absolute monarch, possessing under the heritable jurisdictions and under his special powers of pit and gallows what amounted to power of life or death over them. For a chief to have a clansman (or clanswoman) put to death, should he so decide, was normal practice. Thus it is recorded of Macdonald of Clanranald that, when a woman of his clan was brought before him, accused of stealing his money, he simply gave orders for her long hair to be tied to the seaweed growing on the rocks on the shore and for her to be left there for the rising tide to drown her.

Skye crofters, John Macleod and his wife about 1812.

But, while a chief wielded far-reaching authority over his clanspeople, he also possessed no less well-defined duties and responsibilities towards them. By age-old tradition it was his duty as chief to care for his people's welfare and security, to the extent even of helping a widowed clansman find a new wife, should he feel the need for one.

In peace as in war, a Chief made full use of the services of the Gentlemen of the Clan, as they were known, in other words of the men of his own blood, however distantly related to him, and of the leading members of the Clan's different septs and branches. In wartime, the Gentlemen of the Clan served as officers in the clan regiment; in peacetime as counsellors and administrators by helping their Chief settle disputes within the clan and deal with the numerous problems of everyday life. (The Camerons, characteristically enough, claimed that their clan "were all Gentlemen".) For such purposes many clans possessed regular councils, while the MacDonalds, as Lords of the Isles, had their own Parliament, ready if necessary to assume the conduct of Clan Donald's affairs.

Shinty players. Detail from J. & F. Tallis Map of Scotland, 1851.

The Curlers, by George Harvey, 19th century. Curling was the great winter sport, popular since the 16th century and still played today.

Cattle (anonymous painting c.1892). The Highland economy was once based on the trade in Highland black cattle. During the 17th century, more than 20,000 animals per year were herded along the drove roads to fairs at Creiff and Falkirk, and from here to the English markets. This number rose to a peak of 150,000 by about 1850 before trade in sheep took over. Dairy produce was also a currency.

Crossing a burn, by Richard Ansdell, 1863.

Shetland ram, Orkney ewe and Cheviot cross lamb, by William Shiels, c.1835. Sheep flocks, particularly the Cheviot, were brought up from the Scottish borders early in the 19th century by landowners.

When he sallied forth, a Chief, like a reigning prince or commanding general, was accompanied by a retinue or "tail" of clansmen. First came his Henchman or personal Bodyguard, as often as not his own foster brother, bound to him by the common bond of shared mother's milk. Then the Bard or *Seanachaidh*, whose duty it was to chronicle his Chief's heroic deeds and those of his Clan and his forebears. Next came the Piper, whose post, like that of Bard, was hereditary, passing from father to son in the same family. Both Bard and Piper would follow their Chief into battle, the former that he might witness with his own eyes his leader's acts of valour, and the latter to inspire the Clan to yet greater heroism by his playing. Next followed the Chief's *Bladaire* or Spokesman, ready to make proclamations should they be needed or fluently argue on his

behalf the rights and wrongs of any case or dispute that might arise. Then came a ghillie or two, to carry his broadsword and targe, to take his pony's bridle when the road was rough and, when necessary, to carry him dry-shod over a ford or burn.

In the early days the Clan lands were held by the Clan in common. But by general consent or by virtue of some piece of parchment, they later became the personal property of the Chief who would, if he so chose,

A Highland shepherd or drover.

"Wool Waulking", by Keith Henderson, circa 1927-8. "Waulking" is the process of kneading woven cloth to thicken it for tailoring; a laborious task, usually undertaken by women. The work was carried out to the rhythm of one of the thousands of waulking songs which embody a great wealth of Gaelic culture.

Women at the Quern (or handmill). Engraving by Thomas Pennant.

make parts of them over, virtually in perpetuity, to the members of his own family, to the office-bearers of the Clan and to the members of his entourage, the Bard, for example, or the Piper. What remained was usually held by tenants known as "tacksmen" on "tacks" or leases granted to them by the Chief. With the Gentlemen of the Clan, the tacksmen, who often let part of their land to sub-tenants, played a leading part in the life of the Clan, serving as officers in the Clan regiment and busying themselves as required with the affairs of the Clan. To them, first and foremost, fell the all-important duty of bringing out the Clan in time of war, if necessary by the use of force, notably by burning the houses of reluctant clansmen over their heads.

By comparison with the relative prosperity of the Lowlands, the people of the Highlands, scraping a bare existence from their barren hills, lived simply and poorly. Of a total population of some 200,000 Highlanders, less than half were what could be called gainfully employed. A *Clachan* or crofting township consisted of a cluster of bothies or black houses, built for the most part from turf and stone and roughly thatched with heather. Each house had a single room, sometimes divided by a curtain of wattle. In the middle of this burned a peat fire over which hung an iron cooking pot, while the smoke found its way out through a hole in the roof.

The Highlander's diet was sparse. To eat, oatmeal in one form or another, bread when there was any, fish when they were caught, rabbits when they were snared, braxy mutton from sheep found dead on the hill, a little meat, salted usually, from the jealously

Shetland shawl-making. Early photograph. Over the centuries, women developed skills in dyeing, carding, spinning and weaving. Women also traditionally milked, made butter and cheese and worked the land.

Neil Gow (1727–1807),
the famous violinist and
composer of many reels,
by Sir Henry Raeburn.

guarded flocks and herds, which provided the principal if not only source of income. To drink, peaty water from the nearest burn and since the 16th century, when it first appears, *usquebaugh* or whisky, the Water of Life, home distilled from their own malted barley. In 1494 an entry in the Scottish Exchequer Roll took note of "the delivery of eight bolls of malt to Friar John Cor wherewith to make *aquavitae*". Today, it may be observed, whisky contributes more than a billion pounds a year to the British Exchequer, while in France more whisky is drunk in a month than cognac in a year and in the United States a bottle of whisky is consumed every tenth of a second.

When not working or eating or sleeping, a Highland household would, when the mood took them, gather round the peat fire in the half-light to tell and listen to endless stories of fairies and witchcraft and the second sight, or to poems and tales handed down from generation to generation, celebrating the valorous deeds, the stratagems, the victories and defeats of their forebears; to sing the old songs and listen to the music of the *clarsach* and the pipes. And yet, to the uncomprehending stranger, to the English Captain Burt, for example, peering into the half-darkness from outside, what he saw of their existence seemed immeasurably dreary and

Charles Leslie (1677-1782), itinerant ballad singer in Aberdeenshire, by James Wales. Ballad singers were an important part of Highland life as their songs eased the hardships of the crofting life.

"Scottish Highland Family". Interior of a house by David Allan. Highland homes were shared by the family and their livestock, centred around the fire. The door often provided the only source of light.

squalid. "They have no diversions to amuse them," he wrote, "but sit brooding in the smoke of their fire."

Nor were incomers immediately attracted by their appearance. Over their shirts most Highlanders wore a long belted plaid of parti-coloured cloth called the *breacan* covering the shoulder and kilted round the waist with rough rawhide brogues on their feet. Stuck in his bonnet the clansman carried the traditional plant-badge of his clan, possessing for those who wore it a mystic significance, a sprig of holly if he was a Maclean, of seaweed from the shore if he was a MacNeil, or of yew if he was a Fraser, cut in this case from the ancient yew tree which still stands in Stratherrick or from the great yews which grew round the Fraser gathering-place of Tomahurich. Dressed with fitting magnificence, in kilt or, if he were riding, tartan trews, the Chief of a Clan wore in his bonnet three eagle-feathers, lesser chieftains two and the gentlemen of the Clan one.

To a stranger, the garb of old Gaul was apt to come as a shock. "The common habit of the Highlander," wrote Captain Burt a trifle censoriously, "is far from being acceptable to the eye. With them a small part of the plaid, which is not so large as the former, is set in folds and girt round the waist to make of it a short petticoat that reaches half-way down the thigh, the rest is brought over the shoulders and fastened before, below the neck, often with a fork and sometimes with a bodkin or sharpened piece of stick, so that they make pretty nearly the appearance of the poor women in London when they bring their gowns over their heads to shelter themselves from the rain. This dress is called the quelt and for the most part the petticoat so very short that in a windy day, going up a hill, or stooping, the indecency of it is plainly discovered." But even Captain Burt discerned the Highlanders' innate dignity. "They walk," he reported, "with a kind of stateliness in the midst of their poverty."

In time of war a clansman carried into battle a broadsword and leather targe, a dirk and *sghiann-dhu* for in-fighting and sometimes a Lochaber axe with its handy hook to help drag a mounted adversary from his horse. To these, with the advent of firearms, were later added a musket and pistol, which each fighting man would discharge and then throw down before charging the enemy. Launched downhill, the Highland charge, to an accompaniment of unearthly yells, had not surprisingly a devastating impact on an enemy accustomed to more orderly and traditional forms of warfare.

Inevitably there were considerable differences of style and circumstance in the way of life of different clan chiefs. Some, disposing of considerable wealth and many possessions, lived on a scale becoming to the great noblemen they were. Other, lesser Chiefs and Chieftains lived in a style approximating more closely to that of their own clanspeople. Thus, while MacFarlane of Arrochar possessed a couple of massive strongholds for purposes of defence, we learn from the Dewar Manuscript that his own dwelling-house at Cladach Mor by Loch Lomond "was but thirty-four feet long and thirteen broad, inside. It contained but three rooms, a kitchen, a sitting-room and a pantry, and the pantry was in the middle of the house. The kitchen fire was on the middle of the floor and a hole right over it in the roof allowed the smoke to escape. A chimney-top made of twigs and daubed with clay was above the fire of the chamber to let out the smoke. The rafters of the house were about three feet asunder. Beams of cleft oak placed close together and covered with sods formed a loft above the laird of

Malt whisky distillery at Glengoyne, near Killearn, Stirlingshire. 19th-century painting.

Collecting seaweed, Skye (inset left). Early photograph. Seaweed was used as a fertiliser in the struggle to cultivate barren soil. In some places, stones would have to be broken down in order to make soil.

Arrochar. There was but a single window with six panels in the chamber. There was one window with four panes in the kitchen, on the front of the house, and there was a window on the back, which was shut with boards when the wind blew through it. There was another window-hole in the pantry shut with boards, which was open when anything was to be done there. The house was thatched with bracken."

On the other hand, MacFarlane's neighbour, Colquhoun of Luss, lived in a handsome castle at Rossdhu not many miles to the south. Which did not prevent MacFarlane, on learning that Colquhoun had seduced his wife and so infringed his dignity, from burning down his fine castle with its owner inside it and serving his unfaithful spouse with her lover's private parts for dinner on a platter, remarking as he did so: "That is your share. You will understand yourself what it is."

Some chiefs, having studied at universities in Scotland or abroad, were highly civilised and sophisticated, speaking foreign tongues and as often as not possessing a good grasp of the humanities. But, whether well educated or not, all, including

innumerable lesser chieftains, displayed the same pride of race and consciousness of their own innate superiority over the people of the plain. "I am far prouder" the Chief of Clan Campbell said the other day to the present author, "of being MacCailein Mor, than of being Duke of Argyll." And there are few Chiefs in the Highlands who, whatever their other ranks or title, would not feel and say the same. "They have a pride in their family," declared the bewildered Captain Burt, "almost everyone is a genealogist."

Centangaval, Barra, photographed by G.W. Wilkinson (main picture).

Cutting peat (inset below right). It took one man 20 days to cut enough peat to heat a croft for a year.

CHAPTER XVI

The 1715: Mar's Rebellion and General Wade

Though many of those responsible for the Treaty of Union sincerely believed they were acting in Scotland's best interest by concluding it, the Union was from the start unpopular and it was only natural that the Jacobites, who since James VII's death in 1701 had regarded his son James Edward as the rightful King, should have felt encouraged. When Queen Anne was first taken ill in 1714, a successful Jacobite coup seemed possible. But on her death in August of that year her place, following prompt action by the Whig administration, was immediately taken by George of Hanover, son of the Electress Sophia, who had narrowly predeceased her cousin.

George I was not only personally unattractive and very German; he clearly took but little interest in his new subjects. When, with James's permission, the Highland Chiefs generously sent him an address of acceptance, he brusquely rejected it. Even in the Lowlands discontent with the Union was rife, and throughout Scotland there were many who drank to "The King over the Water".

After James VII's death in 1701, Louis XIV of France, then on the brink of war with England, had promised to help the dead King's son and in March 1708, less than a year after the Union, a sizeable French fleet had escorted James Edward who, whatever his shortcomings, did not lack courage, to within sight of the Scottish coast with the firm intention of landing him on British soil. But an encounter with some vessels of the English fleet deterred the French commander and, despite James's entreaties, the expedition returned to France without putting him ashore.

Seven years later, in 1715, there was again talk of a Jacobite rising. This time there was less hope of help from France, now at peace with England. But James Edward, who by this time was twenty-seven and had spent all except the first few weeks of his life in exile, decided to make the attempt nonetheless and in the summer of 1715 wrote to the Earl of Mar, with whom he was already in correspondence, calling on him to raise the Clans.

Bobbing John, as Mar was known, had been one of the signatories of the Treaty of Union, had served as Secretary for Scotland under Queen Anne and had at the beginning of the new reign hastened to declare himself the "faithful and dutiful subject and servant" of King George. But he had been disappointed by the latter's cool response and had accordingly made or resumed contact with the exiled Court. On

Field Marshal George Wade, road building through Corrieyairack Pass, attributed to van Diest. Wade was appointed Commander-in-Chief of Scotland in 1724 in order to pacify the Highlanders. He built 235 miles of road and 28 bridges in six years, to serve as links between forts – a prodigious feat on such terrain.

receiving James's letter, he disguised himself, however unconvincingly, as a workman and boarded a collier bound for Scotland. Arriving there towards the middle of August, he summoned his friends and neighbours to a great tinchal or hunting party on the Braes of Mar in Aberdeenshire and there acquainted them with what was afoot. Three weeks later, on 6 September, he publicly proclaimed James VIII and III as King and raised the old Scottish standard at Castletown in Braemar.

Of the Jacobite clans, the Macleans, under Sir John Maclean of Duart, who had returned from France in 1704 under an indemnity from Queen Anne, were among the first to rally to King James's standard. Also the Camerons under old Lochiel's son John, the Stewarts under Robert, Eighth of Appin, and the MacLachlans under their Chief, Lachlan. The MacGregors, still nameless, were led by Alexander MacGregor of Balhaldie, Gregor MacGregor of Glengyle and, most famous of all, the latter's uncle, Rob Ruadh or Rob Roy, a swashbuckling character whose arms were reputed to reach a full two inches below his knees. Black Ruari MacNeil of Barra, who had fought with Dundee at Killiecrankie, again brought out his clan for King James. The MacDonalds came out under Allan, Twelfth Captain of Clanranald and Alastair, Eleventh of Glengarry. Though the Duke of Gordon was already in prison as a potential Jacobite, his eldest son, Huntly, in fact a far likelier leader than Mar, promptly joined the rising with 3000 clansmen, including 500 cavalry. With him was Major-General Alexander Gordon of Auchintoul, recently returned from Russia, where he had gained a considerable reputation as a soldier of fortune under Peter the Great. The Mackenzies were likewise traditionally committed to the Stewart cause. After some years abroad, their chief, William, Fifth Earl of Seaforth, had returned to Scotland in time to attend Mar's *tinchal*. Having travelled to the far north to call out his clan and raised in all some 3000 clansmen, he then successfully fought his way back south despite the combined efforts of the staunchly Hanoverian Earl of Sutherland, the Mackay Chief, Lord Reay, and Sir Hector Munro of Foulis, whose lands lay across his way. Clan Donnachaidh also rallied to Mar's standard. Already in 1689 young Alexander Robertson of Struan, famous as a wit and a poet, had joined the Jacobites. As a result, his lands had been occupied by Government forces and Alexander exiled to France. Returning from exile, he now brought out two hundred and fifty of his clansmen for King James, carrying with him *Clach na Bratach*, the crystal Ensign Stone which his forebear Sturdy Duncan had carried at Bannockburn. While the newly created Duke of Atholl and his second son, Lord James Murray, remained Whigs, his eldest son, William, Marquess of Tullibardine, and third son, Lord George Murray, came out for King James, bringing a number of Athollmen with them. Though

Marquess of Tullibardine, "Duke William of Atholl", who fought in both the 1715 and 1745 risings, living in exile in France.

the remainder of Clan Grant sided with the Government, the Grants of Glenmoriston again showed their independence by backing the Jacobites. Among others who joined Mar were, surprisingly enough, five hundred Campbells sent by wily old Ian Glas of Breadalbane, who no doubt calculated that, if he played his cards right, a Jacobite victory, which he must have regarded as probable, would win him a Dukedom and the much coveted Chiefship of Clan Diarmid.

As loyal Jacobites, the Mackintoshes took from the first an active part in the Rising, none more than William Mackintosh younger of Borlum, who for some time had been living at the Jacobite Court in France and in 1714 had made his way to Scotland. Old Borlum, as he was known, was a character of some note. Described by one contemporary as "a tall Rawboned Man about sixty years old, fair complexioned, beetle-browed, Grey Eyed, speaks Broad Scotch", by another as possessing "an affected Inverness English accent" and by a third as being "remarkable for the grim ferocity of his scarred face", he had for some years been acting as a Jacobite agent. He now set about recruiting all the supporters he could for King James. Once Mar had raised the standard at Braemar, Lachlan Mackintosh, the 20th Chief of Clan Chattan, placed Borlum, a relatively experienced soldier, in command of all the Mackintosh clansmen he could rally and proceeded with him to Inverness, where, proclaiming James King, they seized in his name all the arms and money they could lay hands on. Thence, with 800 clansmen, they marched south to join Mar in Perth, where The Mackintosh assumed command of his own regiment and Borlum took over the brigade of which it now became part.

At first the rising prospered. No less than twelve thousand armed Jacobite clansmen rallied to the Royal standard and many of the northern towns readily declared for King James. By mid-September Mar had without much difficulty established himself in Perth. Between him and the English border there lay only two thousand Government troops based on Stirling. These were, however, commanded by John, Second Duke of Argyll, an experienced soldier, already famous as Red John of the Battles. A colonel at seventeen, Argyll had quickly risen to be one of Marlborough's generals, fighting with distinction at Blenheim, Ramillies and Oudenarde and later becoming General of the British forces in Spain and Ambassador Extraordinary to that country. More recently, he had, as we have seen, successfully promoted the Treaty of Union.

Mar, on the other hand, was no kind of military leader. Having somehow succeeded in capturing Perth, he lingered there for weeks, missing the opportunity thus offered for swift action against an enemy as yet outnumbered and unprepared. Elsewhere

King James VIII, anonymous miniature. He visited Scotland briefly in 1715.

individual clans made independent sorties. The MacGregors, in their haphazard way, tried unsuccessfully to storm Dumbarton Castle, while the Macleans, the Camerons and the MacDonalds of Glengarry boldly marched on the Campbell stronghold of Inveraray in an unsuccessful attempt to repeat their exploits of Montrose's day.

Learning early in November that the border Jacobites were stirring, Mar now despatched Mackintosh of Borlum, his most experienced commander, to make contact with them with two thousand men. While Mar and the rest of his force stayed on in Perth, Old Borlum on his own initiative made a quick dash for Edinburgh in the hope that a spontaneous Jacobite rising would enable him to seize that city. But by this time the city magistrates had caused all the known Jacobites they could find to be arrested and Borlum, having seized Leith and successfully beaten off an attack by Argyll, abandoned his original project and marched on south to join Lord Kenmure, Thomas Forster, the Member of Parliament for Northumberland, and a number of other Jacobite leaders by this time assembled at Kelso.

It was now that Lord Kenmure took the decision to march on into Lancashire in the optimistic belief that he would there be joined by large numbers of English Jacobites. In this, however, he was disappointed, managing to recruit no more than a handful of the local gentry and their retainers. Having entered Preston and there proclaimed King James, they soon found themselves obliged to defend the city against a substantial force of English regulars under the command of General Wills who, on receiving further reinforcements, called upon them to surrender. This, at the instance of Thomas Forster and some other English Jacobites, who seem to have lost their nerve, they did on 14 November. Whereupon Wills reoccupied Preston, taking no less than fifteen hundred Jacobite prisoners, including Borlum and the Mackintosh, who were promptly des-patched to London for trial. But, before he could

Twenty-eight Campbells and twenty-five others signed this petition at Inverary on 11 August 1715, in support of King George and the government.

This snuff mull belonged to Sir John Maclean of Duart who died in 1716 from a bout of consumption caught during the 1715 rebellion.

be brought to trial, Old Borlum escaped to France, while The Mackintosh, pleading that he had been "trepanned into the rebellion by the craft of the Brigadier", was in due course pardoned and allowed to go free.

Mar, for his part, had remained at Perth. Earlier, when Argyll had briefly left Stirling unprotected in order to save Edinburgh from Borlum, he had, it is true, advanced as far as Dunblane, but only to fall back on Perth once Argyll returned.

In the North, meantime, while the Earl of Sutherland rallied the Whig clans for the government, the Fraser Chief, Simon of Beaufort or, as he now claimed to be, of Lovat, having returned from France where he had been in touch with King James, had seized Inverness Castle, hitherto held by the Jacobite Mackenzies, on behalf of King George, thereby to some extent regaining the confidence of the Government, who up to then had, like everyone else, regarded him with deep suspicion.

Simon of Lovat's motives require some explanation. In 1686 Hugh, 9th Lord Lovat, Chief of Clan Fraser, had died without surviving male issue. Under his contract of marriage with a daughter of the powerful house of Atholl, his title and lands had been settled on his daughter and heiress of line, Amelia, now a child of ten. This did not suit young Simon who, as Hugh's cousin and nearest male heir, not unreasonably regarded himself as his cousin's rightful successor. His enthusiasm for his own cause had however led him to overplay his hand. First he had produced what purported to be a will, under the terms of which Hugh, who of late had fallen heavily under his influence, seemed to have disinherited his daughter and left his lands, title and chiefship to Simon. Next, with the help of some Fraser supporters from Stratherrick, he had, for no very good reason, carried off the heiress's mother, the Dowager Lady Lovat, to an island in the river Beauly where, after first going through a form of marriage with her, he had raped her, first cutting her corsets through with his dirk, while a piper played for all he was worth to drown his intended's screams. Finding himself faced with a criminal charge (he had also kidnapped, imprisoned and threatened to hang his own remote kinsman, William Fraser, Lord Saltoun, who had dared seek Amelia's hand for his son in marriage), Simon had next taken refuge in France, where he had been received both at the French Court and at the Jacobite Court at St Germain before being taken in the end into custody at Saumur. During his absence abroad he had duly been outlawed and such lands as he had forfeited.

Hugh's daughter Amelia had by now married a Mackenzie, who, having assumed the somewhat fanciful name and style of Fraser of Fraserdale, had declared himself a Jacobite and at the start of the Rising in 1715 had called out the clan for King James, joining Mar with some three hundred Fraser clansmen. Disturbed by this, a number of the leading gentlemen of the traditionally Whig clan now despatched to France a certain Major James Fraser of Castle Leather to find Simon, whom they regarded, with good cause, as the true MacShimi, and suggest to him that this was an opportunity "to fish in drumly waters", a pastime for which he possessed undoubted aptitude.

Seeing the force of their argument, Simon at once hurried home and, promptly declaring for King George, hastily called back the three hundred Frasers who, under Fraserdale, had joined the Jacobite army. He then seized Inverness Castle for the Hanoverians. As a consequence of which, he was a year later granted a royal pardon for any crimes he might have committed, his forfeited estates were restored to him and some time after this he was formally recognised as the 11th Lord Lovat. Fraser of Fraserdale had meanwhile been forfeited for his part in the Rising.

In addition to the Frasers, who had defected at Simon's instance, a number of Gordons now did the same, being followed in due course by their Chief's son Huntly who, withdrawing to the North, managed to surrender, without too much unpleasantness to his friend and kinsman, the staunchly Hanoverian Earl of Sutherland. Thereafter command of the remaining Gordon contingent passed to Alexander Gordon of Auchintoul. By this time the situation of the Jacobites in the North was fast deteriorating. Soon the traditionally Whig clans, Sutherlands, Frasers, Mackays, Rosses and Munros, were in more or less complete control there.

At length, in the second week of November, more than two months after the start of the Rising, Mar and his main force slowly set out from Perth in the direction of Stirling, "*a la bonne aventure*", wrote one of them, "the blind leading the blind, not knowing whither we were going or what we were to do". Argyll moved to meet him and on the morning of 13 November the two armies met at Sheriffmuir in the Ochil Hills, a couple of

John Erskine, 11th Earl of Mar, by Kneller. Erskine was known as "Bobbing John" because he changed his allegiances so often.

miles to the north of Dunblane. In the engagement that followed, the Macleans and MacDonalds occupied the right of the line. For them something more was at stake than the future of this dynasty or the other. They were fighting once again for their existence as clans against their hereditary enemies, the all-pervading Campbells. "Gentlemen," said Maclean of Duart, a veteran of Killiecrankie, placing himself at the head of his Clan and looking across to where Argyll had drawn up his troops over against them, "this is a day we have long wished to see. Yonder stands MacChailein Mor for King George. Here stands Maclean for King James. God bless Maclean and King James. Gentlemen, charge." Throwing off their plaids, they then charged the enemy in the traditional manner with the claymore.

In the ensuing encounter the opposing Hanoverian infantry were quickly put to flight by the violence of the Highland charge. But such was the enthusiasm of the clansmen on the right of the line that they scarcely noticed that their own centre and left had in the meantime been broken by Argyll's cavalry and driven back to Allan Water. In the event, neither side saw fit to risk a second round. Argyll fell back on Dunblane, while Mar withdrew once again to Perth. "There's some say that we wan," runs a contemporary ballad, "And some say that they wan, And some say that none wan at a', man."

Though militarily indecisive, the battle of Sheriffmuir amounted in effect to a defeat for the Jacobites. Argyll still held Stirling, thus effectively blocking the way to England, whence news was soon received of the Jacobite surrender at Preston. The longer Mar

The Battle of Glenshiel, 1719, at which the Spanish gave support to the Jacobite cause. The battle ended the 1715 Jacobite Rebellion. This painting is by Peter Tillemans.

195

sat at Perth, the worse his position became. His Highlanders, with nothing to do and little hope of plunder, soon began, as was their way, to fade back into the hills in ever larger numbers. By now Argyll's army had been joined by reinforcements from Holland as well as by the troops released by the Jacobite surrender at Preston. From being themselves heavily outnumbered, the Government forces now outnumbered their opponents by nearly three to one. Only heavy snow stopped them from at once attacking in strength.

Such was the situation when, on 22 December, 1715, James Edward landed at the bleak Aberdeenshire port of Peterhead. "Old Mr Melancholy" was not the man to redeem a situation already as good as lost. Some gold sent him by the Spaniards had been lost at sea off Dundee. He himself was suffering from fever and ague. "For me," he told his officers with gloomy resignation, "it is no new thing to be unfortunate, since my whole life from my cradle has been a constant series of misfortunes." It was

Master James Fraser of Castle Leathers, 1723. Fraser was sent to France to collect Lord Lovat for the 1715 rising.

John, 4th Duke of Argyll who, as General John Campbell of Mamore, commanded the Government forces in the Rising of 1745. In the 1715 rising he was ADC to the 2nd Duke of Argyll.

not a speech to raise the spirits of already downhearted men. "If he was disappointed in us," wrote one of those present, "we were tenfold more so in him."

Another month went by and at the end of January 1716 came the news that Argyll was advancing to the attack. Simultaneously, Mar's Highlanders learned to their dismay that it was their leaders' intention to abandon Perth and retreat northwards. Worse still, on reaching nearby Montrose, James Edward and Mar, slipping away secretly, took ship

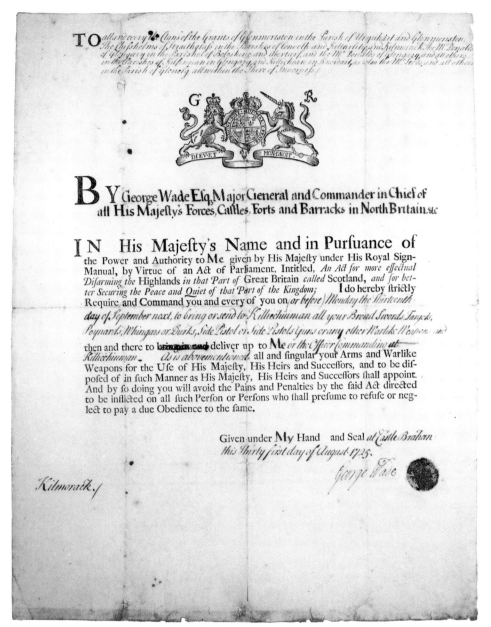

TO all and every the Clans of the Grants of Glenmoriston in the Parish of Urquhart and Glenmoriston, the Chisholms of Strathglass in the Parishes of Conveth and Kiltarlity and Kilmorack, the McDonalds of Glengary in the Parishes of Boleskine and thereof, and the McKenzies of Glengary, and all others in the Parishes of Kiltarman in Glengary, and Kilichoan in Knoidart, as also the McLeods, and all others in the Parish of Glenelg, all within the Shire of Invernesse.

BY George Wade Esq, Major General and Commander in Chief of all His Majesty's Forces, Castles, Forts and Barracks in North Britain, &c

IN His Majesty's Name and in Pursuance of the Power and Authority to Me given by His Majesty under His Royal Sign-Manual, by Virtue of an Act of Parliament, Intitled, *An Act for more effectual Disarming the Highlands in that Part of Great Britain called Scotland, and for bet-ter Securing the Peace and Quiet of that Part of the Kingdom;* I do hereby strictly Require and Command you and every of you on *or before)* Monday the thirteenth day of September next, to bring or send to Killichuiman all your Broad Swords, Targets, Poynards, Whingars or Durks, Side Pistol or Side Pistols Guns or any other Warlike Weapons and then and there to ~~bring and~~ deliver up to Me *or the Officer Commanding at Killichuiman. As is abovementioned* all and singular your Arms and Warlike Weapons for the Use of His Majesty, His Heirs and Successors, and to be dis-posed of in such Manner as His Majesty, His Heirs and Successors shall appoint. And by so doing you will avoid the Pains and Penalties by the said Act directed to be inflicted on all such Person or Persons who shall presume to refuse or neg-lect to pay a due Obedience to the same.

Given under My Hand and Seal at Castle Braham this Thirty first day of August 1725.

George Wade

Kilmorack.

General Wade's proclamation of 31 August 1725 to Grants, Chisholms, etc., ordering the forfeiting of their weapons.

Sword inscribed "Prosperity to Scotland and no Union", circa 1707.

to France. When the remaining Highlanders reached Aberdeen under Alexander Gordon of Auchintoul, who had taken command after Huntly's surrender, a message from James entitled *A letter of Adieu to the Scotch* was read out to them, advising them in so many words to shift for themselves.

On reaching Ruthven in Badenoch, the decision was accordingly taken by the Jacobite leaders to dismiss those of their followers who had not already gone home. After first escaping abroad, Auchintoul was in due course lucky enough to be able to return to his estates in Scotland, which, owing to a clerical error (the Act of Attainder gave his name as Thomas instead of Alexander) had, it emerged, never legally been confiscated. Huntly, who succeeded his father as Second Duke of Gordon in 1716 and had only made a half-hearted contribution to the Rising, also escaped retribution. His wife Henrietta, an exceptionally strong-minded young Englishwoman, and, strangely enough, an enthusiastic Jacobite, brought up all their eleven children as Protestants, thereby finally severing that family's connection with the Church of Rome.

Leaving some of their clansmen to hold Inverness for King James, the Mackenzies, under Seaforth, had arrived in time to fight at Sheriffmuir, where they had suffered severe casualties. After the battle Seaforth and his surviving clansmen returned north in the hope of raising a fresh force, only to find that with the help of the Sutherlands, Munros, Rosses and Mackays, Lovat had retaken Inverness for King George, while their own strongholds of Brahan and Eilean Donan had both been occupied by the Hanoverians.

The Rising was now as good as over. After Seaforth had escaped to France, his lands were formally sequestrated by the Government, who, however, owing to their inaccessibility and to the unco-operative attitude of the inhabitants, encountered such difficulty in actually taking possession of them that in the end they were obliged to abandon the attempt. At least one notorious rebel was to survive the Rising unscathed. Rob Roy MacGregor had for his part used the occasion to conduct a private war of his own, wisely keeping out of the battle of Sheriffmuir and spending most of his time harassing the Duke of Montrose and extorting "black-mail" or protection money from the latter's tenants, possibly, it seems, at the instigation of the Duke of Argyll. Twice he was captured, once by the Duke of Montrose and once by the Duke of Atholl, but both times managed to escape. To explain his behaviour, he later claimed, probably not without some justification, that he had all the time been acting as a Government agent, gathering intelligence for the Duke of Argyll. Even so, the MacGregors' part in the Rising did nothing to endear them to their country's new rulers. Under the Hanoverians as under the Stewarts their name was proscribed and they were expressly excluded from the General Pardon granted in 1717. "Plunder and booty," remarked a contemporary, "is their Bussiness."

Warned by the Fifteen, the London Government now took drastic steps to prevent another rising. Hundreds of Jacobites were sent to the plantations, two of the leaders who had failed to escape abroad were executed and nineteen peerages and a number of estates forfeited. Individual Whigs took vengeance on individual Jacobites. Lachlan MacLachlan of that Ilk had been one of the first to join Mar. His neighbour on Lochfyneside, Campbell of Ardkinglas, now "followed him like a sleuth hound for five years

"Rent Day in the Wilderness", by Edwin Landseer, showing Donald Murchison collecting rent from the Ross-shire estates to send to the exiled Earl of Seaforth. After the 1715 rising, Murchison resisted Government attempts to regain the Seaforth estates.

and shot him dead in 1720". An attempt to disarm the clans was only partly successful. Those clans whose loyalty was to London obediently handed over their weapons: the others turned in any obsolete weapons they no longer needed and hid the rest for future use. By this time the Union was more unpopular than ever and even those Scots who supported the Hanoverians had come to resent the London Government's attitude to their country; with the result that Jacobite hopes remained high.

A couple of years later a fresh opportunity for action presented itself. In December 1718 the British Government had declared war on Spain. In Cardinal Alberoni, the Spanish King's Chief Minister, the Jacobites found an enthusiastic supporter. At a meeting in Madrid, it was decided that in March 1719 the Duke of Ormonde would invade England with the support of a Spanish force of twenty-seven ships and five thousand men. Simultaneously the Earl of Seaforth, the Marquis of Tullibardine and the Earl Marischal would land on the West Coast of Scotland to raise the clans.

In accordance with this plan, Seaforth, who was in France, set sail for Scotland in March, accompanied by Campbell of Glendaruel, a fellow Jacobite. Landing at Stornoway in Lewis in April, they found there two Spanish frigates with some three hundred Spanish soldiers and a supply of money, arms and ammunition, under the

command of the Earl Marischal, who was accompanied by Tullibardine and the latter's younger brother Lord George Murray. From Stornoway they then sailed together to Lochalsh on the mainland, setting up their headquarters in Mackenzie country at Eilean Donan.

By this time, however, Ormonde's fleet had been scattered by a storm and the proposed invasion of England had been abandoned. Nor was it long before a strong force of Government troops under the English General Wightman arrived on the scene from Inverness, while a number of Government warships made their appearance off Eilean Donan. At this, the two Spanish frigates, afraid of being bottled up in Loch Duich, weighed anchor and sailed for home, leaving to their fate the landing party, who by now had advanced some way up Glen Shiel in the vain hope of capturing Inverness, while Seaforth scoured his own country in search of recruits.

Having seized Eilean Donan, the Government troops at once blew up the Castle, destroying it completely. Early in June Seaforth returned at the head of five hundred of his own clansmen and several hundred more recruits from neighbouring Jacobite clans. But a few days later, on 10 June, General Wightman attacked in strength and, coming on his adversaries in the pass of Glenshiel, eventually succeeded in dispersing them. In the course of the battle Seaforth was severely wounded and it now became clear to the Jacobites that their situation was desperate. It was accordingly agreed that the Spaniards, who under international law would count as prisoners of war, should surrender, while the Highlanders who, if captured, would be treated as traitors, vanished into the hills and Seaforth and the Earl Marischal escaped by sea. By this time the rising was over and the Hanoverians were, in the words of their commander, "taking a tour through all the difficult parts of Seaforth's country to terrify the Rebels by burning the houses of the Guilty". As for the six thousand muskets that had been landed from Spain, they seem in due course to have found their way into the hands of those for whom they were intended, for possible use on some future occasion.

Among those who took part in the Nineteen was Mackintosh of Borlum. Undaunted by his experiences in the Fifteen, Old Borlum had returned to Scotland less than four years later, landing at Eilean Donan in March 1719 with Tullibardine and the Earl Marischal. Nor did he escape to France after the Jacobite defeat, but took to the hills and skulked there for a number of years, eluding capture until finally hunted down by the Hanoverians and put in jail, where he died twenty-four years later at the age of eighty-four, a staunch Jacobite to the last.

Barracks at Ruthven in Badenoch, built in 1718 to garrison the Highlands.

Rob Roy MacGregor, who was also out again in 1719, fared better. After surrendering in the end to the English Commander, General Wade, in 1722, he narrowly escaped transportation to the West Indies, but somehow managed to get himself pardoned. After which he joined the Church of Rome and settled down peaceably to spend the rest of

his days in Balquiddher, where he had been born and where his house still stands.

After this second warning, the Government continued more assiduously than ever their measures for the pacification and subjection of the Highlands. The native Gaelic tongue had long been a target for English and, more especially, for Lowland Scottish reformers. Already in 1695 an Act had provided for the "erecting of English Schools for rooting out of the Irish language and other pious uses" and in 1720 we are told that it was the firm design of the Society for the Propagation of Christian Knowledge "not to continue the Irish language, but to wear it out, and learn the people the English tongue". A new and more stringent Disarming Act was passed and for a time many Highlanders abandoned the habit of carrying arms in public.

In the past the inaccessibility and impenetrability of their country had given the Highlanders considerable advantage over potential invaders. In 1725 General Wade, the newly appointed English Commander-in-Chief for Scotland, embarked on a ten-year programme of military road-building, designed to penetrate the more important regions of the Highlands and link together the strategic strongpoints of Fort William, Fort Augustus and Fort George. His roads which, when completed, covered a total of over two hundred and fifty miles, gave the central government a greater measure of control over the Highlands than ever before and, by thus opening them up, in the end did as much as anything to destroy the old order which still prevailed there. At the same time, a number of Independent Highland Companies, recruited from Whig clansmen and later formed into a regular regiment known from the dark colour of their kilts as *An Freiceadan Dubh*, the Black Watch, were raised by General Wade, in the first place for police duties. In view of his local influence and standing the command of one of these companies was entrusted for a time to Lord Lovat, but later, much to his disgust, withdrawn.

In 1727 George II succeeded George I. But there was no marked change in the Government's attitude to Scotland. Nor was the new King any more popular there than his father had been. Up to 1725 Scottish affairs had been handled in Whitehall by a separate Secretary for Scotland. Now, under the long premiership of Sir Robert Walpole, they passed into the province of the Home Secretary. For most purposes, however, executive power resided with the Duke of Argyll or with Duncan Forbes of Culloden, the Lord Advocate. In the Highlands, friction of one kind or another was constant.

The Pinch of Snuff, by William Delacour, 1750, an important picture of early military uniform.

CHAPTER XVII

The '45

In Europe, tensions were by now building up which in 1739 were yet again to involve Britain in war with Spain and in the following year with France. Once more there was every hope that a Jacobite rising might attract active French support. The Jacobites had, moreover, another asset. In James's elder son, Prince Charles Edward, to be known in the Highlands as Bonnie Prince Charlie, they possessed a potential leader, a young man of energy, courage and personal magnetism, more than ready, if the chance offered, to fight for his rights and for those of his house. Messages passed between Jacobites in Scotland and the Jacobite Court in Rome, and in January 1744 Prince Charles took leave of his father and set out for France. By this time the French were planning to invade England with a considerable fleet and an invasion force of ten thousand men had been assembled at Dunkirk under the formidable Marshal Manfriede Saxe, one of the great military commanders of his age. In March, however, storms dispersed the invasion fleet before it could set sail and the whole project was in the end abandoned or at any rate postponed.

To Charles it now became clear that the best, if not the only hope of success lay in bold action on his own part. Only thus, he believed, could the Jacobite clans be persuaded to rise and the French convinced that his cause was worthy of active support. And so, with money raised by pawning his mother's rubies, he fitted out a frigate, the *Doutelle*, and a ship of the line, the *Elizabeth*, with which in July 1745 he set sail from Nantes for Scotland. After a sharp encounter with an English warship off the Lizard, the *Elizabeth* was disabled and forced to put back, but the *Doutelle* escaped her pursuers, and on 2 August 1745 Prince Charles landed on the isle of Eriskay in the Outer Hebrides with just seven supporters, including William Murray, Marquess of Tullibardine, since 1724 titular Duke of Atholl.

His reception on landing in Scotland was far from encouraging. Despite past professions of loyalty, two leading West Coast Chiefs, Macleod of Macleod and MacDonald of Sleat, refused to have anything to do with him. Indeed Macleod shrewdly passed on the news of his arrival to the Government. MacDonald of Boisdale, summoned from neighbouring South Uist, anxiously urged him to go home. "I am come home," replied the Prince and set sail with his seven companions for Moidart on the mainland where he was at once joined by young Macdonald of Clanranald in the heart of whose country he now was.

"Incident in The Battle of Culloden", copy of original painting by David Morier. It depicts the charge of the Right Wing of the Jacobite army against Berrell's Regiment. It is said that Jacobite prisoners held in Carlisle Castle were used as live models by the artist.

Prince Charles on the shore of Loch nan Uamh, with Antoine Walsh, who had conveyed him across the Minch from Eriskay. Contemporary drawing by Moidart.

The news of Charles's landing filled many of the mainland Jacobites with concern. Donald Cameron, Younger of Lochiel, begged him for his part to abandon the enterprise. But without success. "Be the issue what it will," Charles replied, "I am determined to display my Standard and take the field with such as may join in. Lochiel, whom my father esteemed the best friend of our family, may stay at home, and learn his Prince's fate from the newspapers."

The Camerons had long been loyal supporters of the House of Stewart. Thirty years before, in 1715, the aged Sir Ewen Cameron, the Great Lochiel, had stayed behind at Achnacarry, but his son John had joined Mar and had been forfeited for so doing. John was now Chief. In his absence in France, his son Donald, the Gentle Lochiel, as he became known, was serving as Chief in his place. In the end, despite his misgivings, Donald allowed Prince Charles to convince him. "I'll share the fate of my Prince," he said, "and so shall every man over whom nature or fortune hath given me any power." When, some days later, Prince Charles raised the Royal Standard at Glenfinnan and proclaimed his father King, it was the arrival of seven hundred Camerons and four or five hundred MacDonalds of Clanranald and Keppoch that first gave the rising reality.

From Glenfinnan, the Prince now set out boldly for Edinburgh, gathering support as he went. Soon some three thousand clansmen from the West had joined him. MacDonell of Glengarry, who had earlier sent his elder son Alexander (later a Government spy) to France to try to stop the Prince from coming, remained aloof. But for all that a day or two later his second son Angus and his kinsman Donald of Lochgarry joined Charles with four hundred clansmen, as did a hundred and twenty MacDonalds of Glencoe and some of the Grants of Glenmoriston.

At Invergarry the Prince also found Fraser of Gortleg with a message of encouragement from his Chief, Lord Lovat who, though in 1715 he had supported the Hanoverians now strongly urged him to march north through Stratherrick to Inverness. If he did this, said Lovat, whose right to his peerage had been confirmed a dozen years before by King George, but who was now angling for a Jacobite dukedom, the Frasers would rise to a man for King James and would in all probability be joined, not only by Sir Alexander MacDonald of Sleat, but by the Macleods, the Mackenzies, the Grants and the Mackintoshes. Just how seriously this message deserved to be taken, coming from such a source, was hard to say. In the event, Charles let himself be persuaded by Tullibardine that a wiser course would be to march southwards through Atholl (where, he assured him, every Athollman would rise) and thence to Perth and Edinburgh. Before leaving Invergarry, the Prince was joined by two hundred and sixty Stewarts of Appin, led in their Chief's absence by Charles Stewart of Ardshiel.

From Garvamore, where General Wade's new bridge now crossed the Spey and which the Prince reached on 28 August, Lochiel sent a party of Camerons to Cluny to bring in his cousin (and Lovat's son in law) Macpherson of Cluny, then serving with the Government forces. Cluny had in fact returned home to raise his clan for King George, but, after meeting Prince Charles, decided in the end to raise it for him instead, observing that "An angel could not resist the soothing close applications of the rebels." Which meant several hundred more recruits for the Prince. A couple of days later came the news that a number of nameless and landless MacGregors had joined the Prince's army, seized the newly built barracks at Inversnaid on the eastern shore of Loch Lomond and already taken eighty-nine enemy prisoners.

On 31 August the Prince arrived with Tullibardine or, as he now styled himself, Duke William of Atholl, at Blair Atholl, the latter's ancestral home, hastily evacuated a few days before by his Hanoverian younger brother, Duke James. Thence he marched via Dunkeld to Perth, where he remained until 10 September. In Perth he was joined by the young Drummond Duke of Perth and by Atholl's other brother, Lord George Murray, both of whom he appointed Lieutenant-General. These brought with them several hundred clansmen or followers, whom the Prince now inspected along with several hundred more newly arrived MacGregors, brought in by Glencarnaig and Glengyle. While in Perth he was also joined by Old Robertson of Struan with two hundred of his clansmen who, with Duke

Locket with miniature of Prince Charles Edward Stewart, Jacobite wine glass (1775) and white silk cockade, the badge of the Jacobites in 1745–6.

Prince Charles Edward Stewart, by Giles Hussey.

"Duke James" of Atholl, who supported the Government against his two brothers: "Duke William" and Lord George Murray.

William of Atholl's followers and those of Lord Nairne and Menzies of Shian, formed an Atholl Brigade, which was appropriately enough placed under the operational command of Lord George Murray who had been out in the Fifteen and was not without military experience. On belatedly receiving news of what was happening, the English Commander-in-Chief, Sir John Cope, had chosen to withdraw northwards towards Inverness, thus leaving the way to Edinburgh open to the Jacobites. Accordingly, from Perth the Prince's army now made straight for the capital. It was mid-September.

At Coltbridge, on the outskirts of the city, they encountered two regiments of Government dragoons whom they put to flight. In the city itself there was panic. The City Guards and Volunteers melted away and, while the Netherbar Port was being opened to let a coach pass through, Lochiel with a party of Camerons rushed the sentries and gained control of the sleeping city, which woke next day to find itself in Jacobite hands, though the Castle and its garrison of Government troops still held out for King George. Later that day, 17 September, King James VIII was proclaimed at the Market Cross and Charles entered Holyrood in

Lord George Murray, who proved an able Lieutenant General. He was the first officer to wear the kilt instead of trews, in order to march with his men.

triumph. In Edinburgh he was joined by more supporters. From remote Cowal, MacLachan of MacLachlan, giving his Campbell neighbours the slip, brought in a hundred and fifty men and Lord Nairne two hundred and fifty more from Atholl. A few days later came more Grants from Glenmoriston.

General Cope, meanwhile, had reached Aberdeen. Not wishing to be cut off completely, he rather shamefacedly piled his soldiers into some ships and, landing them at Dunbar, marched on Edinburgh. At Prestonpans he encountered the Prince who had come out to meet him. As so often before, the regular British infantry could not, when it came to the point, withstand the onset of the Highland charge. The thin red line wavered and broke; the Government artillery missed their opportunity; and Cope's two regiments of dragoons, accompanied by their commanding general, once again sought safety in flight. One Jacobite who benefited personally by General Cope's hurried departure was the aged Robertson of Struan, who, having led his clan thus far in person, now handed over command to a younger kinsman and himself left for home in Cope's own travelling carriage, warmly wrapped in the General's fur-lined nightgown to protect him against the autumn chill.

Lord Ogilvy, by Allan Ramsay, another of the leading Jacobite supporters.

Charles's victory at Prestonpans had given him a high opinion of the troops under his command and of their potentialities. It also brought him fresh reinforcements: Lord Ogilvy with six hundred men; Gordon of Glenbucket with four hundred; four hundred and eighty from Strathbogie and Enzie under David Tulloch and John Hamilton; two companies of foot under Gordon of Aberlour and Stewart of Tinninnar; Alexander Forbes, Lord Pitsligo with a hundred and thirty horse and two hundred and fifty foot from Banffshire and Aberdeen; two troops of Life Guards, as they were called, under Lord Elcho and Arthur Elphinstone, Lord Balmerino; and, from the West, a further contingent of Camerons and MacDonalds of Keppoch, and a hundred more MacGregors from Balquhidder.

It had been the Prince's original intention to land in the first place on Mull where, though the island was now in Campbell hands, he knew he could count on loyal Maclean support. But in the event things had turned out differently. In the summer of 1745 Sir Hector Maclean of Duart had come over to Edinburgh from France on Jacobite business, but had lingered there longer than was prudent and, before he could leave, had been arrested and consigned first to Edinburgh Castle and later to the Tower of London. Without their Chief, seven hundred Macleans from Mull, Morvern and Ardgour had nevertheless set out to join Prince Charles under old Maclean of Drimnin and a younger son of Maclean of Ardgour. Long before reaching Edinburgh, however, they had encountered strong opposition from the all-encompassing Campbells as well as from regular Government troops under Lord Loudon, and it was not until later that they eventually managed to break through and join the Prince's army.

In the East, meanwhile, the Duke of Gordon's younger brother, Lord Lewis Gordon, leaving his less enthusiastic elder brother behind, had by now gone north as Lord Lieutenant for the Prince to raise as many of his clan as he could. Like her son Lewis,

Prince Charles entering Edinburgh after the Battle of Prestonpans, in 1745. A painting by T. Duncan, 1840. Edinburgh was the high point of the Jacobite campaign.

Ring given to Clementina Wharton by Prince Charles.

their mother Henrietta remained a staunch Jacobite and had breakfast laid out at her gates when she heard the Prince might pass that way. (Charles never ate the breakfast, but for this misdemeanour old Henrietta's modest pension was later stopped by the London Government.) Finally, before the end of October, the Prince was re-joined by Duke William of Atholl with another six hundred Athollmen and some gunners who had arrived from France under James Grant. Cluny Macpherson, by this time a committed supporter, also brought in four hundred more of his Clan. But, despite these reinforcements, Charles did not immediately follow up his early advantage, lingering on instead in Edinburgh for more than a month and so leaving time for George II's Government, now seriously disturbed, to bring back more regular troops from Flanders and send them north to join old General Wade, by now a Field Marshal, at Newcastle.

In the Highlands the Whig clans were by this time also gathering their strength, first and foremost the Campbells. Their Chief, Archibald 3rd Duke of Argyll, had succeeded his father in 1743, two years before the Rising, the suppression of which quickly became his principal preoccupation. As was to be expected, the Duke

gave the London Government his total support, at once placing all his very considerable resources at their disposal. To his influence and power Prince Charles himself paid significant tribute. "There is one man in this country whom I could wish to have my friend," he wrote to his father from Perth in September, "and that is the Duke of Argyll, who I find is in great credit amongst them, on account of his great abilities and quality, and has many dependents by his great fortune; but I am told I can hardly flatter myself by the hope of it."

Though a lawyer by profession, Argyll now actively concerned himself with military matters. From the first his Argyll Militia took an active part in the campaign. Since 1730 he and his friend Lord President Forbes of Culloden had been busy raising from clans known to be loyal to the House of Hanover the six independent companies of local militia known as the Black Watch. By now these had been formed into a regular infantry regiment, the Forty Second Foot, which in April of that year had fought bravely for the English at Fontenoy. A no less important part in marshalling the resources and directing the military operations of Clan Campbell fell to the Duke's cousin and heir, General John Campbell of Mamore, and his son John. While raising fresh levies and gathering supplies throughout the Western Highlands, neither of them as Highlanders born and bred showed quite the same vindictive spirit in the ensuing campaign as did many of the London Government's other Scottish supporters.

Basket-hilted broadsword given to Prince Charles by the Duke of Perth, as part of the accoutrements of Highland dress, and sent out to him in France. The sword went into the Royal collection after the 1745 rising until it was given to the Clan Ranald by George IV on his coronation in 1822.

Once the news of the Prince's landing had been received, the Chiefs of the Whig clans and other leading adherents of the House of Hanover had started calling out their clans and assembling their forces with varying degrees of enthusiasm. By the middle of September 1745 John Campbell, 4th Earl of Loudon, was seeking to recruit as many as twenty companies for service with the regiment which bore his name. In this task he enjoyed the active support of the Mackays and Munros, of the renegade Macleod of Macleod and MacDonald of Sleat, of the Earl of Sutherland and, curiously enough, of Lord Seaforth's son, Lord Fortrose. Lord Cromartie and Lord Lovat, it was reported, were also engaged in a recruiting drive, though on whose behalf was not as yet altogether clear.

Despite his clan's Whig traditions, and the urgings of Forbes of Culloden, Sir James Grant of Grant seems to have evinced no great enthusiasm for either side, advising Ludovick, his son and heir, "to stay at home and take care of his country and join no party". While readily staying at home, as his father had suggested, Ludovick, for his part, made every effort to prevent his clansmen, some of whom had strong Jacobite sympathies, from joining the Prince. Even so, a number of Grants, including the Grants of Glenmoriston, had managed to do so, after which Ludovick made it his

209

"The March to Finchley",
by William Hogarth,
1750.

business to hunt down as many of them as possible and hand them over to the Government.

Of all the Government's supporters in Scotland none played a more active or more important part at this time than Duncan Forbes of Culloden, the able and humane Lord President, who, convinced that the Rising would be a disaster for all concerned, used his very considerable influence with many of the traditionally Jacobite clans to restrain them from joining it, while at the same time urging his Whig friends, his neighbour Lovat in particular, to give the Government all the help they could.

Charles, in that autumn of 1745, was still hoping for active French support. Supplies came from France and money, but as yet no men. For Charles to delay any longer would have been disastrous. Accordingly at the beginning of November he crossed the border into England and started his advance on London. Though he met with little resistance, he was joined by only two or three hundred English recruits, while some of his Highlanders, feeling homesick, were already beginning to desert.

For the Jacobites the outlook was anything but reassuring. From the north-east Wade was now threatening the Prince with one army; George II's plump young son, the Duke of Cumberland, was advancing through the Midlands with another, while a third was drawn up at Finchley for the defence of the English capital: in all some thirty thousand regular troops against no more than five thousand badly equipped Highlanders and a couple of hundred men from Manchester.

By early December the Highland army, still undefeated, had reached Derby. There Charles held a council of war to decide on his next move. He was now only 130 miles from London. He had not suffered a single set-back. Morale was high. In the English capital there was panic. There was a run on the Bank of England, who, to gain time, were

"The Highland Visitors", engraving by J. Dubois, showing the Scottish soldiers en route for Derby. The Jacobite army were tougher and fitter than the Government troops, but lacking disciplined tactics.

paying it was said in red-hot sixpences, and George II, with the Royal yacht standing by in the Thames, was getting ready to go back to Hanover. It was a moment when boldness offered the best, indeed the only hope of success. Counsels of prudence could only be counsels of despair. Realising this, Charles pleaded with his commanders to be allowed to continue his advance. "I can see nothing," he said, "but ruin and destruction to us in case we should retreat." But his advisers, led by Lord George Murray, only saw the obvious dangers of advancing further. In the end it was they who won the day and, to Charles's vigorously expressed disgust, the fateful decision was taken to withdraw to the Highlands.

Fowling piece given to "Gentle Lochiel" by Prince Charles.

A Mackenzie fleeing Culloden. Print by McIan

On 19 December the retreating Jacobite army reached Carlisle where Charles insisted on leaving behind a token garrison. The following day they were back on Scottish soil, though not necessarily among well-wishers. In Glasgow their reception was far from friendly. In the Highlands, however, more clans had by now come out for the Prince, so that his numbers were again on the increase, reaching eight thousand by the end of the year. With no help from his brother the Duke, Lord Lewis Gordon had managed to bring out eight hundred Gordon clansmen as well as a considerable number more from Aberdeenshire as a whole, including a whole regiment under Moir of Strongwood and a further unit under Gordon of Avochy and Farquharson of Monaltrie. Lord Lewis had also occupied the city of Aberdeen for the Jacobites. Late in November Perth's brother, Lord John Drummond, had arrived from France with some artillery and seven hundred men of the French Royal Scots and Irish Brigades.

In the north, Lovat, despite the entreaties of Forbes of Culloden, had, while reserving his own position, in the end encouraged his reluctant son to bring the Frasers out for Prince Charles. Of the Mackenzies, Seaforth's son and successor, known since the attainder as Lord Fortrose, had under Forbes's influence joined the Government forces under Lord Loudon. "*He, Mon Dieu!*", exclaimed the Prince on hearing this, "*et Seaforth est aussi contre moi*". Lady Fortrose, on the other hand, had displayed her independence by bringing out a number of Mackenzie clansmen for Charles, while Lord Cromartie had joined the Jacobite army with five hundred more Mackenzies.

Despite his clan's strongly Jacobite antecedents, the Rising had found The Mackintosh commanding a company of the Black Watch under Lord Loudon. His wife Anne, on the other hand, the twenty-year-old daughter of Farquharson of Invercauld and a Jacobite born and bred, made it her business to bring out Clan Chattan for Prince Charles, herself inspecting their regiment of eight hundred men before they marched south under the MacGillivray Chieftain of Dunmaglas. Some more reinforcements under MacDonell of Barrisdale and Young Glengarry, some more Camerons and some more MacGregors had by this time also joined the Prince's forces in the north under the command of Lord John Drummond.

On 3 January, 1746, Charles reached Stirling with his main force and, conscious of its strategic importance, laid siege to the castle. At Falkirk he encountered the English General Hawley with a strong force of Government troops. Once more the Highland charge put the regulars to flight. But again Charles did not follow up his advantage when the opportunity offered. Instead, having raised the siege of Stirling, he continued his march north and, crossing the Tay, made for Inverness.

On 16 February 1746, Prince Charles arrived at Moy, some ten miles from Inverness, where he was made welcome by Colonel Anne, as Lady Mackintosh was now known, while five hundred of Lochiel's Camerons camped nearby at Moybeg. Inverness itself was held at the time by seventeen hundred Government troops under Lord Loudon who, learning of the Prince's arrival, marched that very night on Moy. Colonel Anne meanwhile had posted Donald Fraser, the village blacksmith, with four other men to watch the Inverness road. On the approach of the Hanoverians the five of them rushed out from among peat-stacks, firing their muskets and calling out at the top of their voices to imaginary clan regiments, Mackintoshes, Camerons, and MacDonalds, to advance. At this Loudon's seventeen hundred men at once fell back in confusion. Almost the only casualty in the Rout of Moy, as it came to be called, was MacLeod of MacLeod's personal piper, Donald Ban MacCrimmon, of the famous family of pipers from Skye, whose Chief had sent him against his will to serve against Prince Charles and who, having the second sight and foreseeing his own death in a cause which he abhorred, composed for the occasion the haunting lament *Cha till, Cha till, Cha till MacCraimein*, MacCrimmon will not return.

Convinced that he was heavily outnumbered, Loudon now hastily abandoned Inverness and with-

Portrait traditionally thought to be of Donald Cameron of Lochiel, "The Gentle Lochiel", by Sir George Chalmers, 1762.

Sad remnants of a defeated army – Jacobite sword-blades from the Culloden field, given as trophies to the Duke of Cumberland. He had them made into a fence around Cumberland House. When the house was demolished at the end of the 19th century, the sword-blades were purchased and taken to Inverary Castle.

Targe made for Prince Charles, given to Cluny Macpherson after Culloden.

drew rapidly into Ross-shire; the Jacobites occupied the town and Prince Charles established himself for a time in old Lady Mackintosh's house in Church Street, then one of the very few stone-built houses in the Royal Burgh and famous as the only one which could boast a sitting-room without a bed in it. Once the rest of his troops had reached Inverness, the Prince sent out a column under the Duke of Perth to attack Loudon's force, putting it to flight and taking a considerable number of prisoners, including The Mackintosh, who was promptly handed over to his wife for safe-keeping. On being greeted by Anne with the words "Your servant, Captain", he is said to have replied, no less succinctly if a trifle shamefacedly, "Your servant, Colonel."

All this time the Government had been bringing back more and more troops from Flanders. On their arrival in Scotland these were assembled at Aberdeen under the command of the Duke of Cumberland, and in April 1746, two months after his own arrival in Inverness, Charles learned that Cumberland was advancing on that town with a well equipped, well trained and well fed force of regular troops twice the size of his own. Faced with this disturbing prospect, Charles now sought to rally his troops, assembling some five thousand hungry, ill-equipped Highlanders on the bleak expanse of Culloden Moor, some five miles outside Inverness. While on their way there, they were joined by some three hundred Frasers under Charles Fraser of Inverallochy, who brought the news that a further Fraser contingent led by the Master of Lovat were even now on their way to Inverness from further North. But neither they nor Lord Cromartie's Mackenzies, who had been intercepted in Sutherland by the Mackays, ever reached the battlefield.

Favourable to regular troops, the site chosen for the forthcoming encounter was as ill-suited as it could be to the semi-guerilla tactics of the Highlanders. On 14 April Cumberland's army, having crossed the Spey, pitched their camp twelve miles away, outside the town of Nairn. On the night of 15–16 April, Lord George Murray, who quite rightly "did not like the ground", and could only hope that surprise might somehow help to redress the balance between the two armies, agreed to attempt a night attack on Cumberland's camp. But the plan miscarried badly. The Highlanders, who the day before had eaten only one biscuit apiece, spent half the night wandering about in the dark without ever finding the enemy. By the time they had made their way back to their camp, they were worn out and slept where they dropped. At first light Cumberland gave his well fed, well trained and well rested regulars the order to attack and the starving and exhausted Highlanders were dragged from their sleep by the sound of the enemy's drums beating to arms.

Private, 43rd Regiment, 1742, from the "Cloathing Book" engraved by order of the Duke of Cumberland.

At the outset of the battle the Prince's army of five thousand men was drawn up in two lines, facing north-east. On the right of the line were the Athollmen. Next came Lochiel's Camerons; then the Stewarts of Appin under Charles Stewart of Ardshiel; then the Frasers, the Mackintoshes, the Farquharsons, the Maclachlans and the Macleans. On the far left were the MacDonalds of Clanranald, Keppoch and Glengarry. In the second line were what remained of Lord Ogilvy's, Lord Lewis Gordon's and the Duke of Perth's regiments.

Cumberland opened his attack with a heavy artillery barrage to which the Highlanders could make no effective reply. After this had lasted for an hour and ever more gaps were showing in their ranks, they began to grow restive, the Mackintoshes in particular, and the Prince told Lord George Murray to give the order to charge. To make way for Lord George Murray's Athollmen, the MacDonalds, who since Bannockburn had traditionally claimed the right of line, had been placed on the left and were therefore disgruntled and, despite the gallant example of their chieftains, inclined to hang back. In the centre, the Camerons, the Mackintoshes with the Macphersons, the rest of Clan Chattan and the little regiment of Macleans and Maclachlans came first to the shock. "Nothing," wrote an English officer afterwards, "could be more desperate than their attack and more properly received."

But this time the Government troops were better prepared for the Highland charge and the Highlanders, rushing forward, died in their hundreds on the Hanoverian bayonets. Seeing the men of his clan waver, MacDonald of Keppoch himself ran forward, sword in hand towards the enemy, crying, as he fell beneath a hail of bullets: "*Mo Dhia, ando threig clann ma chinnidhmi?*" "My God, have the clansmen of my name deserted me?" In less than half an hour the battle was over. Soon all over the field the English cavalry were riding down and butchering the Highland wounded. After watching the rout of his army, Prince Charles let himself be led from the field by one of his officers.

Later that evening Charles, now a fugitive, stopped for refreshment at the house of Fraser of Gorthleck, whose aged Chief, Lord Lovat, also happened to be sheltering there and offered him such hospitality as he could. It was thus that, by an irony of fate which was to cost him his life, Simon Lovat, who had himself until then managed to avoid direct involvement in the Rising, but could not in the circumstances refuse the Prince hospitality, became at last, whether he liked it or not, irretrievably committed to the Jacobite cause.

Engraving by Richard Cooper, 1745, which appeared on the advertisement for the arrest of Prince Charles.

The Mackintoshes, without their Chief, had led the Highland charge, suffering, it is said, the heaviest casualties of any clan. That night Cumberland, in his turn, stayed uninvited in old Lady Mackintosh's house in Inverness, sleeping in the bed previously occupied by Prince Charles. "I've had two King's bairns living with me in my time," the old lady would say afterwards, "and to tell you the truth, I wish I may never have another." At Moy, Colonel Anne was arrested by the Hanoverians and brought back under guard to Inverness, where she was held for six weeks as a prisoner. She was an attractive young woman and, while under arrest, received frequent visits from Cumberland's officers. "I drank tea yesterday with Lady Mackintosh," wrote one of them to his brother. "She is really a very pretty woman, pity she is a rebel!"

Leaving what remained of his army to disperse as best they could, Prince Charles now set out with two or three companions for the West Coast in the hope of eventually being picked up there by a French ship. From Gorthleck he made his way by Invergarry and thence by Loch Arkaig and Glen Pean to Arisaig where he had first landed nine months before. But there the news was not of French but of English ships patrolling the coast in search of him. On hearing this, Charles arrived at the improbable decision that his best hope was to make for Skye and there throw himself on the mercy of MacLeod of MacLeod and Sir Alexander MacDonald of Sleat, both of whom had from the start of the Rising made it more than clear that they wished to have nothing to do with him, indeed that their loyalty lay strongly with the Government. However at Borrodale in Arisaig he encountered Donald MacLeod, an old seaman from Skye with Jacobite sympathies who from his knowledge of his own Chief and of Sleat swiftly disillusioned him. "Ye mauna do it," he kept repeating. "Ye mauna do it." Instead, Donald offered to carry him himself in an eight-oared boat to the Outer Islands, an alternative which in the end the Prince accepted. It was thus that, after a stormy crossing, Charles and his companions landed at dawn on Sunday 27 April at Rossinish on Benbecula, just across the island from Nunton, the house of the older MacDonald of Clanranald, whose son had fought for him throughout the Rising.

After consulting old Clanranald and his half-brother MacDonald of Boisdale, the Prince and his companions now left Benbecula for Stornoway in Donald's boat under the guise of shipwrecked merchants in search of a sizeable vessel with which to carry on their trade. Next day they were driven ashore on the Island of Scalpay, off Harris, where they were hospitably entertained by Donald Campbell, the tenant of Scalpay. Meanwhile from Benbecula the local Minister, the Revd. John Macaulay,* who had happened to be dining with Clanranald when news of the Prince's arrival was brought to him, had sent an urgent message to his father, the Rev. Aulay Macaulay, Minister of Tarbert in Harris, urging him to have the Prince seized on his arrival there. But when the Revd. Aulay made his appearance with a boat-load of parishioners keen to seize the Prince and claim the reward of £30,000 offered for his capture, they were chased away by Donald Campbell who, although a Whig and a Campbell, put the laws of hospitality before mere political expediency. In the end, after an arduous journey by land and sea, the Prince reached Stornoway, only to learn from old Donald MacLeod, who had gone on ahead in search of a larger vessel, that his attempts to hire a ship had been unsuccessful and that a company of the local Mackenzie militia were by now already on the look out for him.

There was clearly no time to be lost and so, piling back into old Donald's little boat, they headed south again for Benbecula. After a hair-raising journey and a narrow escape from enemy warships, they eventually landed on a little island off the east coast of Benbecula, just to the south of Rossinish, where they found shelter in a bothy. Here they were visited next day by Old Clanranald, bringing with him from Nunton his family's tutor, Neil McEachain.** Neil, he said, would guide

* grandfather of Lord Macaulay, the Whig historian

** Neil McEachain's son, Alexander, born in exile in France, became Napoleon's Marshal MacDonald, Duke of Taranto. By birth they were Macleans, but this seems somehow to have been overlooked by all concerned.

After a warrant had been issued for his arrest, Prince Charles' riposte was to offer a reward of £30,000 for the capture of George II, 1745.

CHARLES
Prince of *Wales,* &c.

Regent of the Kingdoms of *Scotland,* *England, France* and *Ireland,* and the Dominions thereunto belonging.

WHEREAS We have seen a certain scandalous and malicious Paper, published in the Stile and Form of a Proclamation, bearing Date the 1st instant, wherein under Pretence of bringing Us to Justice, like Our Royal Ancestor King *Charles* the I. of blessed Memory, there is a Reward, of Thirty Thousand Pounds *Sterling,* promised to those who shall deliver Us into the Hands of Our Enemies : We could not but be moved with a just Indignation at so insolent an Attempt. And tho' from Our Nature and Principles We abhor and detest a Practice so unusual among Christian Princes, We cannot but out of a just Regard to the Dignity of our Person, promise the like Reward of Thirty Thousand Pounds *Sterling,* to him or those who shall seize and secure, till Our further Orders, the Person of the Elector of *Hanover,* whether landed, or attempting to land, in any Part of His Majesty's Dominions. Should any fatal Accident happen from hence, let the Blame ly entirely at the Door of those who first set the infamous Example.

CHARLES, P. R.

Given in Our Camp at *Kinlocheill,* *August* the 22d, 1745.

By His Highness Command,

JO. MURRAY.

Opposite,
Flora MacDonald of
South Uist, wearing the
white Jacobite rose, by
Allan Ramsay.

The Isle of Skye, where
Prince Charles stayed
during his five month
flight in the Highlands
after Culloden.

them to Glen Corrodale in South Uist, where, under Clanranald's protection, they could for the time being be safe from enemy visitations.

Setting out on the night of 14 May, the Prince and his companions walked the fifteen miles across rough country to Glen Corrodale, where they found "a famous palace" in the shape of a forester's bothy, lying in an idyllic spot between two sizeable hills, Ben Hella and Ben More. Here they spent three weeks undisturbed. But it was not long before even Corrodale became unsafe for the fugitive. There were disturbing stories of militia companies in the vicinity and of enemy warships off the coast, and on 6 June the Prince set out once more on his travels. After a couple of days in a cave on an island off Benbecula and a few more near Rossinish, he made his way south to Loch Boisdale, where he had barely installed himself in the ruins of an old tower on the islet of Calvey, when a party of the enemy landed within a mile of him. Alarmed by this, he at once sent a messenger to the nearby house of MacDonald of Boisdale, only to find that Boisdale had himself been carried off by the enemy.

By this time it was all too clear that the Prince could no longer safely remain on the Long Island and, with the help of Lady Clanranald, a plan was made for him to go to Skye, en route for the mainland where, it was hoped, he would have a better chance of hiding until a ship could be found to take him to France. The plan was that with Fionnghal or Flora Macdonald, a young kinswoman of Clanranald, he should travel by boat to Skye, somewhat improbably disguised as Flora's Irish serving-maid, Betty Burke. Having successfully avoided the enemy soldiers who were by now closing in on him, the Prince took leave of Lady Clanranald and on 28 June embarked for Skye in a twenty-four foot yawl with Neil MacEachain and Flora, who carried an official letter of pass from her stepfather, Hugh MacDonald of Armadale, an officer of the local militia, who were supposed to be searching for him. After numerous adventures and one very narrow escape from capture, they landed next afternoon at Kilbride on Skye not far from Monkstadt, the residence of the renegade Sir Alexander MacDonald of Sleat.

Sir Alexander himself was at the time at Fort Augustus, paying his respects to the Duke of Cumberland. Unlike her husband, however, his wife Lady Margaret, a friend of Flora's, was at least sympathetic to the Jacobite cause. She herself did not meet the Prince, but their factor, MacDonald of Kingsburgh, likewise an officer in the militia, who, observing of the inadequately disguised Prince that he was "the worst Pretender

Warrant against Mackay for wearing Highland dress, 1751. As part of the Government's measures to quell Scotland after Culloden, Highland dress was proscribed.

he ever saw", readily provided the party with food, drink and lodging for the night, setting them next day on their way to Portree. There, in a room at the Inn, Charles bade farewell to Flora. "For all that has happened, I hope, Madam," he said as he left her, "we shall meet in St James's yet."

From Portree Charles, believing he could count on help from MacLeod of Raasay, now crossed to that island, recently sacked by the Red Coats, but, finding it offered no real cover, returned immediately to Skye, where this time he took refuge near Strathardle in the south of the island with the staunchly Jacobite Mackinnons, whose old Chief John readily escorted him back across stormy seas from Elgol to Mallaig on the mainland.* In Morar, after yet another narrow escape from some militiamen, the Prince had a disheartening encounter with old Clanranald, who happened to be in the neighbourhood. "What muckle devil has brought him to this country again?" exclaimed the old Chief, whose enthusiasm for the Prince and his cause was by now beginning to wane. Nor was he much better received by MacDonald of Morar, Lochiel's brother-in-law, who, on meeting him, "became very cool and backward". But Mackinnon remained staunchly loyal, staying with him until he could hand him over to Angus MacDonald of Borrodale, who had helped him when he landed in Morar the year before, and since his own house had been burned down, had been skulking nearby in a hut in the woods.

Almost immediately after this came the news that old Mackinnon, whose clan had been out in the Fifteen as well as the Forty-five, had been taken. The pursuit was closing

* Originally natives of Mull, the Mackinnons, having lost most of their land there to the Macleans, had moved to Skye in the fourteenth century.

Tombstone of Duncan McKenzie, showing him killing a Dragoon at Prestonpans, 1745. It was erected by his grandson in the early 19th century at Eilean Munde, Argyll.

in on every side. In the knowledge that to landward side they were by this time cut off by a regular line of militia posts, while out at sea naval vessels patrolled the coast, the decision was now taken to try somehow to break through to the East. Guided by Borrodale's son and by MacDonald of Glenaladale who had served as a major in Clanranald's regiment, the Prince in the end somehow managed to slip between two enemy posts and reach the neighbourhood of Loch Arkaig. There they were joined by Lochiel's brother, Dr Archibald Cameron, who led them through Chisholm and Fraser territory to Strathglass, some twenty miles to the west of Inverness.* In Strathglass the Prince took shelter in a cave, where he was joined by young Clanranald, who from the first had shown himself a stauncher Jacobite than his father. It was now, at Corriegoe, in the hills between Loch Cluanie and Glen Affric, that the Prince first met the Seven Men of Glenmoriston, as they were called, all of whom had fought in his army and who now became his devoted bodyguard, foraging for him and guiding him from hiding-place to hiding-place.

There were still at this time in the Western Highlands places where a man, if he so chose, could skulk in relative safety, provided he had food and was timeously informed of the enemy's movements. In the woods near Achnacarry a group of Camerons were guarding the wounded Lochiel, who had somehow been brought there from Culloden, while Cluny Macpherson, too, dwelt in relative security, hidden in Badenoch or on the slopes of Ben Alder. Another Jacobite fugutive at this time was Lord Pitsligo who, thanks to the loyalty of his Forbes clansmen, was able to hide in his own country on Donside from 1746 until his death in 1762.

On 14 August the Prince and Glenaladale and some of the men of Glenmoriston went by Glengarry to Achnasaul at the eastern end of Loch Arkaig, where they were joined by MacDonald of Lochgarry. Thence they made their way to the neighbourhood of Achnacarry, where they received a message from Lochiel by his brother Dr Archie to say that the Prince would be safe where he himself was now hiding in Badenoch, to the east of the Great Glen. Glenaladale now took his leave of the

Simon, Lord Lovat, 1746, the last peer in the U.K. to be beheaded. The English jibe was "Scots seldom return home if they really have a head on their shoulders".

* The Chisholms first came to the Highlands from further south when Robert Chisholm became Constable of Castle Urquhart in 1359.

Prince, handing him over to Lochgarry and Dr Cameron. On 30 August, by Loch Ericht on the south-eastern slope of Ben Alder, some twenty-five miles east of Fort William, they finally met Lochiel, who entertained them there and then to a much needed meal of mutton and whisky and minced collops.

Two days later, on 1 September, they were joined by Cluny Macpherson and with him moved two days after that higher up Ben Alder to "a romantic comical habitation", a kind of hut, built into the hillside in a wood on the upper slopes of Ben Alder and known as Cluny's Cage. Here the Prince was to spend a week in relative comfort in the company of Cluny, Lochiel, Lochgarry and Dr Cameron, and here on 13 September they at last received the news that there were French ships at anchor in Loch nan Uamh.

Setting out that same night, they marched north between Ben Alder and Loch Ericht, then west through the Ben Alder forest and past the south end of Loch Laggan towards Glen Roy and the River Lochy. Crossing the Lochy by moonlight in a leaky old craft, they came again to Achnacarry, where they stopped for a day, continuing the following night by Loch Arkaig to Borrodale and Loch nan Uamh, where Charles had landed fourteen months before. There at long last the Prince boarded the French ship *L'Heureux*, which soon after weighed anchor and set sail for France. With him went Lochiel, Dr Archie Cameron and Lochgarry. Cluny, for his part, did not accompany the Prince, but continued for the next eight years to skulk undisturbed in his cage before in his turn finally escaping to France.

For five months the Prince, a hunted fugitive with a price of £30,000 on his head, had wandered with only two or three companions through the Western Highlands and Islands. Thanks to the loyalty and resourcefulness of his friends, and possibly to the half-heartedness of some of those who were supposed to be searching for him, he was never captured. *Bliadhna Thearlaich*, Charlie's Year, as they called it in Gaelic, was over. It was to bring a heavy toll of suffering to the Highlands.

CHAPTER XVIII

Highlanders Post Culloden

The Rising of 1745 gave the Government in London and their numerous friends in Scotland the opportunity they had long been seeking for a final reckoning with the Highlanders. In Cumberland, aptly named the Butcher, they found the ideal instrument for this task. After Culloden no quarter was given. Hundreds of Highland wounded were shot, bayoneted or, where it was more convenient, burned alive. Such prisoners as were taken were treated in such a way that they died by hundreds and detachments of Government troops were sent out into the territory of the clans who had been loyal to Prince Charles to hunt down the fugitives, loot and burn the houses, drive away the cattle and devastate the country. To crown the Duke's triumph, he received in May a loyal address from the General Assembly of the Church of Scotland which spoke in fulsome terms of the "public blessings" he had conferred "on mankind".

Badly frightened by the extent and initial success of the Rising, the London Government followed up Cumberland's efforts with a number of acts of policy deliberately designed to prevent any risk of a Jacobite revival by crushing the spirit of the Highlanders and methodically destroying the Highland way of life. The Episcopal Church, which was suspected of favouring the Jacobite cause, was savagely persecuted. Most of the Jacobite leaders who had not died in battle or escaped abroad were tried and executed and hundreds of clansmen sent to the plantations. Even the aged Lovat who, after his brief encounter with the Prince had taken refuge on an island in remote Loch Morar, was eventually hunted down by the Redcoats and carried off to London for trial and execution. At the same time the lands of the Jacobite chiefs were forfeited and a determined attempt made to destroy the clan system once and for all. A special Disarming Act, passed in 1746 by Lord Chancellor Hardwicke, imposed severe penalties not only for carrying or possessing arms, but for wearing the kilt, plaid or any other tartan garment. The pipes were prohibited as "an instrument of war". The heritable jurisdictions of the chiefs were abolished and a number of other measures taken to break their power and destroy their old patriarchal relationship with their clans.

For all this, spies sent out by Lord Albermarle, who had succeeded Cumberland as Commander-in-Chief in Scotland, reported that, if only help could be obtained from France, the Macleans, Grants of Glenmoriston, Macphersons, Macdonells of Glengarry and Camerons, were all eager "to do it again". On 15 May 1752, Campbell of Glenure,

"Lochaber No More", by John Watson Nicol, 1883.

while engaged in evicting tenants from the forfeited Jacobite lands of Lochiel and Ardshiel in Appin, was shot dead in broad daylight by a marksman who, thanks to good planning and to the widespread sympathy his action commanded, got clean away, though the Duke of Argyll and a Campbell jury saw to it that another, innocent man, James Stewart of Acharn, was hanged in his place. Even as late as 1770 secret agents were to report to an anxious Argyll that the Macleans were still "stirring".

But by this time there was no longer any real hope for the Jacobite cause. Prince Charles, since 1766 in his turn "King over the water" and by now a belated convert to Protestantism, was living in a

Colonel Alasdair Macdonnell of Glengarry.

The Hon. William Gordon in Huntley tartan, by Pompeo Batoni, 1766.

fusty Italian palace, a pathetic, rather drunken, elderly gentleman with a pretentious, unfaithful German wife and no legitimate child. On his death in 1788 he was succeeded as head of the House of Stuart by his younger brother Henry, Cardinal York, who by entering the Church had effectively destroyed the prospects of his dynasty, but nevertheless now assumed the style of Henry IX. In 1807, he too died, leaving his remote cousin King George III with at least as good a claim to the British throne as anyone else.

While the Jacobites continued to suffer for another forty years for their loyalty to the Stewart cause, life was somewhat easier for clans who had consistently supported the London Government. Among these, and in some ways typical of them, were the Brodies of Brodie. Over the centuries the Brodies had no more than their neighbours entirely escaped the vicissitudes of Highland history. In the 1560s the lands of Alexander Twelfth of Brodie had been briefly forfeited for his apparent hostility to Mary Queen of Scots, but duly restored to him in 1566, by when his offence seemed more readily excusable. It was now that, feeling more confident, he added the handsome southwest tower to his castle. In 1638 Alexander's great-grandson, the 15th Chief, another Alexander, signed the National Covenant. Having, though a strong Puritan and a keen Covenanter, attended Charles II's coronation at Scone, and having, it was claimed, shown himself "resolved and determined in the strength of the Lord to eschew and avoid all employment under Cromwell", Alexander had visited London shortly after the Restoration to seek reparation for the financial losses he had sustained during those difficult times, but only to be rebuffed and, worse still, fined a further £4800. Perhaps not surprisingly, the 18th century had in consequence found the Brodies disgusted with the Stewarts and firm adherents of the House of Hanover. In 1715 Brodie was

The Blind Ossian singing, by Alexander Runciman. Ossian poetry did much to revive Gaelic culture, in spite of the fact that it turned out to be fraudulent.

227

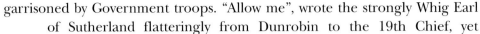

Dr Johnson walking in the Hebrides. Engraving by T. Trotter.

garrisoned by Government troops. "Allow me", wrote the strongly Whig Earl of Sutherland flatteringly from Dunrobin to the 19th Chief, yet another Alexander, "to call your seat Castle Brodie instead of house, since it has been garrisoned in so good a cause." And thirty years later Cumberland was likewise to find in him a loyal friend. In the 18th century great gardens were in vogue. Appointed Lord Lyon King of Arms in 1727, Alexander Brodie spent everything he had on laying out a truly magnificent formal garden and died in 1754 leaving his estate heavily burdened with unpaid debts to the tune of 18,268 pounds fifteen shillings and fourpence halfpenny. Luckily, later Brodies managed to restore the family fortunes by good marriages and successful commercial ventures in India, whence, like other hard-up Highlanders, they returned in due course as nabobs, with the happy result that the 19th Laird's magnificent garden has survived to this day as one of the glories of Nairnshire.

In the last quarter of the eighteenth century some attempt was made to redress the wrongs which had been done to the Highlands. In 1782 the Disarming Act of 1746, which proscribed the wearing of Highland dress and the playing of the pipes, was repealed, and in 1784 many of the forfeited Jacobite estates were returned to their rightful owners, while during the Seven Years War the Government took regiments, recruited from clansmen who barely a dozen years before had fought for Prince Charles.

But by now the ancient Highland way of life had disappeared for ever. By the legislation with which they sought to break the clan system and by destroying the old patriarchal links between chief and clan, the London Government had succeeded in turning the surviving chiefs, whether Jacobite or Whig, into mere landed proprietors, some of whom no longer felt the same sense of responsibility for their clansmen and dependents as formerly but, in appallingly difficult times, were desperately concerned to make their estates pay.

The easiest method of doing this, they now discovered, was to turn them over to sheep farming. For this purpose large areas of land were required; and so, at the end of the eighteenth and during the first half of the nineteenth century in many parts of the Highlands, farms were cleared and taken over and the tenants evicted. Some of these turned, where it was possible, to crofting or fishing. Others emigrated to North America or

Fingal's Cave, an engraving from Thomas Pennant.

enlisted in the new Highland regiments. Thousands more drifted into the already overcrowded cities. Soon in the glens little heaps of stones amid the grass and nettles were all that remained of what had once been sizeable *clachans* and townships.

Much has been written about the clearances. While there can be no doubt that some landed proprietors in the Highlands, many of them by now incomers, behaved with heartless brutality, others did all they could to avoid hardship to local communities. For example, Lovat and Mackenzie of Cromartie not only refused to clear but gave shelter to the victims of neighbouring clearances. Lord MacDonald, Robertson of Struan and Macleod of Macleod literally ruined themselves in their efforts to give relief to the victims of economic stress. Others, like the Macnab who, it should be said, seems to have brought his clansmen over with him as bond servants, themselves emigrated to North America with their clansmen, while yet others, like the Campbell Lord

Breadalbane, were attacked by Robert Burns for actually seeking to prevent their clansmen from emigrating. Ironically enough, the landlord usually held responsible for the worst clearances of all, the high principled, Liberal, English Marquess of Stafford who, having married the Sutherland heiress, was later created first Duke of Sutherland, was firmly convinced that, as a Liberal, he was acting in a thoroughly progressive and enlightened manner in evicting his tenants from their substandard homes. But, despite his well-intentioned experiments in social engineering, the fact remains that the population of Sutherland continued even so to increase and was actually larger after the clearances than before.

Meanwhile, with the arrival of thousands of uprooted Highlanders, the population of the cities and industrial areas increased by leaps and bounds. From 12,000 at the time of the Union, the population of Glasgow, now very largely of Highland origin, had risen by 1830 to over 200,000, reaching a million in 1931. The result, not unnaturally, was fearful

"Honours of Scotland", by Denis Dighton. Clan Gregor formed the guard of honour when the Scottish Regalia were carried in procession from the Crown Room, during the visit of George IV.

overcrowding and appalling living conditions. Soon the simple, mainly rural economy of Scotland had been replaced by a more complex one. People no longer lived from the produce of their own districts. In the Clyde Valley, in particular, industrial areas, matched by corresponding concentrations of population, were fast beginning to grow up. With increasing economic development, better means of transport became a necessity and in the Highlands General Wade's strategic roads were used as a starting point for a more comprehensive road system.

"Discovery of the Honours of Scotland", by David Wilkie. Sir Walter Scott found the Scottish Regalia in the Crown Room.

BONNIE WILLIE.

And now, by an odd quirk of fortune, the Highlands, "that vile spot" as Cumberland had called them, suddenly became fashionable. The trend had started in the second half of the eighteenth century with Ossian, an ancient Celtic bard of doubtful identity, whose poems, collected or possibly fabricated by the Rev. James MacPherson, a kinsman of Cluny's, had an immediate vogue, leading to the rediscovery of a hitherto largely unsuspected Celtic culture and folklore, while at the same time setting off a prolonged and acrimonious literary controversy. Not long after this the "great Cham of literature" himself, Dr Samuel Johnson, hitherto notorious as a detractor of Scotland and the Scots and of Ossian in particular, undertook a

"Bonnie Willie", by Cruikshank. George IV's coronation was a gift for the caricaturists. Here Sir William Curtis is lampooned.

Sir John Sinclair of Ulbster, by Raeburn. Sinclair was the leading Scottish agriculturist who helped prepare the first "Statistical Account" of Scotland.

journey of investigation through the Highlands and Islands, of which he later published an interesting and not unsympathetic account, as did his companion James Boswell. Indeed, it is to Johnson that we owe the acid and painfully apt comment that "to govern peaceably by having no subjects is an expedient that argues no great profundity of policy". Over the years other travellers followed. This was the age of the Romantic Revival. By the turn of the century the Highlands had, with the ready help of two Lowlanders, Robert Burns, himself a Jacobite in retrospect, and, better still, Sir Walter Scott, begun to appear in an increasingly romantic and attractive light.

The ensuing cult reached a climax when in 1822 King George IV himself paid a State visit to Edinburgh, picturesquely attired in full Highland dress, the first reigning monarch to set foot in Scotland since Charles II's short but eventful sojourn in 1650. Though the twenty-stone King did not actually venture into the Highlands, the visit was with Sir Walter Scott's help made memorable by an

unprecedented display of gaily coloured tartans and other Highland gear, especially produced for the occasion by the enterprising tradesmen of the capital, while General David Stewart of Garth, a direct descendant of the Wolf of Badenoch, gave much valuable advice to all concerned on matters military, sartorial and historical. In his enthusiasm Sir Walter even took to addressing the solidly Lowland Duke of Buccleuch as "my beloved chief"; and in the course of the proceedings, which lasted for several days, a number of normally self-respecting Lowland lairds proudly displayed themselves in Highland costumes, which their fathers and

Plan of Thurso, 1802, by Sir John Sinclair..

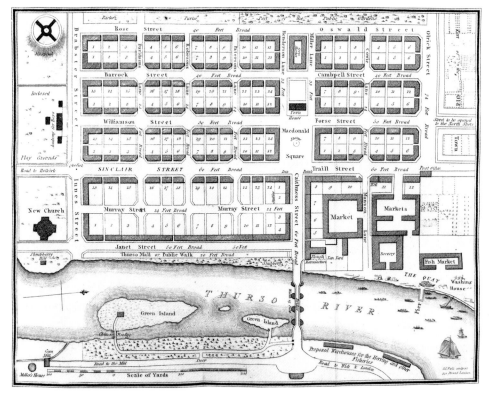

Tobermory, Mull, by William Daniell.

Portree, by William Daniell. After improvements, 130 ships were known to have anchored off its pier, including Baltic traders, in the 19th century.

grandfathers, who regarded Highlanders as being akin to Hottentots, would not willingly have been seen dead in. Even so, few excelled the Lord Mayor of London, a biscuit-manufacturer from Wapping, who, loyally following his sovereign's example, dutifully draped himself from head to foot in what both had been assured was the Royal Stewart tartan.

Eviction of tenants. Early photograph.

With what can only be termed poetic justice, a leading part in these colourful ceremonies was played by Major General Sir Evan MacGregor of MacGregor, a former Governor of the Windward Isles and Father of those same Children of the Mist, whom successive Kings and governments had over the centuries sought so assiduously to exterminate. It was he who, rising to his feet at a banquet held in that same Parliament House where his forebears had been outlawed and prosecuted, proposed on behalf of his fellow chiefs the toast, "the King – the Chief of Chiefs"; and it was his clan, ironically enough, who were privileged to escort the Honours of Scotland to and from Edinburgh Castle. In recording this latter-day apotheosis of Clan Gregor, who in 1822 founded one of the earliest Clan Societies in

"The Last of the Clans", by Thomas Faed, 1865. A romantic view of Highland emigration.

Black house in ruins, North Uist. The Scots dispersed abroad as a result of the clearances.

John Murray, 4th Earl of Dunmore, Mayor of New York, Governor of the Bahamas, by Reynolds, 1765 (far right).

existence, it is perhaps worth recalling that over the years no less than twenty-two of Sir Evan's forebears had been hanged, four beheaded, three murdered (two shot in the back), five killed in battle and one, who had prudently emigrated to America, scalped by Red Indians not long after his arrival there.

Another Highland phenomenon, scarcely less remarkable than the Royal Visit of 1822, was the sudden appearance, at about this time, of two mysterious, bearded brothers, who emerged from nowhere, calling themselves Sobieski Stewart and claiming, without the slightest justification, to be descendants of Bonny Prince Charlie. No doubt under the impression that he was carrying on a family tradition and somehow striking a last blow for a lost cause, the Lord Lovat of the day generously provided the brothers with a handsome residence on the same island in the Beauly River, where his forebear Simon had a century before raped his first cousin's widow, and where rather more recently the present author spent his honeymoon. There the brothers, known locally as the Princes, passed their time in mediaeval pageantry and in compiling a register of clan tartans, which, while it bore but little relation to historical reality,

Archibald Macnab of Macnab, coloniser of Upper Canada, circa 1781–1860.

indirectly made a useful and enduring contribution to the national economy and provided all and sundry with a clan tartan which they could without too painful a stretch of the imagination call their own. From their *Vestiarium Scoticum,* allegedly based on a 16th century manuscript, "formerly in the Library of the Scots College at Douay", and other works, are drawn with few exceptions the setts worn to this day by the majority of Highland clans, another generally accepted authority being James Logan, whose *Scottish Gael* was published in 1831. More usefully still, a descendant of the same Lord Lovat has in our own time compiled one of the best available books on the subject.*

Much has been written about "the garb of old Gaul". In fact, some individual clan and family tartans may possibly have existed in the eighteenth century and a few even earlier. For instance, we know that, under a charter dated 1597, in the days of Sir Lachlan Mor, the feu-duty payable on certain Maclean lands in Islay took the form of sixty ells of green, black and white cloth, the colours of the present Maclean hunting tartan. But until the raising of the Highland Regiments, most Highlanders seem to have worn belted tartan plaids of whatever colours came handy or caught their fancy or blended best with the local landscape, and it was not until much later that different specific setts and colours were used by individual clans. Thus none of the unfortunate Jacobite prisoners so conveniently used by Morier as models for his carefully painted

* Christian Hesketh. *Tartans.* London 1981.

First gathering of the Bendigo Caledonian Society, in January 1890, by George Lacey. The Scots abroad established flourishing clan societies.

contemporary picture of Redcoats bayoneting Highlanders at Culloden are wearing any recognizable clan tartan. What in fact seems probable is that after the raising of the Black Watch and the introduction of the dark blue, black and green Government tartan, when it was specifically laid down by General Wade that "the plaid of each company is to be as near as they can be of the same sort and colour", a number of Whig clans, notably the Campbells, took to wearing this as their own clan tartan with or without added stripes of one colour or another. And not, as is sometimes suggested, the other way round. In particular, the Gordons added a yellow stripe to the Government tartan and the Seaforths a red and a white. The kilt as worn today appears to have been invented in the late eighteenth century by an English iron-master, Thomas Rawlinson, who, while living and working in the Highlands, hit on the novel and quite practical idea of dividing the original all-enveloping belted plaid into two halves, an upper and a lower, the lower being stitched into neat pleats.

Any previous neglect of Scotland by her monarchs was more than made up for by Queen Victoria, who, with her brightly kilted consort, Prince Albert of Saxe-Coburg-Gotha, regularly spent her summer holidays in the Highlands, describing them day by day and in great detail in her *Journal of Our Life in the Highlands.* "We were always," she wrote, "in the habit of conversing with the Highlanders – with whom one comes so much in contact in the Highlands. The Prince highly appreciated the good-breeding, simplicity,

and intelligence which make it so pleasant and even instructive to talk to them." And again: "The view was so beautiful over the dear hills: the day so fine; the whole so *gemuthlich*." It is a tradition which has been most happily continued by her descendants.

As a result of massive and often enforced emigration, numerous colonies of expatriate Highlanders have over the last three hundred years sprung up in North America and, more recently, in Australia and New Zealand, bringing with them to the New World the habits, traditions and native culture of their forebears. To realise the full extent and endurance of this Highland heritage it is only necessary to visit one or other of the Gaelic-speaking villages of Nova Scotia or Cape Breton Island, to take one of many examples.

Settlers from the Highlands reached the New World in a number of different ways. As early as 1685, Sir Aeneas Macpherson of Inverestrie possessed five thousand acres in Pennsylvania. The Great Lochiel, likewise, owned land in the West Indies and in 1734 one of his grandsons took "a cargo of people" from Lochaber to Jamaica. As founder and Governor of Georgia, the English General Oglethorpe brought a hundred and thirty Highlanders from Inverness-shire, wearing tartan plaids and armed with broadswords and targes to help defend that colony's southern frontier against the Spaniards. In 1739 three hundred and fifty colonists from Argyll settled in North Carolina. In the 1730s too, a Captain Lachlan Campbell from Islay went to New York to arrange for several hundred settlers to go to the colony from the Hebrides and elsewhere, while not long after some Mackintoshes of Borlum led two hundred of their clan to Georgia, where they settled to the south of Savannah. From a Mackintosh of Borlum who reached America at this time and married a Creek redskin is descended Waldo E. Mackintosh, principal Chief of the Creek Nation – who number over twenty thousand and live for the most part in Oklahoma. In 1802 a MacNeil chieftain from Barra led three hundred and seventy clansmen to North America, whence in our own century one of his descendants returned as Chief of the Clan to rebuild and restore his ancestral castle. After the Risings of 1715 and 1745, hundreds of Jacobite prisoners were transported to the American Colonies and the West Indies to work on the plantations or as indentured servants. Of the thousands of Highlanders who served in North America in the Seven Years War many, both officers

93rd Sutherland Highlanders, by R. Poate, 1852.

and other ranks, were given grants of land in Prince Edward Island and the Hudson River Valley and stayed on there after the war was over, thereby strengthening the colony's northern defences. Altogether between the end of the Seven Years War and the outbreak of the American War of Independence some twenty thousand people seem to have left the Highlands for North America.

In the latter conflict large numbers of Highland immigrants were involved on both sides, many former Jacobites fighting, ironically enough, for the Duke of Cumberland's nephew, King George III. Thus Colonel Allan Maclean of Torloisk in Mull raised the Royal Highland Emigrant Regiment which fought throughout the war, wearing Highland uniform, and were later rewarded with grants of land in Canada. Flora MacDonald and her husband Allan MacDonald of Kingsburgh, who had emigrated to Cumberland county in 1772, were, surprisingly enough, likewise loyal to King George, with the result that Allan and one of their sons were taken prisoner, losing in the end all their possessions and eventually returning home penniless, thoroughly disgusted with what they had seen of the American Revolution.

After the war was over, many American colonists of Highland descent, whose loyalty was to the old country, moved from the United States to Canada, settling in Nova Scotia, New Brunswick and Ontario, where in the years that followed they were joined by fresh waves of Highland settlers. In the early years of the nineteenth century Australia likewise became a fresh outlet for Highland settlement. In particular, Lachlan Macquarrie, an early Governor, did much to encourage settlers from his native isle of

"The Thin Red Line". 93rd (Sutherland) Highlanders at Balaclava, by Gibb.

241

Mull and from the Western Highlands and Islands in general.

Over the last two hundred years and more the Highland Regiments of the British Army have played a vital part in keeping alive clan feeling and the Highland tradition, reflecting in a sense the special spirit and special characteristics of the clan regiments who fought for the last time at Culloden. One early Highland Regiment was the Earl of Argyll's Regiment, raised by the Tenth Earl in 1689, a company of which under Campbell of Glenlyon were almost immediately used to carry out the notorious massacre of Glencoe. The first Highland regiment to be formed after the Union was the Black Watch. This grew out of the Independent Companies which the Government had raised from Whig clansmen after the Rising of 1715 primarily for the purpose of keeping order in the Highlands. In 1725 six such companies were raised with the help of the Earl of Atholl, Cluny Macpherson and Lord Lovat, who himself for a time commanded one of them. They wore the dark green, blue and black Government tartan and, to distinguish them from *Saighdearan Dearg* – the Red Soldiers – in other words, regular troops, were known as *Am Freiceadan Dubh* – the Black Watch. This name passed to the regular regiment which in 1739 was formed from them at the suggestion of Duncan Forbes of Culloden. A War Office manual published in 1742 explained how Highland Dress should be worn. Four years later, following Lord Hardwicke's edict, soldiers in the Highland Regiments became the only Highlanders entitled to wear it. Originally raised for service at home in a counter-insurgency role, the Black Watch were nevertheless, much to their disgust, sent overseas in 1743 and fought bravely with the British Army at the battle of Fontenoy in Flanders in 1745. That same year the Government, encouraged by the success of the Black Watch, authorised the Campbell Earl of Loudoun to raise another Highland regiment, Loudoun's Highlanders, who, however, after serving with no great distinction against their fellow Highlanders in the Forty-five, were disbanded in 1748.

In 1757, despite the sustained opposition of Lord Chancellor Hardwicke, who declared it "an act of imprudence", the elder Pitt, needing troops for the Seven Years War which had broken out the year before, took the bold and imaginative step of authorising the formation of two more Regiments from Highlanders, many of whom had been directly or indirectly involved in the recent Rising. One of those to whom the Government entrusted this task was Simon Fraser, Master of Lovat, son of the Lord Lovat who had been forfeited and executed ten years earlier for high treason and who as a young man had himself taken part in the Forty-five. "Without estate, money or

Pipes played at Waterloo by George Mackay and at entry of George IV into Edinburgh.

influence," wrote General Stewart of Garth, "beyond that influence which flowed from attachment to his family, person and name, this gentleman (Simon Fraser) in a few weeks found himself at the head of eight hundred men recruited by himself. The gentlemen of the country and the officers of the regiment added more than seven hundred and thus a battalion was formed of thirteen companies of one hundred and five rank and file each, making in all one thousand four hundred men, including sixty five sergeants and thirty pipers and drummers." There could scarcely have been a better illustration of enduring loyalties to a family and clan. A story still told in a family of Canadian Frasers illustrates as well as anything the kind of relationship that existed between clansmen and Chief. In 1759 the Fraser Highlanders were amongst the British troops who with General Wolfe stormed the Heights of Abraham. Having landed with his men at the foot of the high cliffs that needed to be climbed, the Master of Lovat called for "the man who stole a cheese from the tower of Fairburn", adding that anyone who could climb the tower of Fairburn could scale the Heights of Abraham. On stepping forward, the cheese-stealer was detailed to lead the way up the cliff and others followed. Having reached the top, they stormed the French battery they found there and by first light the Heights had been secured. Interestingly enough, when, almost a century and a half later, the 16th Lord Lovat called for recruits for the Lovat Scouts which he raised to fight in the Boer War, the response from all over Inverness-shire was equally prompt and enthusiastic.

Major Archibald Montgomerie, who raised another new Highland regiment, Montgomerie's Highlanders, seems to have been scarcely less successful. Though himself a Lowlander, he had Highland connections and, we are told by General Stewart

"The Reel of Tulloch",
19th-century photograph.

of Garth, "mixed much with the people", and, "being a high spirited young man with a considerable dash of romantic enthusiasm in his composition and with manners cheerful and affable, made himself highly acceptable to the Highlanders".   Among those who served in his regiment was old Allan Maclean of Ardgour's son James, who a score of years earlier had fought at Culloden for Prince Charles and who, on 1 June 1767, was killed at sea in an action with a privateer, fighting, this time, for King George.*

From the Government's point of view the experiment was to prove an outstanding success. In the first place, it gained for the British Army some of the finest soldiers in the world. "I sought for merit," declared Pitt, "wherever it was to be found. It is my boast that I was the first Minister who looked for it and found it in the mountains of the north. I called it forth and drew into your service a hardy and intrepid race of men....they served with fidelity as they fought with valour and conquered for you in every part of the world."

The Highland Regiments served another purpose, too. They helped remove a potential threat to the House of Hanover. "The Highlanders," wrote General Wolfe, who had fought against them at Culloden and had them under his command in Canada, "are hardy, intrepid, accustomed to rough country, and no greater mischief if

* It was his sister Lady Margaret MacDonald of Sleat who had helped Prince Charlie on his way in 1746.

they fall. How can you better employ a secret enemy than by making his end conducive to the common good?" While to the still unconvinced Lord Hardwicke, Pitt privately commended his decision on the grounds that "not many of them will return". In the long run many former Jacobites fell fighting for King George. Thus old Maclean of Ardgour's son James, who had fought at Culloden, was in 1761 killed fighting in the West Indies with Montgomerie's Highlanders, while Simon Fraser of Inverallochy, whose wounded father had been shot in cold blood on the battlefield of Culloden, was killed scaling the heights of Abraham with the Fraser Highlanders in 1759. Others who survived the war settled, as we have seen, in North America after it was over. Altogether more than 12,000 Highlanders are said to have served in the Seven Years War.

Whatever the London Government's motives in raising the Highland Regiments, there can be no doubt that in the long run their decision to do so helped in its way to heal the wounds left by Culloden. During the four decades which separated the passing of Lord Hardwicke's Disarming Act from its eventual repeal, they afforded many Highlanders an opportunity to consort with their fellow-countrymen in a familiar spirit of comradeship which bore at any rate some resemblance to that of a clan and even allowed them to wear their forbidden national dress under the guise of military uniform.

During the second half of the eighteenth century more Highland Regiments came into being. In the words of a contemporary, "battalions on battalions were raised in the remotest parts of the Highlands, Frasers, MacDonalds, Camerons, Macleans, Macphersons and others of disaffected names and clans were enrolled; their chiefs or connections obtained commissions; the lower class, always ready to follow, they with eagerness endeavoured who should be first enlisted".

Individual Highland Regiments had close links with individual families and clans. Thus between 1793 and 1827 no less than eleven officers of the Cameron Highlanders were sons, brothers, nephews or grandsons of Allan Cameron of Erracht who had originally raised them, while in protesting to the Commander in Chief in 1786 about the proposed disbandment in India of the Second Black Watch, their Commanding Officer, MacLeod of MacLeod, was able to write: "My own company are all of my own name and Clan and if I return to Europe without them I shall be effectually banished from my own home."

In 1775 Simon Fraser, who by then had become a general and managed to regain his father's forfeited estates, though not his title, was invited by George III to raise another regiment of two battalions for service in America, where the War of Independence had just begun. This he did "with equal care and expedition", raising within weeks over two thousand men for the 71st Fraser Highlanders. Among his officers were no less than six other chiefs, Macdonell of Lochgarry, Cluny Macpherson, MacLeod of MacLeod, The Chisholm, The Mackintosh and Cameron of Lochiel, each of whom brought in his train large numbers of his clansmen. By the time the regiment embarked for America, Lochiel, who had brought with him 120 of his own clansmen from his forfeited estates, had fallen seriously ill and could not accompany them, but thanks, we learn, to Lovat's "persuasive eloquence" in the Gaelic tongue, the Cameron contingent, after some initial hesitation, in the end agreed to sail notwithstanding.

Many of the Highland Regiments then raised were in due course disbanded, including Montgomerie's and the Fraser Highlanders, but several have survived until our own times. Of these, the Seaforth Highlanders were raised by Lord Seaforth in Ross-shire and the Hebrides in 1778 and the Cameron Highlanders (with whom they were eventually amalgamated as the Queen's Own Highlanders) by Cameron of Erracht in Lochaber in 1794. The Argyll Highlanders, raised in Argyll by the Duke of Argyll in 1794, and the Sutherland Highlanders, raised in Sutherland and Ross-shire in 1800, were in 1881 amalgamated as the Argyll and Sutherland Highlanders. Recruiting for the Gordon Highlanders in Badenoch in 1784 was greatly expedited by the beautiful Duchess of Gordon who, wearing her own version of their uniform, is said to have kissed each recruit as he enlisted. They were in 1994 amalgamated with the Queen's Own Highlanders to form the Highlanders.

Perhaps the best account of what he calls the military character of the Highlands is given by General Stewart of Garth in a book published in 1822 and directly drawn from his own considerable military experience. "As the simplicity of his life," he writes of the Highland soldier, "gave vigour to his body, so it fortified his mind. He was taught to consider courage as the most honourable virtue, cowardice the most disgraceful failing; to venerate and obey his chief and to devote himself for his native country and clan.... With such principles and regarding any disgrace he might bring on his clan and district as the cruellest misfortune, the Highland private soldier had a

Photograph of a Highland couple dancing, late 1890's.

peculiar motive to exertion. The common soldier of many other countries has scarcely any stimulus to the performance of his duty than the fear of chastisement.... With a Highland soldier it is otherwise. When in a national or district corps, he is surrounded by the companions of his youth and the rivals of his early achievements; he feels the impulse of emulation strengthened by the consciousness that every proof which he displays, either of bravery or cowardice, will find its way to his native home. He thus learns to appreciate the value of a good name; and it is thus that in a Highland regiment, consisting of men from the same country, whose kindred and connections are mutually known, every individual feels that his conduct is the subject of observation and that, independently of this duty, as one member of a systematic whole, he has a separate and individual reputation to sustain, which will be reflected on his family or district or glen. Hence he requires no artificial excitements. He acts from motives within himself; his point is fixed and his aim must terminate either in victory or in death." As anyone who has served in or been associated with a Highland Regiment will know, this is as true today as when it was first written.

Epilogue

The Battle of Culloden is often said to have marked the end both of the clan system and of the old Highland way of life. In a sense, of course, this is true, but for my part I am constantly struck by how much has survived and by the enduring strength of the old loyalties.

The reasons for this are not far to seek. The Clan system, and with it the Highland way of life, was patriarchal and therefore in its essence enduring. The Chief was father of his people. Highlanders are still less concerned than, say, the English with socially divisive questions of class. Possessing as they do a keen sense of history and knowing that they can trace their ancestry back through countless generations of Norse or Celtic Kings, they realise that they are at least as well born as the next man. "For that," wrote Robert Louis Stevenson, "is the mark of the Scot of all classes: that he stands in an attitude towards the past unthinkable to Englishmen, and remembers and cherishes the memory of his forebears, good or bad; and there burns alive in him a sense of identity with the dead even to the twentieth generation." As Chief of Clan Fraser, my wife's father enjoyed reminding his parlour-maid that if by some mishap he and his family were to be wiped out, her brother would have as good a claim as anyone to the Chiefship of their Clan.

I have written of the Highland Regiments and of the part they played in preserving Clan loyalties. Though this may not have been what William Pitt had in mind when he first raised them, there can be no doubt that in the heartrending half century that followed Culloden they did much to keep Highland traditions alive and so won time for some of the bitterness it had engendered to die down and be replaced among Highlanders by a new readiness to make common cause.

In the Highland revival that followed George IV's visit to Scotland in 1822, a multitude of Clan Societies came into being, designed to keep the clan spirit alive, to bring clansmen and clanswomen together and to help them help each other. These were quickly matched by corresponding societies overseas, as well as by St Andrew's and Caledonian Societies, which multiplied, nowhere more than in North America. In the Carolinas and in Georgia, I believe, there are Caledonian Societies that even predate the Union.

During the eighteenth and nineteenth centuries many thousands of Highlanders left Scotland for the New World, some of their own accord, some under pressure of one

Kilchurn Castle,
Loch Awe, Argyll.

Lord Lovat with the Lovat Scouts, 1st contingent, in South Africa until the end of the Boer War.

Opening of the Stables, Clan Donald Visitor Centre, Skye, 1984.

kind or another. But, whatever its causes, the results of this Highland *diaspora* are I believe something that we can take pride in, offering as they do plentiful proof of our native resilience and resourcefulness in the shape of a formidable array of statesmen, administrators, soldiers, sailors, men of letters and captains of industry, all sharing the same enduring pride in their Highland origins.

A year or two ago I was lucky enough to be asked to preside over the Grandfather Mountain Highland Games in North Carolina. I have been to a good many Highland Games, but I can honestly say that I have never seen Games on a more magnificent scale or in a more beautiful setting. What is more, the piping, the dancing and all the other events were of the very highest standard. But what struck me most of all was the enthusiasm these tens of thousands of expatriate

Highlanders felt for their own clans and the land of their forebears to which they flock back whenever the opportunity offers. Here, for all to see, is convincing proof that "the blood is strong, the heart is Highland".

F.M.
Strachur, Argyll

Highland Games at Grandfather mountain, North Carolina.

Glossary

BRODIE

One of the ancient tribes of Morayshire, the Brodies take their name from Brodie near Forres. Malcolm was Thane of Brodie in the time of Alexander III and his son Michael received a Charter from Robert the Bruce in about 1311 erecting the old Celtic Thanage into a Barony. Alexander Brodie of Brodie, born in 1617, was an enthusiastic supporter of the reformed religion. In 1640 he destroyed the carvings and paintings in Elgin Cathedral regarding them as idolatrous. Another Alexander, born in 1697, became Lord Lyon King at Arms and attended assiduously on the Duke of Cumberland throughout the campaign of 1746.

BUCHANAN

The progenitor of the Buchanans, Ansalen O'Cain, son of a King of Ulster, is said to have received from King Malcolm II the lands of Buchanan on Loch Lomondside for his services against the Danes. The island of Clarinch later became the Clan's gathering place in time of war. The Buchanans supported Bruce in the War of Independence and fought at Flodden, where their Chief lost his life. They also took an active part in the battles of Pinkie and Langside. In 1746 Buchanan of Drumnakill betrayed Lord Tullibardine to the Government. The Buchanan lands were sold in 1682 and the principal line became extinct in 1762.

CAMERON

The territory of Clan Cameron has long been mainly in Lochaber. The first Chief of the Clan to be found in historical records is Donald Dhu, reckoned the 11th Chief, who is known to have fought as an ally of the Lord of the Isles at the Battle of Harlaw in 1411. The Camerons were vassals of the Lords of the Isles until their defection with Clan Chattan in 1429. The lands of the Captain of Clan Cameron were erected into the Barony of Lochiel by a Charter from King James V. Achnacarry has been the seat of Cameron of Lochiel, the Chief of the Clan, since the time of Sir Ewen Cameron, 17th of Lochiel, known as The Great Lochiel. The Camerons were among the most loyal supporters of the Jacobite cause and the Cameron lands were forfeited after the Rising of 1745 but later restored. Achnacarry remains to this day the seat of Cameron of Lochiel. The Clan regiment, the Cameron Highlanders, raised by Cameron of Erracht in 1793 and later amalgamated with the Seaforths to form the Queen's Own Highlanders, was always closely connected with the Clan.

CAMPBELL

Through the centuries, the Campbells have been a dominant influence in the Western Highlands. From Diarmid O'Duine they derived their original Celtic name of Clan Duihne. In the thirteenth century Archibald Campbell obtained by marriage the Lordship of Lochow. Sir Colin, progenitor of the Campbells of Argyll, was knighted in 1280. From him successive Chiefs derive the patronym MacCailein Mhor. Colin's son, Sir Neil, married Lady Marjorie Bruce and thereafter the Campbells played a leading part in national affairs, in the main as supporters of the national government. In 1464 Colin, 1st Earl of Argyll, became Master of the Royal Household and in 1483 Lord High Chancellor of Scotland. Since 1472 Inveraray Castle on Loch Fyne has been the seat of the Campbell Chiefs. Archibald the 4th Earl was a leading supporter of the Reformation. In 1701 Archibald the 10th Earl was created Duke of Argyll. Clan Campbell played a vital part in defeating the Jacobite movement. By the middle of the eighteenth century the Campbells were by far the most powerful Clan in Scotland.

Next to the Earls and Dukes of Argyll the most important branch of Clan Campbell were the Campbells of Glen Orchy. John Campbell of Glen Orchy was created Earl of Breadalbane in 1681. From Sir John Campbell, 3rd son of the 2nd Earl of Argyll, spring the Campbells of Calder or Cawdor, Earls of Cawdor.

CLAN CHATTAN

Clan Chattan was in its origin a tribal community or confederation of clans under Mackintosh hegemony in Lochaber, Strathnairn and Badenoch, which included the Farquharsons, the Shaws, the Macphersons, the MacGillivrays, McBains, Macqueens and Macleans of Dochgarroch. During the Rising of 1745 Alexander MacCillivray of Dunmaglas commanded the combined forces of Clan Chattan and was killed at Culloden.

CHISHOLM

The Chisholms take their name from Chishom in Roxburghshire. They moved to the Highlands in 1359, when Robert Chisholm of that Ilk succeeded his maternal grandfather, Sir Robert Lauder, as Royal Constable of Castle Urquhart, at the same time inheriting from him lands in Moray near Elgin and Nairn. His son Alexander married the heiress of Erchless and Strathglass in Inverness-shire, which had originally belonged to the Anglo-Norman Bissets. By the 17th century the Chisholm Chief had come to be known as *an Siosalach* or The Chisholm. In the Jacobite Rising of 1715 the Chisholms supported Lord Mar and in 1745 Roderick, a younger son of the then Chief, was killed at Culloden. In 1887 the Chiefship passed through an heiress to James Gooden-Chisholm whose descendant is recognised as Chief.

COLQUHOUN

The Colquhouns took their name from the lands of Colquhoun on Loch Lomondside. These were granted to Humphrey of Kilpatrick in the time of Alexander II. Sir Robert Kilpatrick of Colquhoun married the daughter of the Laird of Luss, since when Colquhoun Chiefs have been known as Colquhoun of Luss, their residence being at

Rossdhu (the Black Headland) on Loch Lomond. In 1602 the Colquhouns suffered severe losses in a savage encounter with the MacGregors in Glenfruin. In 1702 Anne the daughter of Sir Humphrey Colquhoun 17th of Luss married James Grant of Pluscardine, second son of Grant of that Ilk, who assumed the name and arms of Colquhoun, and succeeded his father-in-law as Sir James Colquhoun of Luss. Sir James later became Chief of Clan Grant in his own right. Their eldest son carried on the line of Grant of Grant while their second son became Colquhoun of Luss.

CUMMING

The Cummings, Comyns or Cummins were of Norman origin. The first to settle in Scotland was William Comyn who became Chancellor of Scotland in the time of King David and received a grant of land in Roxburgh. After 1230 the Comyns became Lords of Badenoch and also held much of Lochaber and the Great Glen. In 1242, as a result of marriages to Celtic dynastic heiresses, Alexander Comyn was Earl of Buchan, Walter was Earl of Menteith and John was Earl of Angus. By this time nearly one quarter of the Scottish Earls were Comyns and they had come to have as much Celtic as Norman blood. Their Chief, the Black Comyn, was one of the competitors for the Crown of Scotland. His son, the Red Comyn, was stabbed to death by Robert Bruce who during and after the long war that followed very largely managed to destroy the Comyns. Since the Middle Ages their Chiefs have held the Barony of Altyre near Forres, where they now reside. In 1804 Sir Alexander Cumming of Altyre was created a baronet. On succeeding to the estates of Gordon of Gordonstoun he took the name of Gordon-Cumming.

DRUMMOND

The Drummonds take their name from Drymen or Drummond in Stirlingshire. Sir Malcolm Drymen or Drummond fought for Robert the Bruce at Bannockburn, greatly contributing to Bruce's victory by strewing the field of battle with caltrops or spikes which helped disable the English cavalry. The Drummond motto "Gang Warily" is an allusion to this. In the 14th century John Drummond became John Drummond of Stobhall, still the present Chief's home. The Barony of Drummond was created in 1488 in favour of Sir John Drummond and in 1605 the 4th Lord Drummond was created Earl of Perth. The Drummonds were loyal supporters of the Stewart cause. James the 4th Earl was appointed Lord High Chancellor of Scotland in 1684. On the accession of King James VII he openly declared himself a Roman Catholic. He was made a founder Knight of the Order of the Thistle on its revival in 1687, as was his brother Lord Melfort, and made a Duke by King James VII after his flight to France. In the Jacobite Rising of 1715 the 2nd Duke of Perth commanded the Jacobite cavalry at the Battle of Sheriffmuir while the 3rd Duke was one of the principal Jacobite leaders in the Rising of 1745.

FARQUHARSON

The Farquharsons of Invercauld in Aberdeenshire are a prominent branch of Clan Chattan. They trace their descent from Farquhar, son of Shaw of Rothiemurchus, owner of the Braes of Mar. Farquhar's son Donald married Isobel Stewart, heiress of Invercauld. Their son Finlay who was killed at the Battle of Pinkie in 1547 is reckoned progenitor of the Clan. Strong supporters of the Stewart cause, they played a leading part in the Jacobite Risings of 1715 and 1745. In 1715 John Farquharson of Invercauld was Colonel of the Clan Chattan Regiment. In the '45 Anne Farquharson, known as Colonel Anne, wife of Angus 22nd Chief of Clan Mackintosh, raised Clan Mackintosh for Prince Charles, while her husband fought on the Hanoverian side.

FORBES

Clan Forbes trace their descent from Ochonachar. In the Middle Ages the Braes of Forbes in Aberdeenshire were in thrall to a savage bear which made that part of Donside uninhabitable, slaying nine maidens by the Nine Maidens Well in the Parish of Forbes. Having slain the bear, Ochonochar settled in the territory he had won from it. Sir John Forbes of Forbes, who lived during the reigns of King Robert II and King Robert III, had four sons. The eldest, Alexander, was raised to the peerage by King James I in 1442 as Lord Forbes. From his three younger sons sprang the families of Pitsligo, Culloden, Waterton and Foveran. The Braes of Forbes became the *duthus* of Forbes and still belong to their Chief, Lord Forbes, the premier Baron of Scotland, who resides at Balforbes on Donside. His arms are three bears' heads muzzled. The bear was sacred to the ancient Celts. The old Celtic word for bear was *arth*. Arthur has long been a popular Forbes name.

FRASER

The Frasers are of Norman origin. In the 11th century a knightly family in Anjou named Frezel gave their name to the signeurie of La Frèzelière. In 1160 Simon Fraser held lands in East Lothian. His descendant Simon was a leading supporter of both Sir William Wallace and King Robert the Bruce. Captured by the English he was taken to London and executed "with great cruelty". His successor, Sir Andrew, acquired the lands of Lovat in Inverness-shire through his wife, daughter of the Earl of Orkney and Caithness, through her descent from Sir David de Graham and the Bissets. From Sir Andrew's eldest son, Simon, the Chief of Clan Fraser of Lovat is styled *MacShimi*, son of Simon. In the 15th century Sir Hugh Fraser of Lovat was raised to the peerage as Lord Fraser of Lovat. The famous Simon Lord Lovat was beheaded for his part in the Jacobite Rising of 1745 and the Lovat peerage attainted. On the extinction of the direct line in 1815 the Chiefship passed to Fraser of Strichen. In 1837 the peerage was restored and Thomas Fraser of Strichen, who was descended from a second son of the 4th Lord Lovat, created Baron Lovat. The present Chief, Simon, Lord Lovat played an important part in raising and training the Commandos and was an outstanding military leader in World War II. Of him Winston Churchill wrote to Stalin, quoting Byron, that he was "the mildest mannered man that ever scuttled ship or cut a throat". The present head of the Lowland branch of the Frasers is Flora Fraser, 20th Lady Saltoun.

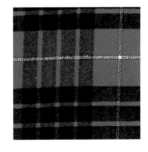

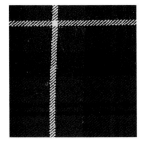

GORDON

The name Gordon is derived from the Parish of Gordon in Berwickshire. The Gordons are of Norman origin and settled in the South of Scotland in the 12th century. In the early 14th century Sir Adam de Gordon was granted lands in Strathbogie in Aberdeenshire by King Robert the Bruce. In 1449 Alexander Gordon was created Earl of Huntly. George, 4th Earl of Huntly became Chancellor of Scotland in 1547. George (6th Earl of Huntly) who defeated Argyll at the Battle of Glenlivet was created Marquess in 1599. The 2nd Marquess, a loyal supporter of Charles I, was beheaded in 1649. In 1684 George, the 4th Marquess, was created Duke of Gordon by King Charles II. In the Jacobite Risings of 1715 and 1745 the Gordons fought on both sides. The 2nd Duke was out for the Jacobites in 1715. In 1745 the 3rd Duke supported the Hanoverians, though his brother raised a regiment for Prince Charles. The Gordon Highlanders were raised in 1794 with the help of the celebrated 4th Duchess.

GRAHAM

The Grahams are of Anglo-Norman origin. William de Graham witnessed the Charter of the Abbey of Holyrood in 1128 when he was granted the lands of Abercorn and Dalkeith in Midlothian. Sir John de Graham fought for Wallace and was killed in 1298 at the Battle of Falkirk. In the reign of King James I Sir William Graham married Mary Stewart, daughter of King Robert III. From this union spring the Grahams of Claverhouse. In 1504 William Lord Graham was created Earl of Montrose. James 5th Earl, born in 1612, was in 1644 created Marquess of Montrose. A great military leader, his campaign of 1644-45 for the King, though it ended in defeat, was a truly remarkable one. Another famous soldier was John Graham of Claverhouse, Viscount Dundee, who died in his hour of victory at Killicrankie in 1689. In 1707 James the 4th Marquess was created Duke of Montrose. From him is descended the present Duke of Montrose, Chief of Clan Graham.

GRANT

The Grants are of Norman origin. Sir Laurence le Grant was Sheriff of Inverness in 1258. The Grants, who supported Wallace, were to become the dominant Clan in Glen Moriston, Glen Urquhart and Strathspey. Their gathering-place is Craigellachie and their slogan "Stand Fast". Originally styled Grant of Freuchie, in the sixteenth century they became known as Lairds of Grant. When offered a Peerage by James VI the then Chief refused politely, asking "And wha'll be Laird O'Grant?" In the Jacobite Rising the Clan supported the House of Hanover with the exception of the Grants of Glenmoriston who supported the Jacobites. The Chief of Clan Grant is Lord Strathspey.

GUNN

The Norse name-father of the Gunns was Gunni, a Norse Orcadian whose wife Ragnhild brought with her great estates in Caithness and Sutherland. The Gunns claim descent from Olave the Black, Norse King of Man and the Isles. They were a warlike Clan, feuding with Clan Keith, the Mackays and the Earls of Caithness and Sutherland and were in the end heavily defeated in 1585 at Loch Broom by the Earl of Sutherland.

In the Jacobite Rising of 1745 the Gunns fought on the Hanoverian side. An early stronghold of the Gunn Chiefs was the old Castle of Hallburg. Later they had as their seat the Castle of Killearnan which, however, was destroyed by fire in 1690.

LAMONT

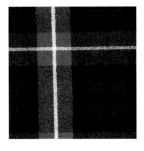

The Lamonts, descended from Aodh O'Neill, King of Northern Ireland in the eleventh century, at one time owned a great part of Cowal in Argyll but, like other clans, suffered from the proximity of the Campbells who in 1646 massacred two hundred Lamonts in one day at Dunoon. After their Castle of Toward had been destroyed by the Campbells, Ardlamont became the Chief's residence. The present Chief of Clan Lamont lives in Australia. The Lamonts of Knockdow are the only branch still possessing clan lands.

LINDSAY

The Lindsays, of Anglo-Norman origin, sat as Barons in the Scottish Parliament from the mid-twelfth century. Sir Alexander de Lindsay was knighted by King Edward I of England, but did not let this prevent him from fighting with both Wallace and Bruce against the English which cost him all his lands in England. David Lindsay of Glenesk was created Earl of Crawford in 1398 and married a daughter of King Robert II. He was overlord of the Highland district of Strathnairn and also Admiral of Scotland. The Lindsay holdings in the Highlands have since been lost. In his day Sir David Lindsay of the Mount, Lord Lyon King of Arms, belonging to a cadet branch, was a famous Scottish poet.

MACDONALD

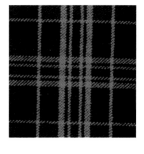

Long the mightiest of all the clans, Clan Donald sprang from Donald, grandson of Somerled King of the Isles and Lord of Argyll and Kintyre. In the fourteenth century the MacDonalds, who assumed the style of Lords of the Isles, held all the South Isles and part of the North Isles. Good John of Islay is reckoned First Lord of the Isles from 1354. From his first marriage to the heiress of the MacRuaris he held the Outer Isles and Garmoran, including Moidart, Knoydart and Morvern. This inheritance he passed to his elder son Ranald, to be held under the suzerainty of his younger son Donald, the son of his second marriage to Margaret, daughter of King Robert II. Donald he appointed Lord of the Isles and High Chief of Clan Donald. From Donald's younger brother, Iain Mor the Tanist, who married the heiress of the Bissets from the Glens of Antrim, sprang the MacDonalds of Islay and Kintyre and the McDonell Earls of Antrim. From Ranald sprang the MacDonalds of Clanranald with their younger branch the MacDonells of Glengarry. In the late seventeenth century High MacDonald of Sleat in Skye was recognised by the Privy Council as Laird of MacDonald. After the Jacobite Rising of 1715 the Barony of Sleat was forfeited. In 1766, however, Sir Alexander MacDonald of Sleat was created Baron MacDonald of Slate in the Peerage of Ireland. In 1947 the present Lord MacDonald's father was recognised as High Chief of Clan Donald.

MACDOUGALL

The MacDougalls descend from Dougall, the eldest son of Somerled, King of the Isles. Dougall styled himself "King of the South Isles and Lord of Lorne". After 1164 Dougall held Argyll and Lorne with Mull, Lismore, Kerrera, Tiree and Coll. His son Duncan and his grandson Ewan built a number of castles in strategic positions including Dunstaffnage, Dunollie, Duntrune and Dunchonnel. The third MacDougall Chief was Eoghan of Argyll, King in the Hebrides and Lord of Lorne. Eoghan's son Alexander married a daughter of the Red Comyn who was slain by Robert the Bruce at Dumfries, with the result that the MacDougalls became bitter enemies of Bruce and after his victory were promptly forfeited. But the 6th Chief married Bruce's grand-daughter, when they recovered the Lordship of Lorne. In 1715 the MacDougalls supported the Jacobite cause after which the Chief's lands were forfeited. His son Alexander took no part in the Rising of 1745 and his lands were subsequently restored to him. The ruins of Dunollie Castle still belong to the present Chief.

MACDUFF

Traditionally MacDuff was the patronymic of the ancient Earls of Fife. In addition to the lands they held in the Lowlands, the Chiefs of Clan MacDuff had extensive possessions in the Highlands. It is said that it was MacDuff, 1st Earl of Fife and name-father of the Clan, who vanquished MacBeth and restored Malcolm Canmore to the throne of Scotland. By tradition it was the privilege of the Chief of Clan MacDuff to crown the King of Scots. The MacDuffs were the premier clan in mediaeval Scotland and their Chief, the Earl of Fife, accordingly bore a red lion on his Coat of Arms. The younger son of the 4th Earl, who died in 1139, was Hugh founder of the great Lowland family of Wemyss of Wemyss.

MACFARLANE

The MacFarlanes are descended from the Celtic Earls of Lennox. Their name-father Parlane lived during the reign of King David I. Their territory lay at the Head of Loch Lomond. They seem to have been as troublesome as their neighbours the MacGregors and like them eventually suffered proscription. Sir Iain MacFarlane, "Captain of Clan Pharlane", was killed at Flodden. His grandson Duncan MacFarlane of Tarbet, in command of one hundred and fifty men, "well armed in shirts of mail", fell at the Battle of Pinkie in 1547. The next MacFarlane Chief brought three hundred of his clan to fight against Mary Queen of Scots at the Battle of Langside. Walter MacFarlane of that Ilk fought for Charles I under Montrose. The MacFarlane lands of Arrochar and Tarbet were sold in 1785 when the last MacFarlane Chief emigrated to America.

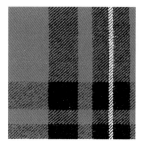

MACGREGOR

The Clan lands of Clan Gregor originally lay in the three glens, Glen Orchy, Glen Strae and Glen Lochy. From Glenstrae they later expanded to Glengyle and Roro. Their name-father was Gregor, said to be a son of King Alpin of the Golden Bridles. Their lands being situated on the borders of Perthshire and Argyll, they suffered severely as neighbours of the Campbells, who in the end absorbed most of their territory. Without a firm base, they took to raiding and soon became outlaws. Following their victory over the Colquhouns at Glen Fruin in 1603 they were outlawed by King James VI who decided to exterminate them. The laws against them as a clan were not repealed until 1774. General Sir John Murray MacGregor was then created a Baronet and recognised as their Chief. His direct descendant, Sir Gregor MacGregor of MacGregor, their present Chief, formerly commanded the 1st Battalion Scots Guards.

MACKAYS

The Mackays are said to descend from the ancient Royal House of Moray. Their territories were in the extreme North West of Scotland. They are thought to have been among the Men of Moray cleared out of Moray by King Malcolm IV in 1160. Their Chief Magnus fought at Bannockburn for Robert the Bruce. In 1427 his successor Angus Dubh could muster as many as 400 men. Sir Donald Mackay was raised to the peerage as Lord Reay by King Charles I in 1628. In the Risings of 1715 and 1745 the Mackays supported the Government.

MACKENZIE

The Mackenzies are said to descend from Gilleon Na H'Airde the progenitor of the O'Beolan Earls of Ross. In 1362 Murdo son of Kenneth was granted a Charter by King David II. The Mackenzies can be said to have risen on the ruins of Clan Donald, whose vassals they were. In 1427 their Chief already had a following of 2000 men. In 1447 King James III granted Alastair Mackenzie of Kintail extensive lands including Strathcoman. Under his son Kenneth the expansion continued. Kintail was erected into a Barony in 1508. The *reddendo* for Kintail was a stag to be rendered to the King. From this came the old motto "*Cuidiche an Righ*" "tribute to the King" and the stag's head in the Chief's Coat of Arms, which gave him his Gaelic title *Caberfeidh* or "Deer Antlers". Mackenzie was originally pronounced Mackingye (thus Sir George Mackenzie of Rosehaugh, Lord Advocate in the seventeenth century was famous as "Bluidy Mackingye"). The Mackenzies continued to extend their lands in Ross, from the Black Isle to the Gairloch and from Kintail to Coigeach. Their Western stronghold, the Castle of Eilean Donan, was usually held for them by the MacRaes. In the seventeenth century they built Brahan Castle near Dingwall, made famous by the prophecies of the Brahan Seer. The Mackenzies were staunch Jacobites and after the Rising of 1745 their peerages were forfeited though later restored to them. Their present Chief, the Earl of Cromartie, descended from Sir Roderick Mackenzie of Coigeach, lives at Castle Leod in Strathconan, granted to the Mackenzie Chief in 1477.

MACKINTOSH

The Mackintoshes derive their name from the Gaelic *Toisech*, meaning Chief. The first Mackintosh Chief was Shaw, the second son of Duncan 2nd Earl of Fife. For his services in suppressing the rebels in Moray in 1160 he was rewarded with wide possessions in the North of Scotland and made Constable of Inverness Castle. The sixth chief supported Robert the Bruce in the War in Independence. Towards the end of the thirteenth century the Chiefs of Clan Mackintosh also became Captains of Clan

Chattan following the marriage of Angus Mackintosh to Eva, the daughter of the then Captain of the confederacy. The original seat of The Mackintosh, as their Chief is known, was on an island in Loch Moy. The Mackintoshes fought for Montrose in support of King Charles I and remained loyal to the Stewart cause in 1715. In the Jacobite Rising of 1745 their 22nd Chief Angus commanded a company of Black Watch for the Government, while his wife, known as Colonel Anne, raised the Clan for Prince Charles.

MACKINNON

Fingon, name-father of the Mackinnons, lived in the thirteenth century. The hand holding a cross in the Mackinnon arms shows him to have been of the kin of St Columba. In the fourteenth century another Fingon, brother of the Mackinnon Chief Niall, was chosen to be Mitred Abbot of Iona. Known as the Green Abbot and described as "a subtle and wicked councillor" he is said to have rebelled against the Lord of the Isles, as a result of which the Mackinnons lost much of their land in Mull to the Macleans who were loyal supporters of the Lordship. The centre of Mackinnon power subsequently shifted to Skye where they acquired the whole of Strathairdale. In 1715 and 1745 the Mackinnons loyally supported the Stewart cause. After 1745 the aged Mackinnon Chief was arrested and confined for a year in Tilbury Fort, after which he was released. On being reminded by the Attorney General of King George's clemency, he made the neat retort: "Had I the King in my power, as I am in his, I would return the compliment by sending him back to his own country."

MACLACHLAN

The MacLachlans take their name from Lachlan Mor who lived by Loch Fyne in the thirteenth century. Castle Lachlan remains the seat of the present Chief. The MacLachlans sprang from the O'Neill Kings of Northern Ireland whose ancestry can be traced back to the fourth century. The MacLachlans were loyal Jacobites. In 1715 Lachlan MacLachlan of MacLachlan signed the address of welcome to King James VIII and III when he landed in Scotland. In 1745 his son "was shot by a cannon ball as he was advancing on horseback to lead on his Regiment". After the Rising a Government ship came up Loch Fyne and bombarded Castle Lachlan. The MacLachlan Chief had been killed before he could be attainted and the Duke of Argyll, who had always been a good friend to his MacLachlan neighbours, intervened to stop his estates being forfeited. In 1942 Marjorie MacLachlan of MacLachlan succeeded her father John as 24th Chief.

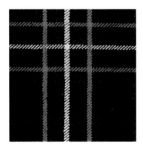

MACLAREN

The MacLarens take their name from Laurence Abbot of Achtow in Balquhidder who lived in the thirteenth century in the ancient Earldom of Strathearn. When the MacGregors were driven out of their own lands by the Campbells, they moved into what had been MacLaren territory. The MacLarens were a warlike clan who fought at Flodden and Pinkie and for Montrose at Inverlochy. In 1745 the MacLarens were out for Prince Charles. Fighting alongside the Stewarts of Appin, they suffered very heavy casualties. "The MacLarens of Achleskine," writes the Chronicler, "were all grand strong men. They were buried inside the Kirk of Balquhidder. When the old Kirk was repaired in 1839 Donald dug up bones at that spot 23 inches long." The MacLarens of Achleskine continued to farm Achtow until 1892. MacLaren of Achleskine was in due course recognised by Lyon King of Arms as Chief of Clan MacLaren. On his death in 1966 his son succeeded him as Chief.

MACLEAN

The Macleans trace their descent from the ancient Gaelic Kings of Dalriada. Their name-father Gillean of the Battleaxe fought at the Battle of Largs in 1263. His descendant Iain Dhu settled in Mull. Iain's son Lachlan Lubanach, who married Mary, daughter of the Lord of the Isles, was the progenitor of the Macleans of Duart, Chiefs of Clan Gillean. From his younger son, Eachan Reganach, sprang the Macleans of Lochbuie, who later adopted the spelling Maclaine. From Eachan Reaganach sprang also the Macleans of Dochgarroch in Inverness-shire who in about 1460 attached themselves for geopolitical reasons to Clan Chattan. The Macleans of Ardgour and Coll were cadets of Duart as were the Keepers and Captains of Dunconnel in the Isles of the Sea. As vassals of the Lords of the Isles, the Macleans fought at Harlaw in 1411, where their Chief Red Hector of the Battles lost his life. After the forfeiture of the Lords of the Isles the Macleans became independent Chiefs. In 1496 their lands at Duart were erected into a feudal barony by King James IV. In 1598 Sir Lachlan Mor Maclean of Duart was killed fighting against the MacDonalds at the Battle of Traigh Ghruineard in Islay. The Macleans loyally supported the Stewart cause and were out in 1715 and 1745. The great stronghold of Duart which dominates the Sound of Mull was for centuries the seat of the Maclean Chiefs and, after various vicissitudes was recovered for the Clan in 1912 by Sir Fitzroy Maclean of Duart. Sir Charles Maclean of Duart, Lord Chamberlain to H.M. the Queen, was Chief of Clan Gillean for more than fifty years and was created a Life Peer. His son, Sir Lachlan, the present Chief, served, like his father, in the Scots Guards.

MACLEOD

The MacLeods are generally believed to be of Norse ancestry, their name-father Leod being the son of Olaf the Black, King of Man and the North Isles. Leod left two sons, Tormod, founder of Siol Tormod, the MacLeods of MacLeod and Harris, and Torquil, founder of Siol Torquil, the MacLeods of Lewis. Glenelg on the mainland is thought to have been the earliest possession of the MacLeods. Leod inherited the Isle of Lewis and Harris with part of Skye. Dunvegan, which has been in the possession of the same family for more than seven centuries, remains to this day the seat of MacLeod of MacLeod. The Siol Tormod supported Bruce in the War of Independence and in 1343 Malcolm son of Tormod received a Charter from King David II granting him lands in Glenelg. John MacLeod of MacLeod fought for the Lord of the Isles at Harlaw in 1411. The eighth MacLeod Chief, Alasdair Crottach, built the famous Fairy Tower at Dunvegan and is buried in a handsome tomb in St Clement's Rodil. Another great MacLeod Chief, Sir Rory Mor MacLeod was knighted by King James VI in 1603 and continued the work of Alasdair Crottach. The famous *piobaireachd*, Rory Mor's lament, was composed in his honour by his hereditary piper, Patrick Mor MacCrimmon. The MacLeods supported Charles I and Charles II and were almost wiped out at the Battle of Worcester in 1651. They played a less prominent part in the Jacobite Rising of 1715. Though individual clansmen were out in 1745, their chief took no part in the Rising.

MACMILLAN

The Macmillans are believed to be of Celtic origin. In the thirteenth century they held lands on Tayside. During the Middle Ages they established themselves in Knapdale by marriage to a McNeill heiress. Macmillan of Knap was Chief of the Clan. A rock at Knap Point in Loch Suibhne bore the inscription "Macmillan's right holds good to Knap, so long as wave beats on the rock". But in 1615 Campbell of Cawdor, on orders from his Chief, the Earl of Argyll, pushed the rock into the sea and the old Macmillan lands have long since been lost to the Clan. Lieutenant General Sir Gordon Macmillan of Macmillan and Knap, the father of the present Chief, was recognised as Chief in 1951.

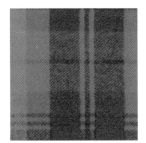

MACNAB

Macnab signifies "son of the Abbot". The Macnab Chiefs claimed descent from Abraruadh, the Red Abbot of Glen Dochart and Strathearn, a descendant of King Fergus of Dalriada. The Clan lands lay on the western shores of Loch Tay and in Strathfillan and Glen Dochart. Angus Macnab was the brother-in-law of The Red Comyn, murdered by Robert the Bruce and accordingly joined the MacDougalls in their campaign against Bruce. After Bannockburn most of the Macnab lands were forfeited except the Barony of Bovain in Glendochart. Under their Chief Iain Min, Smooth John, the Macnabs supported the Stewarts in the Civil War and suffered accordingly. Though many of the Clan supported the Jacobites in 1745, their Chief sided with the Government. Archibald Macnab, the 22nd Chief bought back the Clan lands in 1949. The present and 23rd Chief is James Charles Macnab of Macnab.

MACNAUGHTON

The progenitor of the MacNaughtons is said to be Nachtan Mor who lived in the tenth century. In the thirteenth century the MacNaughtons were in possession of lands bordering on Loch Awe and Loch Fyne. Their strongholds were *Fraoch Eilean*, the Heathery Isle, in Loch Awe and the castles of Dubh Loch in Glen Shira and Dunderave on Loch Fyne. Being related to the MacDougalls of Lorne, their Chief Donald joined that Clan in its resistance to Robert the Bruce and as a result lost many of their possessions. Sir Alexander MacNaughton was killed at the Battle of Flodden in 1513. The MacNaughtons remained loyal to the Stewarts. Their remaining estates were forfeited in the 18th century. One branch had by then moved to Ireland and in 1818 Edmund Alexander MacNaughton of Bushmill, Antrim was recognised as Macnaughton of Dunderave and Chief of the Clan.

MacNeil

The MacNeils descend from Niall of the Nine Hostages, founder of the great U-Neill dynasty in the fifth century. Niall, their first Chief, came to the Isle of Barra in the eleventh century. Neil Og MacNeil fought for Robert the Bruce at Bannockburn. Gilleonan, the 9th Chief, was granted a Charter of Barra and Boisdale by the Lord of the Isles in 1427. The MacNeils remained loyal to the Lords of the Isles until well into the 16th century. MacNeil of Barra is officially recognised as Chief of the whole Clan. When the King of Scots overthrew the Lord of the Isles, MacNeil received a Royal Charter confirming him in possession of Barra and his other territories. The MacNeils had their critics. In 1579 the Bishop of the Isles made a complaint of molestation against Gillean MacNeil of Barra. Gillean's successor Ruari Og MacNeil is described by a contemporary as "a Scot that usuel maketh his summer's course to steal what he can". Under the next Chief, another Ruari known as Ruari the Tatar and described as "a hereditary outlaw", the castle of Kisimul was famous as a nest of pirates. His first wife was the sister of Maclean of Duart. By her he had several sons. Having disowned her, he then married the sister of MacDonald of Clanranald by whom he had several more sons. The two groups of sons subsequently fought each other for the inheritance. In the end the Tatar's eldest son by Duart's sister, Neil Og MacNeil of Barra, became Chief. It was he who with the help of a Catholic missionary, Father Duggan, converted the island to Catholicism in 1652. King James VII made Barra into a feudal Barony. In 1689 Black Ruari brought out his Clan for King James and led them at Killiecrankie. In 1715 he brought them out again in the Jacobite cause. His son, another Roderick, went bankrupt and in 1838 the island had to be sold. In 1937 Robert MacNeill of Barra, a descendant of the old Chiefs, whose great-grandfather had emigrated to America, recovered most of the Clan lands and Kisimul Castle which he subsequently rebuilt and made his home. His son is the present Chief.

Macpherson

In Gaelic Macpherson signifies son of the Parson. The Macphersons descend from Duncan, Parson of Kingussie, who was descended from Ewan Ban son of Muraich, Chief of Clan Chattan in 1173. They belong to Clan Chattan. From several families of Macphersons the Macphersons of Cluny emerged as Chiefs. Andrew Macpherson of Cluny fought for Huntly at Glenlivet. In 1640 Donald Macpherson of Cluny supported King Charles. In 1715 Duncan and in 1745 Ewen Macpherson of Cluny supported the Jacobites and after Culloden Cluny did all he could to help Prince Charles escape. After skulking mostly on his own lands for nine years, he himself escaped to France in 1755. The Cluny lands were forfeited but restored in 1784. They were later sold. The present Chief, Sir William Macpherson, a Judge of the High Court, lives in Blairgowrie.

Malcolm

The Malcolms (or Maccallums) are believed to have settled in Lorne during the thirteenth century. Ranald Maccallum of Corbarron became Constable of Craignish Castle in 1414. In 1562 Donald O'Challum was granted a charter of the lands of Poltalloch in the parish of Kilmartin. His grandson, Zachary 5th of Poltalloch, was a famous swordsman. Corbarron or Corrain was inherited by Zachary Maccallum of Poltalloch towards the end of the seventeenth century. Robin Malcolm of Poltalloch, the present Chief of Clan Malcolm, lives at Duntrune Castle, Argyll.

MENZIES

The Menzies are of Anglo-Norman origin. Sir Robert de Menzies, the first Chief, was Chamberlain of Scotland in 1249. The Menzies supported Bruce at Bannockburn. In 1487 Sir Robert de Menzies received a grant of land which was erected to the Barony of Menzies and in 1665 Sir Alexander Menzies of Castle Menzies near Aberfeldy in Perthshire was created a Baronet of Nova Scotia. The larch was introduced into Scotland from the Tyrol by a Menzies in 1737.

MONCREIFFE

The Moncreiffes take their name from the Hill of Moncreiffe in Perthshire. Sir Matthew Moncreiffe of Moncreiffe was confirmed in the lands of Moncreiffe in 1248. These, with Culdares and Duneaves in the mouth of Glen Lyon, were incorporated in the Barony of Moncreiffe in 1455. Sir John Moncreiffe was killed at the Battle of Flodden in 1513. The 12th Chief, Sir John Moncreiffe, was created a Baronet of Nova Scotia. The House of Moncreiffe was built by Sir William Bruce in 1679. It remained the family seat until destroyed by fire in November 1957, when the 23rd Chief Sir David Moncreiffe of that Ilk lost his life. He was succeeded by Sir Iain Moncreiffe the famous Herald and historian. On Sir Iain's death in 1985 the Chiefship reverted to Sir David's sister Miss Elisabeth Moncreiffe of Moncreiffe.

MORRISON

Of Norse origin, the Morrison Chiefs became hereditary brieves or judges of the Island of Lewis. There is a tradition that their progenitor, Ghille Mhuire, "the Servant of Mary", was a natural son of the King of Norway who, after being shipwrecked off the island of Lewis, was washed ashore on a piece of driftwood. From this the Clan took their plant badge of driftweed. With the end of the brieveship in the 17th century, many Morrisons became Ministers of religion.

MUNRO

The Munros were vassals of the Earls of Ross. The seat of their Chief is at Foulis in eastern Ross-shire. Traditionally they stem from the Siol O'Cairn of North Moray. Hugh, the first Chief to use the style "of Foulis", lived in the twelfth century. Robert Munro fought at Bannockburn for Robert the Bruce. After the downfall of the MacDonald Earls of Ross in 1476 the Munros held the Barony of Foulis directly from the Crown. Sir Henry Munro of Foulis, 6th Baronet was the first Commanding Officer of the Black Watch. After serving with distinction at Fontenoy, he was killed fighting for George II against the Jacobites at Falkirk, as was his brother Duncan. On the death of the 11th Baronet, his eldest daughter Mrs Gascoigne became Heretrix of the Clan. Her son Patrick Munro of Foulis is the present Chief.

MURRAY

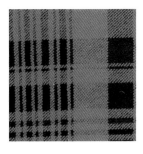

The Murrays take their name from the province of Moray at one time an autonomous kingdom. Their ancestor was Freskin de Moravia from whom were descended the Murrays of Tullibardine, progenitors of the Dukes of Atholl and Chiefs of Clan Murray of Atholl. Freskin's descendant Sir William de Moravia acquired the lands of Tullibardine in Perthshire in 1282. In 1606 Sir John Murray of Tullibardine was created Earl of Tullibardine by King James VI; the second Earl was created Marquess and the 3rd Earl and 2nd Marquess became in 1703 Duke of Atholl. He was a strong opponent of the Union of 1707. In his Memorial to Government in 1745 Lord President Forbes of Culloden wrote a trifle confusingly: "The Murrays is no clan family, though the Duke of Atholl is chief and head of a number of barons and gentlemen of the name of Murray in the Lowlands, but he is deservedly placed here on account of his extensive following of about 3000 Highlanders...." The first Duke's son William Marquess of Tullibardine and his younger brother Lord George Murray took a leading part in the Jacobite Risings of 1715 and 1745. In 1745 Lord George was Lieutenant-General of the Prince's Army. Lord George's descendant, the present Duke of Atholl, still lives at Blair Castle in Blair Atholl.

OGILVY

The Ogilvys sprang from Gilbert of Ogilvy, younger son of Earl Gillebride of Angus, who in the 12th century gave his son Gilbert the lands of Ogilvy in Angus. Sir Patrick Ogilvy, Sheriff of Angus, styled Vicomte d'Angus, commanded the Scottish forces who fought against the English in France with Joan of Arc in 1429. Sir James Ogilvy was elevated to the Scottish peerage as Lord Ogilvy of Airlie in 1491 and James 8th Lord Ogilvy was created Earl of Airlie by Charles I in 1639. The Ogilvys were famous for their loyalty to the Stewart cause. In 1745 David Lord Ogilvy raised a regiment of 600 men for Prince Charles Edward. For this he was attainted. The Earldom was restored in 1823. A ghostly drummer-boy is said to be heard beating his drum whenever an Earl of Airlie is about to die. The family seats are Cortachy Castle and "the Bonnie Hoose of Airlie". The present Chief is Lord Chamberlain to Her Majesty the Queen.

ROBERTSON (CLAN DONNACHAIDH)

The Robertsons claim descent from the old Celtic Earls of Atholl. Their name-father, Donnchadh or Duncan Reamhar, fought for Bruce at the Battle of Bannockburn. In 1451, the lands of their fourth Chief Robert Riach, Grizzled Robert, were erected into the Barony of Struan by King James II as a reward "for the capture of that vile traitor the late Robert of Graham", killer of King James I, an episode thereafter heraldically commemorated in Struan's arms. In 1688 young Robertson of Struan, as a boy, joined Dundee and was consequently attainted. In 1715 he brought 500 of his Clan out for King James and was taken prisoner at Sheriffmuir, but escaped to France. In 1745 he likewise brought the Robertsons out for Prince Charles but was by then too old to do much fighting and returned home after the Battle of Prestonpans in General Wade's coach, wearing his furlined nightshirt.

ROSS

Clan Ross take their name, which in Gaelic signifies "headland", from the province of Ross. Their progenitor, Fearchar Mac-an-t-sagairt of Applecross, joined King Alexander II in crushing the rebellion in Moray in 1215 and was rewarded by being made Earl of Ross. Following a struggle for the Earldom between the Regent Albany and the Lord of the Isles, it later reverted to the Crown, but was subsequently restored to the Lords of the Isles and eventually forfeited, with the Lordship, in 1476. On the death of William, the 5th Earl, in 1372 the Chiefship passed to his younger half-brother Hugh, progenitor of the Rosses of Balnagowan, who for over three centuries remained the principal family of the Clan. In 1632 the Rosses could raise 1000 men. Royalists in the civil war, the Rosses on the whole avoided involvement in the Jacobite Risings of 1715 and 1745. The Chiefship was restored to the old line in 1903, passing in 1968 to David Ross of Ross, a direct descendant of Mac-an-t-sagairt.

SINCLAIR

The Sinclairs are of Norman origin, their name being derived from Saint Clair sur Elle near Saint Lo in Normandy. In the year 1280 their Chief, Sir William Sinclair, Sheriff of Edinburgh, was granted the barony of Rosslyn. His son Henry fought for Bruce at Bannockburn while Sir Henry's son William was slain fighting the Saracens in Andalusia. Through his father's marriage to Isabella Countess of Orkney Sir William Sinclair's grandson Henry inherited the Earldom of Orkney and in 1379 was recognised as Jarl of Orkney by King Haakon of Norway. In 1453 the third Sinclair Earl of Orkney was granted the Earldom of Caithness by King James II of Scotland. Over the years the Earls of Caithness, who were recognised as Chiefs of the Clan, were involved in numerous feuds with neighbouring clans, including the Campbells. George 6th Earl of Caithness was greatly burdened with debt and when in 1676 he died without issue, Sir John Campbell of Glenorchy, who was by then in possession of most of the mortgaged estates, laid claim to the earldom, which was, however, restored to the Sinclairs five years later by Order of Parliament. A prominent Sinclair family were the Sinclairs of Ulbster who possessed great estates in Caithness. Sir John Sinclair of Ulbster (1754-1835), editor of the Statistical Account, was a celebrated agriculturist and improver, while more recently Archibald Sinclair, 1st Viscount Thurso, was Leader of the Liberal Party and Secretary of state for Air during World War II.

STEWART OF APPIN

The West Highland Stewarts of Appin spring from the 4th Steward of Scotland's younger son, Sir John Stewart of Bonkyl, who was killed fighting for Wallace in 1297. By his marriage to the heiress of Lorne one of his descendants secured the Lordship of Lorne. Sir John Stewart of Lorne met his death at Dunstaffnage in 1463 and his son Dougal became the first Stewart Chief of Appin. In the 16th century the Stewarts of Appin fought at Flodden and Pinkie. They fought for Montrose at Inverlochy, Auldearn and Kilsyth, and for Dundee at Killiecrankie. They were out in 1715 and again in 1745, when in their Chief's absence they were led by Stewart of Ardshiel. In 1765 the 9th

Chief of Appin was succeeded by his cousin Duncan, 6th of Ardshiel, who thus became 10th of Appin and from whom the present Chief is descended.

SUTHERLAND

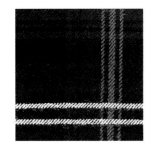

The Sutherlands take their name from Sutherland, in Norse *Suddrland*, the territory lying to the south of Caithness. The ancient Earldom of Sutherland is said to have been granted to William, Lord of Sutherland, a descendant of Freskin, also progenitor of the Murrays, in about 1228. William the 2nd Earl fought for Bruce at Bannockburn and William the 5th Earl was married to Robert Bruce's daughter Margaret. He was killed in 1370 by the Mackays in the course of a feud which was to continue for the next four centuries. Robert the 6th Earl, who in 1389 married a daughter of the notorious Wolf of Badenoch, built Dunrobin, still the seat of the Sutherland Chiefs. When John the 9th Earl died in 1514 without male issue, he was succeeded by his sister Elizabeth, who became the wife of Adam Gordon, second son of the 2nd Earl of Huntly. At the time of the Jacobite risings of 1715 and 1745 the Sutherlands showed themselves loyal supporters of the House of Hanover. On the death in 1766 of William the last of the Gordon Earls of Sutherland, his daughter Elizabeth Countess of Sutherland in her own right married Geroge Granville-Leveson-Gower Marquess of Stafford who in 1833 was made the 1st Duke of Sutherland. A leading English Liberal and keen social reformer, he was, with the best intentions, responsible for the notorious Sutherland clearances. On the death of the 5th Duke, the Earldom of Sutherland and Chiefship of the Clan passed to his niece Elisabeth who became Countess of Sutherland in her own right, while the Dukedom passed to the Earl of Ellesmere, a descendant of the 1st Duke.

URQUHART

The Urquharts are thought to have taken their name from Castle Urquhart at the northern end of Loch Ness, of which they were hereditary keepers. According to Logan "there are records of the Urquharts, who were Chiefs of the name from the year 1306, when we find William Urquhart of Cromartie Sheriff of the county, which was afterwards made heritable in the family." Sir Thomas Urquhart of Cromarty is said to have had no less than twenty-five sons, seven of whom were killed at the Battle of Pinkie in 1547. Another Sir Thomas Urquhart of Cromarty, who showed unwavering devotion to the Stewart cause, was knighted by Charles I in 1641. After the King's defeat and death he went abroad and produced a masterly translation of the works of Rabelais. Returning to this country, he fought at the Battle of Worcester in 1651 and was there taken prisoner. While in the Tower of London he published a family tree tracing his own descent from Adam and Eve. He is said to have died in 1660 in a fit of joyous laughter on learning of the restoration of King Charles II. An American citizen, Kenneth Urquhart, descended from the Urquharts of Braelanigswell, has been recognised as twenty-sixth Chief of the Clan.

Sources of Illustrations

The author and publisher wish to thank all those who have helped to provide photographs, and the many owners of both private and public collections who have given reproduction permission.

The author provided photographs for pages viii and xi

The Abbotsford Collection, Melrose   145 (right), 193 (right) (photo Douglas Corrance)

Aberdeen City Library   246

Reproduced with permission from the George Washington Wilson Collection, Aberdeen University Library   186-187

Trustees of Tenth Duke of Argyll   193 (above left), 196 (right), 202, 214 (above)

Argyll & Sutherland Highlanders Regimental Museum   240

Ashmolean Museum, University of Oxford   144, 219

From His Grace the Duke of Atholl's Collection, Blair Castle, Perthshire   96, 146, 190, 191, 206

National Library of Australia, Canberra   237

Trustees of the Black Watch Regimental Museum   215, 238-239, 239

The Trustees, British Museum   12, 61, 108, 138, 142 (Dept. of Maps), 211, 222, 228

The Marquess of Bute (on loan to the National Museums of Scotland)   23 (above)

By permission of the Syndics of Cambridge University Library   4 (right)

Sir Donald Cameron of Lochiel, KT   154, 155, 212 (above), 213

Kathy Charlton, Photographer   70-71

Clan Donald Visitor Centre, Isle of Skye   250 (below)

By kind permission of the Regimental Lieutenant Colonel, Coldstream Guards (Photo Cranston Fine Arts)   243

Coram Foundation, London (Bridgeman Art Library)   210

The Master and Fellows of Corpus Christi College, Cambridge   iii, 14

Douglas Corrance, Photographer   39, 40-41, 90 (above), 193 (right)

Reproduced by Courtesy of the Faculty of Advocates   76-77, 164 (above left)

Robert Fleming & Co Ltd   224, 234-235

After Friell and Watson *Pictish Studies* 1984   45, 80, 81, 136, 137, 168, 268, 269

Glasgow Museums: Art Gallery & Museum, Kelvingrove   141, 162-163

From H D Graham Antiquities of Iona 1850   16, 44

Grandfather Mountain Highland Games, North Carolina (Photo Hugh Morton)   251

The Guildhall Library, Corporation of London (Bridgeman Art Library)   231 (below)

Dennis Hardley, Photographer   18-19, 32-33, 56, 65, 126

By kind permission of the Baroness Herries and His Grace The Duke of Norfolk   101

Highland Folk Museum, Kingussie   187 (inset)

Inverness Museum and Art Gallery   197 (left), 208 (below), 220

Lang Brothers Ltd   184

From James Logan *The Clans of the Scottish Highlands* 1845   vi, 119, 212 (below)

Lyon Office   29 (above right)

Sir Gregor MacGregor of MacGregor Bt   230

Sir Lachlan Maclean Bt   192 (right)

By kind permission of John MacLeod of MacLeod, Dunvegan Castle, Isle of Skye 54 (above), 73, 74, 128

Mansell Collection   244

Index